# THE ELITES OF BAROTSELAND

## THE AUTHOR

Gerald L. Caplan is a Canadian who gained his Ph.D. at the School of Oriental and African Studies in London. He has held appointments in the history departments of the University of Toronto and the University College of Rhodesia. He collected his oral evidence for this book on three separate visits to Barotseland.

CAPLAN, Gerald L. **The elites of Barotseland, 1878–1969; a political history of Zambia's western province.** California, 1971 (c1970). 270p il map bibl 77-119718. 8.50. ISBN 0-520-01758-7

A political history of Barotseland, this is a study of the interaction between Western imperialism and the tribal aristocracy in this western-most province of Zambia. The rulers of Barotseland, brought under British protection in 1890, retained their traditional form of government. And while the paramount chiefs might occasionally visit England, Barotseland remained largely neglected by British authorities, with the exception of the burdensome hut tax which was imposed upon the Barotse people. Although geographically remote, after Livingstone's journey through Barotseland in the early 1850's, it became the subject of a number of subsequent accounts by missionaries, traders, and hunters. In recent years, the National Museum of Zambia has sponsored the publication of the scholarly Robins series with three of the seven volumes dealing with Barotseland and the Barotse: *Trade and travel in early Barotseland* (1963), edited by E. Tabler; B. Reynolds, *Magic, divination and witchcraft among the Barotse...* (1963); and G. Clay, *Your friend, Lewanika* (1969), a biography of the most important Barotse ruler. Now Caplan's book thoroughly documents the political history from the reign of Lewanika to the incorporation of

Barotseland into Zambia in the 1960's. In the absence of a more general history this is probably the standard work on the Barotse. It is, moreover, written primarily from an African point of view, incorporating extensive oral evidence obtained during the author's three visits to Barotseland. Excellent note on sources.

CHOICE JUL./AUG. '71

History, Geography & Travel

Africa

DT
964
B3
C24

Travel

Africa

THE HISTORY OF MONTESSORI

# THE ELITES OF
# BAROTSELAND

## 1878 - 1969

*A Political History of*
*Zambia's Western Province*

BY

GERALD L. CAPLAN

UNIVERSITY OF CALIFORNIA PRESS

BERKELEY AND LOS ANGELES

1970

UNIVERSITY OF CALIFORNIA PRESS
Berkeley and Los Angeles, California

ISBN 0-520-01758-7

Library of Congress Catalog Card Number: 77-119718

© 1970, by Gerald L. Caplan

Printed in Great Britain

# PREFACE

This study attempts to describe the interaction between western imperialism and the political elites of one African people over the past century. In so doing, however, it hopefully illuminates a number of larger problems. Barotseland today has an international significance such as it has possessed only once before in its long history. In the 1890s, its pacification was among the overriding aims of the British South Africa Company as Rhodes pursued his expansionist policies northward into the heart of the continent. In the 1960s, the integration of Barotseland into the new nation of Zambia became a key to the transformation of an artificial colonial entity into a united and stable state.

During the first half of the 1960s, the process of integration was, outside of Zambia itself, of interest only to those who happened to be shareholders in copper mines or scholars with esoteric interests. This situation, however, soon altered dramatically. By 1969 an astute foreign observer could argue convincingly that

> Zambia is today perhaps Africa's most crucial country. The outcome of the struggle going on inside and around its frontiers will affect much more than the fortunes of its four million inhabitants, or of the big mining companies.[1]

The internal conflict was a power struggle between ethnic and class groupings in which the Lozi were intimately involved. Moreover, Zambia suddenly found itself on the front lines of a racial confrontation with the white south which can hardly avoid becoming a conflagration. Its stability as well as its policies consequently have assumed great significance for the 40 million people of south-central Africa and indeed for all those with interests in the future of the subcontinent. As a further consequence, the tiny Barotse (now Western) Province assumes an international significance it has lacked for more than half a

1. Colin Legum, 'What Kaunda is really up against', *The Observer*, 17 Aug., 1969.

v

century. Forming Zambia's western boundary with Angola, touching the Caprivi Strip and only minutes by plane from Rhodesia; with a traditional elite with strong ties with whites in Southern Africa; and possessing an influence in the republic quite disproportionate to its size and numbers, the fate of Barotseland may well affect millions who are unaware even of its existence.

There is a second reason why Lozi colonial history may be of more than parochial interest. It provides material for the study of certain themes which are important to much of the third world and to scholars in a variety of disciplines. Lozi history demonstrates the consequences for a relatively powerful African kingdom of the attempt to accommodate rather than to resist European power. It is a classic instance of 'indirect rule' in practice. It reveals how structural underdevelopment was built into a colonial territory in order to facilitate the development of imperialist interests. It illustrates the crucial role of formal western education in creating new elite groups. It shows that genuine class conflicts may often underlie so-called 'tribal' animosities. It offers a clear example of a traditional ruling class choosing to ally itself with white imperialists against African nationalists. It indicates how secessionist tendencies develop and how they might constructively be contained.

All of these themes are touched upon in this study. Its central concern, however, is to identify the changing locus of power in Barotseland between 1878 and 1969, and it therefore focusses primarily upon power struggles among elite groups. (I define an elite as a group distinguishable by ascribed or acquired characteristics and which has unusual status and/or decision-making prerogatives in a society.) A number of issues and problems which remain irrelevant or tangential to the central theme are not expanded upon here, however significant they may be in another context.

The largest part of this work was written in 1966–67. It is based on written materials collected in 1964 and 1965, and on oral evidence collected in three visits to Barotseland; by far the longest of these, four months, was undertaken from June to October, 1965. Material for the period from 1966 to 1969 is derived largely from Zambian newspapers and interviews held in Lusaka during a very brief return visit there in March, 1969;

additional sources of information are noted in the text. Besides the usual bibliography, I have appended a critical note on sources and biographies of Lozi informants in the hope that readers will be better able to judge the reliability of the evidence introduced.

I am grateful to those whose financial assistance has made the writing of this book possible: the Commonwealth Scholarship Commissions of the former government of Rhodesia and of the government of the United Kingdom, the University of London Central Research Fund, and the University College of Rhodesia Travel and Research Fund. I would also thank my colleagues and students in the Department of History and Philosophy of the Ontario Institute for Studies in Education (University of Toronto) for generously allowing me the time and funds to return to Zambia in 1969.

I am also indebted to the many people who have given me advice and assistance during the preparation of this work, and above all to my Lozi informants and to several of my teachers and colleagues. Specifically, I want to record my gratitude to Dr. Richard Gray of the School of Oriental and African Studies, University of London, and to Professor Jaap van Velsen of the Department of Sociology, University of Zambia; to Messrs. Mbanga Mtemwa and Arthur M. Zaza, whose friendship and co-operation made my months in Barotseland as enjoyable as they were; and to Miss S. D. Southey, who prepared the maps and organized the bibliography. None of them is of course responsible for what follows, and indeed I know that not all of them agree with certain of my opinions and conclusions.

This book is dedicated to my friend and former colleague, John Conradie.

GERALD L. CAPLAN

*Agincourt, Ontario*
*January, 1970*

# CONTENTS

# PLATES

*Between pages 194 and 195*

1. Lewanika in England, 1902.

2. A Christmas card in honour of Coillard.

3. Bird's-eye view of Lealui village and the flooded plain at 1965 Kuomboka ceremony.

4. The cabinet of the reformed Barotse National Council, after the Katengo elections of 1963.

5. President and Mrs Kaunda and Litunga Mwanawina on royal barge.

6. Litunga Mwanawina arrives at Limulunga, the winter capital, during 1965 Kuomboka ceremony.

7. Litunga Mbikusita Lewanika II.

# MAPS

# ABBREVIATIONS

| | |
|---|---|
| African National Congress | ANC |
| Barotse Anti-Secession Movement | BASMO |
| Barotse Native Government | BNG |
| Barotse National School | BNS |
| Barotse Province File, Mongu Boma | Boma Files |
| Colonial Office | CO |
| National Archives of Rhodesia | NAR |
| National Archives of Zambia | NAZ |
| News from Basutoland and Barotseland | News from B. and B. |
| Northern Rhodesia Native Affairs Annual Report | NRNAAR |
| North-Western Rhodesia | NWR |
| Rhodes–Livingstone Institute (now Institute for Social Research) | RLI |
| Societé des Missions Evangéliques (Paris Missionary Society) | PMS |
| Societé des Missions Evangéliques, Paris Archives | PMSP |
| Societé des Missions Evangéliques, Sefula Archives | PMSS |
| United National Independence Party | UNIP |
| Witswatersrand Native Labour Recruiting Association | WNLA |

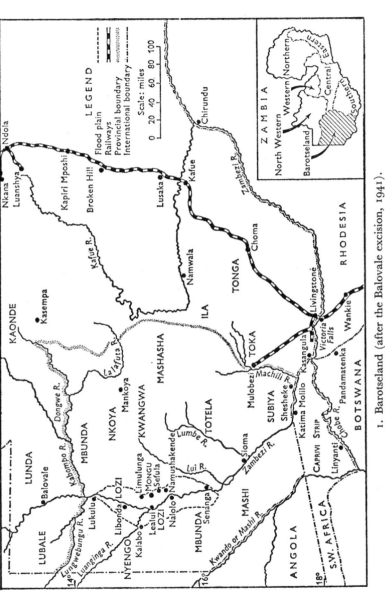

1. Barotseland (after the Balovale excision, 1941).

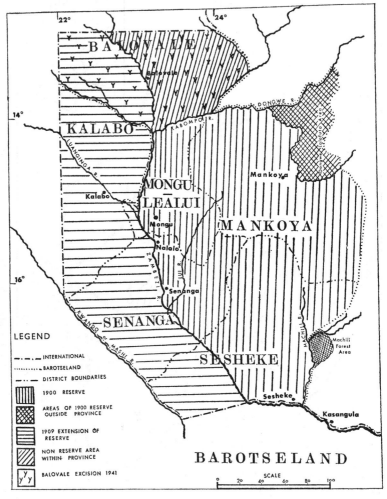

**LEGEND**

—·—·— INTERNATIONAL
············· BAROTSELAND
—··—··— DISTRICT BOUNDARIES

1900 RESERVE

AREAS OF 1900 RESERVE
OUTSIDE PROVINCE

1909 EXTENSION OF
RESERVE

NON RESERVE AREA
WITHIN PROVINCE

BALOVALE EXCISION 1941

SCALE
0    20    40    60    80    100

**BAROTSELAND**

2. An historical map of Barotseland under colonial rule.

# CHAPTER I

# INTRODUCTION

Barotseland is that province of the Zambian republic centred on and extending outwards from the flood plain of the upper Zambesi River. Its name derives from the dominant people of the area, the Lozi (Rozi). The most persuasive, but not definitive, evidence suggests that they split off from the Lunda-Luba empire of the Congo basin, reaching the plain during the latter half of the seventeenth century.[1]

There they were labelled the Luyi (foreigners) by the existing inhabitants whom they conquered, a name they retained until they were conquered from the south in the nineteenth century. According to Gluckman, the anthropologist who in the 1940s carried out intensive research in Barotseland, some twenty-five smaller tribes comprise, with the Lozi themselves, what he calls the 'Barotse nation' as against the ruling Lozi. It is, however, by no means easy to distinguish between Lozi and members of the smaller groupings, who in some senses maintain their original identities yet are to a great extent assimilated. As Gluckman notes, 'These tribes have intermarried considerably, and nowhere has this been more marked than among the Lozi themselves. . . . Today the Lozi themselves say that there is practically no Lozi who is a pure Luyi. Almost all of them point without shame to Nkoya, Kwangwa, Subiya, Totela, Mbunda, Kololo and other blood in their ancestry.'[2] One of my informants, with a Subiya father and a Lozi-Toka mother, speaks Subiya as well as Silozi and told me he was a Subiya, yet added: 'but this is a part of being a Lozi. No one is a real Lozi; this is just a name for all the people of Barotseland.'[3] Yet this too is an over-simplification, for one of the themes of Barotseland history has been the demand by members of the smaller tribes for increased representation in the councils of the nation. Some people clearly were excluded from positions of power, perhaps those who had never intermarried with 'pure Lozi'. This study, therefore, will use the name Lozi when referring to the people who, in the last analysis, remained dominant; Barotseland will be taken as the area over which the Lozi ruled, which included many peoples partly distinguishable from them.

Virtually nothing is known of Lozi history until the end of the eighteenth century. The traditions of the Lozi ruling class, as recorded by an Italian missionary, consist almost entirely of myths, legends, miraculous events and fanciful stories.[4] The function of most of these stories is obscure, but the purpose of one of them at least is apparent. Members of the royal family expounded an autochthonous interpretation for the origin o the Lozi: if Nyambe (God) and his wife-daughter begat the first Lozi King from whom all successive kings are descended, the legitimacy of the royal family's right to reign is not open to challenge.

It is only with the reign of King Mulambwa (1780?–1830?[5]) that some flesh is added to the bare bones of Lozi history. Variously considered to have been the ninth, tenth, or fourteenth Lozi ruler, Mulambwa is universally considered by Lozi to have been their greatest king, and indeed the founder of modern Barotseland. We may presume that during his very long reign, the Lozi political, economic and judicial systems had reached that degree of sophistication which later impressed so many European observers.

Mulambwa's Barotseland, like a number of other nations on both sides of the Zambesi—Ndebele, Ngoni, Bemba and Lunda —clearly falls into the traditional anthropological category of a so-called 'primitive' state, that is, a society with an organized government as opposed to stateless societies such as the neighbouring Ila and Plateau Tonga. Like that of the Ndebele, the Lozi state was essentially a unitary one, in which struggles for power were largely concentrated at the capital. Moreover, for the Lozi ruling class, fissionary tendencies were of little consequence, for they were offset by the centripetal forces, centering on the capital, inherent in the political and economic structure of the kindom.

On the one hand, the extremely complex structure of this highly centralized state produced considerable cohesion and stability; on the other, it created the conditions whereby, as the Lozi themselves say, the state is always on the verge of revolt.[6] The kingship, for example, was the mystical symbol of national unity, but the choice of King was not rigidly fixed: any male descendant in the patrilineal line of the first legendary king was eligible to succeed, thus giving rise to intense competition for the succession. Similarly, any commoner could aspire to become not only an induna (a judge and councillor) but the chief councillor or Ngambela. The King could appoint any commoner to any place in the established hierarchy of council titles, or to the Ngambelaship. This both augmented and diminished the power of the King, for while his subjects depended on him for promotion, he was perpetually open to the threat that, if antagonized, they would rally behind a prince whom they would attempt to substitute for the incumbent. But the induna's freedom of action was also circumscribed. The rewards and perquisites attached to the various titles were considerable in terms of status, land, cattle, followers and further opportunity for promotion; moreover, the more senior the title, the greater were the perquisites. It was therefore in their interests to prove themselves loyal followers of the King, who alone could promote or demote them. Yet by the same token, the rewards of office were a sufficient incentive to support a rival for the throne in the hopes of a higher position should he succeed. Since the Ngambelaship was the highest post in the nation to which a commoner could aspire, it was the obvious object of every ambitious induna; the Ngambela was thus greatly dependent on the King's favour. Yet because constitutionally he was not only the mouthpiece of the King to the nation, but also represented the nation to, and if necessary against, the King, it was his function to oppose a King who ruled unjustly. In this way, then, permanent intrigue at every level of government inhered in the system, no man from King to the most subordinate councillor enjoying secure tenure of office.

Nor was the supreme council of the nation a monolithic body easily able to unite for or against the King. It was, to begin with, divided into three 'mats': on the right of the King in the council sat all the commoner indunas; on his left sat, first, his stewards, who were responsible for his property and who represented his interests (and were also indunas), and, secondly, princes of the royal family who represented the interests of the royal family, if necessary against those of the King. Moreover, the National Council was divided into three sub-councils: the Katengo, comprising minor indunas of the right and the stewards; the Saa, which included all other members of the Council save the Ngambela and the Natamoyo (the 'Minister of Justice' or sanctuary, the only indunaship to which a royal alone could be appointed); and the Sikalo, which consisted of the Ngambela, the Natamoyo, and the senior indunas of the Saa. Each of these sub-councils was considered to represent a different interest: the Sikalo, the King and Ngambela; the Saa, the indunas; and the Katengo, which ceased functioning probably from Lewanika's time to 1947, the mass of the nation.

The sub-councils assembled separately to discuss issues of importance then reintegrated into the full Council for further discussions before the King was called upon to give the final decision. Because of the different interests into which all these members of the ruling class were divided, it was difficult for them to unite against the King. But if they did reach a consensus of opinion, it was hazardous for the King to adopt an opposing policy. Unlike the Zulu and Sotho, the Lozi do not seem to have had regular meetings of the full National Council, except to decide matters of the gravest importance, such as the granting of the concession to the British South Africa Company or the selection of a new King. Ordinary business and court cases at the capital were handled by the Kuta, a smaller body on which representatives of all three mats sat.

In Mulambwa's time (as we are presuming), Lozi political organization was distinguished by a system which largely fell into disuse after the Kololo invasion of 1840. This was its division into both *silalo* and *makolo*, a system unknown to other tribes in southern Africa. The *silalo* were simple territorial divisions, but without the usual administrative functions of such divisions. Far more important for such purposes—jurisdiction, organization for war, labour conscription—were the *makolo*, which Gluckman defines as non-territorial political sectors. Each sector centred in an important title at the capital, and every Lozi was attached to a sector. But the people in one area, even in one village of kinsmen, would be members of different political sectors, and members of any given sector were widely dispersed over the country. As a result, no councillor or prince had accruing to his title a solid localized block of men, with whom he could either break away from or battle against the King.

Several consequences followed from the *makolo* system. It was another element in the extreme centralization of the political system in the capital, and consequently a further reason why the important power struggles were confined to it. It largely precluded segmentation from the larger unit of a dissident block under a councillor or prince, thereby preserving the territorial integrity of the Lozi state. Yet it was a typically Lozi institution in that it simultaneously safeguarded and jeopardized the personal position of the King. For if it prevented a rival prince or an ambitious councillor spurring a prince to mass an army of his dependents against the King, it clearly maximized the possibility of a swift *coup d'état* or assassination.[7]

The Barotse Valley—the flood plain of the Upper Zambesi—floods each year between February and July, compelling in earlier times the people to move during this period each year from the plain to the higher ground surrounding it. This transhumant existence may have prevented the establishment of territorial segments whose leaders with their armies could dominate national politics. The phenomenon of the annual flood was the single most important objective fact of life to the Lozi, and on it was probably based not only part of their political structure, such as the *makolo*, but the greater part of their internal economy as well as the trading system of the larger 'empire' of Barotseland. This profound dependence on the flood and the flood plain continues to be reflected in the annual *kuomboka* and *kuluhela* ceremonies, the ritual voyages of the King from the plain capital to the higher capital in March, and the return in July.[8] These are the most important in Lozi life, and are for them the equivalent of national planting or first-fruits ceremonies such as among the Luvale and the Tonga, which the Lozi do not have.

It is the flood plain which Lozi themselves consider *Bulozi*—Barotseland proper—and within this area there was, besides the 'northern' capital of the King, a 'southern' capital at

Nalolo. Although the 'chief-of-the-south' never possessed the power which attached to the King, he was the latter's equal in terms of ritual honour and prestige, and was the second most powerful individual in the kingdom. The Lozi believe that it was a civil war started by Mulambwa's son, who was prince at Nalolo, which enabled the Kololo to defeat them, and when the Kololo were finally overthrown, the new Lozi King began the practice, followed ever since, of appointing a woman as head of the southern capital. Because a woman could not become king, this *Mulena mukwae* (princess chief) could not be a direct rival for the throne. She had the right to be consulted on all major decisions taken in the King's capital, and the duty to reprove a king she believed was ruling unjustly, but ultimately it was the word of the King which always prevailed. Moreover, in the colonial period, the main link was between the King and the white administration, and the influence of Nalolo steadily declined. Nevertheless, there was a long tradition of competition in the relationship between north and south, which strikingly manifested itself, as shall be seen, in the rebellion of 1884–85.[9]

Local and national politics were also directly affected by the complex and relatively developed economic system which was organized on the substructure of the flood plain. Fishing, cattle and agriculture were the chief elements in the local economy which, if hardly a prosperous one in absolute terms, yet produced in the eighteenth and early nineteenth centuries a higher standard of living in the Barotse Valley than in most other areas of Central Africa. These elements in turn depended upon the control of the numerous though limited mounds which dotted the plain. Although the King was 'owner of the land', his rights of ownership were strictly circumscribed since certain mounds were attached to councillors' names and members of the royal family. When a man was appointed to a title, he acquired temporary control of the highly productive mounds attached to that title. But it was the King who selected his own indunas, and since the more senior an indunaship the greater the amount of land, and thus wealth, status and dependants, which attached to it, the King's power was therefore significantly augmented at the same time that disappointed councillors received even greater reason to rebel.

Moreover, once the Lozi completed their conquest of the Barotse Valley and established their state centred on the flood plain, they were able to extend their domination from that plain in a wide-ranging trading system with its centre at the Lozi capital. For the plain produced goods which were different from the products of the surrounding areas. The Valley and the outlying regions were consequently mutually dependent, giving rise to a certain stability in the kingdom and enhancing the power and influence of the Lozi ruling class which controlled the heart of the network of exchanges. In consequence, the key position of the capital in the overall Lozi polity was yet further consolidated. Moreover, much of the trade and all of the tribute (not always easily distinguishable from trading goods) from the outlying tribes went to the King, who was obligated to distribute it among his councillors, each man's share being contingent upon the seniority of his title. Political status thus led to greater economic status, which in turn created increased opportunity for yet greater political status.[10]

Obviously the control over political and economic resources was reflected in social status, a fact of great significance among a people as conscious of class as the Lozi were and are. All Lozi felt superior to all their vassal tribes, while ruling-class Lozi regarded their less privileged kin with much contempt. Since those in the upper social strata were also the political elite, and since it was in theory and sometimes in practice possible for any commoner to aspire to an induna's title, the rewards of power were very great indeed. In a state characterised by extreme inequality in every sphere, the stakes for which one played were very high.

The extent of the area which may legitimately be considered the kingdom of Barotseland is not easily ascertained. The question was of critical importance on two subsequent occasions in Lozi history. Between 1890 and 1905, Portugal and Britain clashed over the proper boundary between Angola and Northern Rhodesia, a solution requiring the two powers to agree upon the western frontier of Barotseland since its ruler, Lewanika, had granted a concession to the British South Africa Company. More than half a century later, immediately prior to Zambian independence, the Zambian government rejected the Company's assessment of the original eastern limits of Lewanika's dominions, since the Company claimed rights to the minerals of the Copperbelt by virtue of its concessions with Lewanika. On both occasions, a great mass of writing poured forth from the various parties involved, each hoping to validate its own position; for that reason, much of it was tendentious and unreliable.[11]

The problem is unusually difficult because the Lozi did not send princes or senior councillors to govern outlying provinces. Because the Lozi were not threatened by powerful tribes until about the middle of the nineteenth century, and because trade with the Valley was advantageous to many smaller tribes outside it, such direct rule was not considered necessary. Moreover, no king wished to give a potential rival such an obvious opportunity either to establish a secessionist state or to band his subjects together against himself. Outside the Valley, therefore, as for example among the Subiya of Sesheke and the Nkoya of Mankoya, Lozi influence was exerted through *mandumeleti*, Lozi indunas representing the King of Barotseland. So far as we can tell, these representative indunas attempted to exert only so much influence over the area to which they were assigned as to ensure a regular supply of tribute and, perhaps, slaves, to the Valley. Behind them, as their presence constantly attested, lay the sanction of a punitive Lozi military expedition should the expected tribute not be forthcoming.[12]

Like company officials in the 1890s, Lozi informants make extravagant claims as to the extent of the area to which representative indunas were despatched.[13] Yet none of these sources, nor indeed even the royal family itself, have ever suggested that the Lamba people, the aboriginal tribe of the Copperbelt, fell under the Lozi sphere of influence.[14] Nor does it seem, as Lozi say, that permanent residents were attached to the Lunda and Luvale peoples to the north, to all the communities of the Ila and Tonga to the south-east, or to the Mbunda west of the Mashi (Kwando) River, though it is likely that the stronger Lozi did undertake sporadic raids, usually successful, for cattle, tribute and slaves among these tribes.[15] If they did not quite fall within the system of indirect rule, then, they were nevertheless regarded by the Lozi as being within their sphere of influence. Moreover, the evidence is persuasive that representative indunas were stationed in several areas which, under colonial rule, were excised from Lozi jurisdiction: the Hook of the Kafue River, the area between the Mashi River and the 22nd parallel, the Caprivi Strip, and the Zambesi River between Kazangula and Livingstone. The Zambesi between these two latter points was the main entrance to Barotseland from the south, and as all white travellers who attempted to cross the river between 1865 and 1885 discovered, it was effectively controlled by representatives of the Lozi King.

This, then, we presume, was the kingdom of Barotseland over which the great Mulambwa reigned—and ruled—for, so far as we can determine, almost half a century. That he ruled until his death from natural causes at a very old age is eloquent testimony to the potential for stability inherent in the structure of the state, if its institutions were controlled by a King with great wisdom, shrewdness and justice; that is to say, if he satisfied the royal family and important indunas by timely grants of land and suitable promotions and by seeking their advice before taking important decisions (such as, for example, undertaking a raiding party or making an appointment), if he properly preserved the traditions and prestige of the nation, and if he were able to check the ambitions of those not thus satisfied.

On the other hand, that potential instability was equally intrinsic in the institutional structure was reflected in the struggle for the succession between his two sons which followed Mulambwa's death. Silumelume was in fact chosen by the council of the nation, but he was soon assassinated, perhaps on the instructions of his brother Mubukwanu, who thereupon succeeded him.[16] But the fraticidal rivalry had so shattered national unity that only the followers of Mubukwanu rallied behind him against the invading Kololo,[17] and, according to the royal family, when the invasion appeared imminent, 'Mubukwanu sent messengers to those of the Barotse people who refused to recognize him, to tell them to stop fighting and killing each other, because the nation's enemies had arrived'.[18]

The implication that a unified nation might have withstood the Kololo attack is obviously a more palatable explanation to the Lozi for their crushing defeat than the logical alternative, that the size and strength of their empire has been exaggerated.

Yet even had the Lozi kingdom been as great as they enjoy believing, which is not likely, it is doubtful that it would have been a match for the Kololo.

The Kololo were a powerful Sotho group which migrated from the Transorangia area of South Africa to escape the turbulence which resulted from the military revolution of Shaka Zulu. Under their remarkable leader, Sebituane, they adopted a highly centralized political and military organization which soon forced the Lozi, internally divided and militarily much weaker, into retreat. During the early years of the 1840s, Sebituane organized a systematic campaign of conquest north from the Zambesi, through which, despite sporadic but ineffectual Lozi opposition organized by King Mubukwanu, he extended Kololo hegemony over Barotseland as far the northern edge of the Barotse Valley.

Twice during this period the Kololo had to face attacks from south-east of the river by Mzilikazi's Ndebele, and, though successful, Sebituane concluded that the stability of his new empire depended upon winning the loyalty of the defeated Lozi. He therefore integrated important Lozi into his administration, and decided to spare the lives of several members of the royal family including Sibeso and Sipopa, sons of King Mulambwa. In consequence, they and many of their dependents reconciled themselves to a ruler who, though alien, appeared to be liberal and just.[19]

But by no means did all Lozi become collaborators. Imbua, another son of Mulambwa, fled with his followers to Nyengo country along the present Angola–Zambian border. Mubukwanu himself escaped with his son Imasiku to Lukulu, where the King was poisoned in mysterious circumstances. Imasiku, now ruler-in-exile, was soon attacked by Sebituane's forces and was forced to flee. Moving north-east, he and his followers crossed the Kabompo River to hide east of the Manyinga River in what came to be known as the Lukwakwa. The Lozi royal family was thus split into three groups, each of which, when and if the Kololo were expelled from their nation, would inevitably try to assert the right of its own leader to claim the kingship.[20]

The occupation, however, meant far more than an eventual conflict over the succession, for the Kololo made significant changes in the structure of Lozi society. Above all, they disregarded the *makolo* as the key mechanism of the administration and political organization, substituting for it the simpler device of territorial divisions. Moreover, Sebituane distributed large tracts of land to his own followers, much of which was apparently reclaimed by Lozi who had no legitimate right to it after the Kololo were defeated, thus creating considerable hostility between them and the self-professed rightful owners.[21] Finally, the Kololo language, a variant of Sesuto, became the *lingua franca* of the kingdom; language can of course have important social consequences, and it may have acted as a unifying factor in Barotseland, and may have introduced new concepts into Lozi life, but these questions cannot yet be answered.

In order to secure their new empire against Ndebele invasion, the Kololo desperately needed guns. In building up an adequate arsenal, their policy was characterized by complete pragmatism. Sebituane traded Lozi as slaves in exchange for weapons to Mambari half-castes from the west, Arabs from the east, and to Silva Porto, the famous Portuguese slave trader and the first white man to enter Barotseland.[22] Similarly, Sebituane warmly welcomed David Livingstone when the missionary appeared in 1851. 'He had the idea', Livingstone realized, 'that our teaching was chiefly the art of shooting and other European arts, and that by our giving him guns he would thereby procure peace', since the Ndebele would be 'deterred from continuing their unwelcome visits'.[23]

Sebituane's son and successor, Sekeletu, later made the point more explicitly: in 1860 he begged Livingstone and his family to remain and live with his people 'as Mosilikatse [Mzilikazi] would not attack a place where the daughter of his friend Moffat [Livingstone's father-in-law and a favourite missionary of Mzilikazi] was living'.[24] For this reason, Sekeletu had already attempted to use Livingstone as an ambassador to the Lozi royals in exile in the north.[25] The missionary's efforts toward this end proved futile, however, perhaps as a result of the serious internal conflicts which, between 1855 and 1860, had broken out in both the Kololo and Lozi camps.

In the north, Imbua, the son of Mulambwa who had fled to Nyengo country, had attacked his half-brother Imasiku and his supporters at the Lukwakwa. Beaten off, Imbua returned to his Nyengo exile,[26] where those who had replaced him in his absence fled in fear to the Kololo; they included among their number Litia, another son of Mulambwa, and his son Lubosi (later Lewanika). In the next few years, however, most of these men were murdered by the Kololo. By 1863, only two members of the royal family, including Lubosi, remained alive in Barotseland. During the same period, internecine rivalries among the exiles led to the murder of Imasiku and the installation of Sipopa, yet another son of Mulambwa, in his place as Lozi King-in-exile.[27]

The strains within the Kololo camp at the same time were even more serious, undermining as they did the invaders' hegemony on the Upper Zambesi. To a very large extent, this was the responsibility of Sekeletu, Sebituane's son who succeeded when his father died in 1851. It is true that Sekeletu consistently pursued Sebituane's shrewd policy of attempting to use Livingstone to prevent wars with both the Ndebele and the exiled Lozi. Not all his actions were, however, as rationally conceived. He contracted a horrible illness, probably leprosy, and became morbidly possessed by the belief that he had been bewitched.[28] Perhaps for this reason he reversed his father's prudent policies and took only Kololo wives, created only Kololo chiefs, and chose only Kololo advisers.[29] Yet even of these he was suspicious, fearing his death at the hands of those wishing to succeed him. He therefore had murdered not only most Lozi royals but many of his important councillors as well.[30]

Sekeletu's brutal reign has as its most important function the reconciliation of those Lozi remaining in Barotseland with those who had fled to the Lukwakwa.[31] To be sure, it is possible that a united Kololo ruling class might have been able to check a Lozi uprising. But the bloody power struggle consequent upon Sekeletu's death in 1863 irrevocably undermined Kololo might. Grasping the opportunity, the Lukwakwa exiles organized an armed attack against the occupiers of their country, timed to coincide exactly with an uprising of their kin still in Barotseland. The plan worked perfectly; the Kololo were utterly defeated, and in the following weeks virtually all Kololo males were slaughtered.[32] Women and children were, however, spared, some of the former being enslaved, although many were taken in marriage by Lozi men, one result of which being that the Kololo language remained the *lingua franca* of the liberated kingdom.[33]

Liberation, however, as other Africans discovered a century later, by no means meant salvation. The unity of purpose which the Lozi were able to show in the face of a common enemy was soon shattered as a result of a host of new problems which now presented themselves: the return of the emigrés, rights to land, reconstruction of the political system, struggles for the throne and for the senior indunaships, the continuing threat of the Ndebele, and, not least, the question of how to deal with the white traders, hunters and missionaries who were beginning to seek access to the kingdom. In their attempts to come to grips with these problems, inevitable disagreements and disputes among the Lozi leaders over the succeeding three decades certainly endangered the stability of the state.

Yet the turbulence of this period must not be exaggerated. The hysterical accounts by the first white missionaries of a savage state saved from its own destruction by the intervention of the gospel and 'European civilization', hardly squares with the known data. Sipopa, after all, ruled for twelve years; Mwanawina, it is true, was deposed after fewer than three years; Lewanika was in power for seven years before rebels forced him to flee, and once he regained the throne a year later, he retained it (albeit with some difficulty) for another dozen years before the first officer of the British South Africa Company permanently settled in Barotseland.

Although he began by murdering those Lozi who refused to recognize him as King,[34] and had to fight off a serious attempt to depose him in 1870,[35] the first half of Sipopa's twelve-year reign was largely stable and popular. He and his Ngambela, Njekwa, the hero of the rebellion against the Kololo, agreed that the Ndebele still constituted the greatest threat to the nation's security. To meet this threat, weapons were imperative, yet the obvious source of guns was effectively closed to them. For the Mambari traders wished to exchange guns for slaves, while the Lozi wished to use captured slaves as workers in the Barotse Valley.

Like the Kololo, therefore, the Lozi rulers turned in their need to a white man—one of the very few they were prepared to allow into their kingdom. George Westbeech was an English trader who, during the 1860s, worked among the Ndebele where he gained the confidence of Mzilikazi and his successor Lobengula. In 1871, with elephants rapidly disappearing from the country south of the Zambesi, Westbeech and his partner George Blockley appeared on the Zambesi, where they were welcomed by Sipopa who quickly realized their usefulness in serving Lozi ends. For Westbeech's good relations with Lobengula probably made him, like Livingstone, seem capable of preventing Ndebele raids on Barotseland. He was, moreover, a source of firearms for the Lozi, and preferred in exchange for his guns ivory, a commodity then in abundance in Barotseland. For these reasons, Sipopa and his successors allowed Westbeech a virtual monopoly of trade in the kingdom for almost two decades.[36]

In the event, however, Sipopa's mortal enemies proved to be internal. His relations with his new Ngambela, Mowa Mamili, who replaced Njekwa in 1872, were strained from the outset. A number of petty indunas were now beginning to turn against him in response to promises by Mwanawina, a paternal grandson of Mulambwa, of important promotions were he to become king.[37] Moreover, Sipopa himself seems to have grown generally unpopular. He was at worst considered cruel and capricious, at best indifferent; he 'had no ideas', a missionary was later told, 'above hunting, selling ivory and amusing himself, the care of the country being a secondary consideration with him'.[38]

By 1876, Westbeech was able to report that 'the disposition to revolt and the determination to dethrone the King was fast gaining ground among the chiefs. . . .'[39] The danger to the King had increased since the estranged indunas now found a leader in the Ngambela. Sipopa and Mowa Mamili both mobilized their forces, but before the two armies met the King was assassinated by one of his bodyguards who was in the service of his enemies.[40]

Sipopa dead, Mowa Mamili supported Mwanawina's candidature as successor to the throne. Mwanawina apparently enjoyed considerable popularity and his appointment was approved by the leading councillors. Little is recorded of his brief reign, and not much more is recalled in oral tradition. He seems to have made two key errors which led to his downfall.

Mowa Mamili, considering himself a king-maker, is said to have tried to usurp excessive powers to himself; as a result, Mwanawina had him, his children, and his elder brother put to death. The murder of the Ngambela apparently made other indunas fear for their own lives, and these early seeds of tension soon bloomed into outright hostility as nepotism became rife in the administration. Mwanawina came from the Senanga district (that is, he was a 'southerner', considering the flood plain as 'Barotseland proper' or *Bulozi*), and began distributing important titles as well as land to his southern kin. The latter soon demanded that the people of the north be excluded from all positions of power, and finally order the King to kill all 'northern' indunas.[41]

With this, the indunas of the north, led by Mataa, a minor but ambitious councillor, and Numwa, a famous Lozi warrior, assembled and armed their supporters, and succeeded in driving the King from the country. When Mwanawina and his soldiers returned the following year (1879), they discovered that the army of the new king, Lubosi, was prepared for them. Mwanawina's warriors suffered great casualties and soon retreated. The former king managed to escape and died in exile.[42]

In the same year that Lubosi became King, François Coillard of the Paris Missionary Society first arrived in Barotseland. Lubosi (later Lewanika) died in office in 1916; Coillard became one of the two most important white men in Barotseland, a position he maintained until his death in 1904. The year 1878 is thus a climacteric in Lozi history, and may be said to have ushered in the modern historical period.

## REFERENCES

1. This is the broad conclusion reached on the basis of Lozi oral tradition by myself as well as by Mutumba Mainga, 'The Origin of the Lozi: Some Oral Traditions', and L. S. Muuka, 'The Colonization of Barotseland in the 17th Century', in E. Stokes and R. Brown (ed.), *The Zambesian Past: Studies in Central African History* (Manchester, 1966); Max Gluckman, 'The Lozi of Barotseland in North-Western Rhodesia', in E. Colson and M. Gluckman, *Seven Tribes of British Central Africa* (Oxford, 1951), pp. 2–4; C. G. Trapnell and J. Clothier, *The Soils, Vegetation and Agricultural Systems*

16 THE ELITES OF BAROTSELAND

*of North-Western Rhodesia* (Lusaka, 1937), p. 48. For other interpretations, see J. D. Clark, *Pre-History of Southern Africa* (London, 1959), p. 291, and I. G. Cunnison (ed. and trans.), *Historical Traditions of the Eastern Lunda* (Rhodes–Livingstone Institute Communications No. 23, 1962).

2. Gluckman, *op. cit.*, pp. 7–8.

3. Mr. Mbanga Mutemwa.

4. Adolph Jalla, *Litaba za Sicaba sa Malozi*, first printed 1909 and translated as *The History of the Barotse Nation* (Lusaka, 1921).

5. Gluckman, *op. cit.*, pp. 2–3.

6. Max Gluckman, *The Ideas in Barotse Jurisprudence* (New Haven, 1965), p. 57.

7. This very brief summary of the essentials of the Lozi political system is largely based on the extensive writings of Gluckman, especially his chapter on 'The Lozi' in *Seven Tribes; Jurisprudence*, ch. 2; *Economy of the Central Barotse Plain*, Rhodes–Livingstone Papers No. 7 (Livingstone 1941), pp. 94–101; *Politics, Law and Ritual in Tribal Society* (Oxford, 1965), pp. 144–7; *Essays on Lozi Land and Royal Property* (Livingstone, 1943), pp. 13–14; A. F. B. Glennie, 'The Barotse System of Government', *Journal of African Administration*, Vol. IV, No. 1, Jan. 1952; Report on the Barotse by Colin Harding to CO, 30 April, 1901, CO African South 659.

8. These ceremonies continue to this day. Lewanika established Lealui as the permanent flood plain capital between 1878 and 1884, and his son, Yeta III, built Limalunga, the present capital during the flood, in the 1930s.

9. Gluckman, *Seven Tribes*, pp. 26–9.

10. Gluckman, *Politics, Law and Ritual*, pp. 142–4; *Economy*, pp. 29, 33, 90, 93, 104; *Seven Tribes*, p. 14; Report from Coillard, 25 July 1902, in *News from Barotseland*, No. 17, Dec., 1902; F. S. Arnot, *Garenganze, or Seven Years Pioneer Mission Work in Central Africa* (London, 1889), p. 73. For an illuminating account of the means by which a king was able to enhance (and, by implication, to undermine) the status of a commoner, see François Coillard, *On The Threshold of Central Africa*, trans. by C. W. Mackintosh (2nd edition, London, 1902), p. 444.

11. Of the voluminous material on the dispute between Britain and Portugal, the most important is A. St. H. Gibbons, *Africa from South to North Through Marotseland* (London, 1904); Colin Harding, *In Remotest Barotseland* (London, 1904); Report by Harding to CO, 30 April, 1901, CO African South 659, pp. 213–37, 267–70; Report by Major Goold-Adams, 27 Aug., 1897, CO, African South 552, pp. 146–64; Goold-Adams to FO 7 Feb., 1897, FO 403, Vol. 245, No. 108. For a devastating critical attack on what he considers the serious distortions of Harding and Gibbons, see C. M. N. White, 'The Ethno-History of the Upper Zambesi', *African Studies*, Vol. 21, No. 1, 1962, pp. 23–4.

12. Gluckman, *Essays on Lozi Land*, pp. 13–14; Memorandum on Barotse Representative Indunas by Frank Worthington, 5 June, 1908, CO, African South 899.

13. Messrs. Mupatu, Simalumba and M. Mutemwa.

14. See The Frontiers of the Barotse Kingdom as defined in a Council

by King Lewanika and recorded by François Coillard, 25 June, 1890, reproduced in Maxwell Stamp Associates, *op. cit.*, Vol. 2, pp. 24–6.

15. Report of the Commission Appointed to Examine . . . the Past and Present Relations of the Paramount Chief of the Barotse Nation and the Chiefs Resident in the Balovale District. . . . (Luska, 1939), pp. 1–53; White, *op. cit.*; E. W. Smith and A. M. Dale, *The Ila-Speaking Peoples of Northern Rhodesia* (2 Vols., London, 1920), Vol. 1; also from an analysis of the evidence cited in fn. 11.

16. Jalla, *op. cit.*, pp. 17–18.

17. Mr. Zaza.

18. Jalla, *op. cit.*, p. 19.

19. J. D. Omer-Cooper, *The Zulu Aftermath: A Nineteenth Century Revolution in Bantu Africa* (London, 1966), p. 115; A. T. Bryant, *Olden Times in Zululand and Natal* (London, 1929); E. Ritter, *Shaka Zulu* (London, 1955); Editors' introduction, Stokes and Brown, *op cit.*, p. xviii; White, *op. cit.*, p. 25; E. W. Smith, 'Sebituane and the Makololo', *African Studies*, Vol. 15, No. 2, 1956, p. 67–9; David Livingstone, *Missionary Travels and Researches in South Africa* (London, 1857), pp. 86–7, 186, 197; Messrs. Simalumba and Zaza; William Waddell's Diary, 27 Dec., 1885. NAR Hist. mss. WA 1/1/2.

20. Jalla, *op. cit.*, pp. 19–20; White, *op. cit.*, p. 18; Smith, *op. cit.*, pp. 69–70; Messrs. Zaza, Mupatu and Simalumba.

21. Gluckman, *Jurisprudence*, pp. 69–70; this point was not made by Livingstone, Jalla or any of my Lozi informants.

22. Jalla, *op. cit.*, pp. 28–9; George Seaver, *David Livingstone, His Life and Letters* (London, 1957), p. 141; Livingstone, *op. cit.*, p. 92; Isaac Shapera (ed.), *Livingstone's Private Journals*, 1851–53 (London, 1960), p. 16; W. E. Oswell, *William Cotton Oswell* (2 Vols., London, 1900), Vol. 1, p. 245; James MacQueen, 'Journey of Silva Porto with the Arabs from Benguela to Ibo and Mocambique through Africa', *Journal of the Royal Geographical Society*, Vol. 30, 1860; H. M. Hole, *The Passing of the Black Kings* (London, 1932) p. 292; V. W. Brelsford, *Generation of Men: The European Pioneers of Northern Rhodesia* (Luska, 1965), p. 6. No Lozi informant remembered Silva Porto.

23. Schapera, *op. cit.*, 16–17, 25.

24. Cited in Seaver, *op. cit.*, p. 372. For an elaboration of this point, see article by Gluckman in *The Listener*, 22 Sept., 1955.

25. Livingstone, *op. cit.*, p. 177

26. *Ibid.*, p. 497; Jalla, *op. cit.*, p. 35.

27. Jalla, *op. cit.* It is possible that not all those Lozi who claimed to be descendants of Mulambwa could justify their claims. But no Lozi informant challenged them.

28. James I. MacNair (ed.), *Livingstone's Travels* (London, 1956), p. 227.

29. *Ibid.*; Jalla, *op. cit.*, p. 33.

30. Seaver, op. cit., p. 372; David and Charles Livingstone, *Narrative of an Expedition to the Zambesi and its Tributaries* (London, 1865), p. 272.

31. Messrs. Mupatu, Simalumba and Njekwa. Mr. Njekwa is the grandson of the Njekwa who led the successful uprising against the Kololo.

32. Jalla, *op. cit.*, pp. 33-4.

33. Messrs. Njekwa, Zaza and Simalumba.

34. Jalla, *op. cit.*, p. 34 and Mr. Simalumba. One of the most serious problems in the reconstruction of Lozi history is that literally every living literate Lozi has read Jalla's history, which was largely based on the evidence of Lewanika and his closest advisers. It follows that an interpretation by an informant which agrees with that of Jalla cannot necessarily be taken as independent confirmation of Jalla. Nevertheless, I shall in such instances record the existence of both sources, if only to indicate that a source outside the royal family shares (but does not necessarily corroborate) its version of a given situation. When an informant disagrees with Jalla, the conflicting testimonies must be assessed functionally in an attempt to determine whether the former of Jalla's informants among the royal family had more to gain from a particular interpretation; as will emerge, however, the conflicting interests are not always apparent.

35. Gluckman, *Jurisprudence*, p. 69; Jalla, *op. cit.*, pp. 36-7; White, *op. cit.*, p. 19.

36. L. H. Gann, *A History of Northern Rhodesia, Early Days to 1953* (London, 1964), p. 41; Editor's Introduction to E. C. Tabler (ed.), *Trade and Travel in Early Barotseland: the Diaries of George Westbeech and Captain Norman MacLeod* (London, 1863), pp. 4-7; S. Le Roux, *Pioneers and Sportsmen of South Africa, 1760-1890* (Salisbury, 1939), pp. 143-5; Emil Holub, *Seven Years in South Africa* (2 Vols. London, 1881), Vol. 2, pp. 103-4.

37. Mr. Mupatu.

38. Jalla, *op. cit.*, p. 38.

39. Cited in Holub, *op. cit.*, p. 134. Holub was a Czech missionary doctor who Sipopa, on Westbeech's recommendation, allowed to remain in Sesheke for several months in 1875.

40. *Ibid.*, pp. 284-5; Jalla, *op. cit.*, pp. 37-9; and Messrs. Njekwa and Zaza.

41. Messrs. Zaza and Simalumba. Gluckman was also told that the conflict between northerners and southerners led to Mwanawina's downfall; see his *Jurisprudence*, p. 69.

42. Jalla, *op. cit.*, pp. 39-40, and Messrs. Mupatu and Simalumba.

# CHAPTER II

# LUBOSI

Lubosi, later called Lewanika, was born on the western fringes of Barotseland in the 1840s. At the moment of his birth, his father, Litia, son of the great King Mulambwa, was taking refuge from the Kololo invaders; the name Lubosi means 'the escaped one'. Around 1856, Litia decided to ally himself with the Kololo, and returned with his family to the Valley to join Sekeletu. Litia was among the Lozi royals later killed by Sekeletu, but Lubosi was spared. On Sipopa's accession to the throne, he accepted the young man as a member of the royal family, and adopted him as part of his personal entourage,[1] perhaps because he was one of the few remaining descendants of Mulumbwa.[2]

Lubosi appears to have been implicated neither in Sipopa's assassination nor Mwanawina's deposition. After the former's death, he returned from Sesheke to his own village north of Libonda, where he was when the latter was forced to flee the country. Years later, the mature Lewanika reminisced 'with pleasure' about these good years, when he could carve and hunt and be free of the responsibilities of office.[3]

After Mwanawina's escape, the National Council assembled to select his successor. Some of its members may have supported Sikufele of the Lukwakwa, nephew of the late Imbua,[4] but the two major candidates were Lubosi and Musiwa, younger brother of the deposed Mwanawina. Lubosi believed that his rival was sponsored by induna Mataa,[5] but Lubosi's chief supporter, the older and more respected induna Nalabutu, persuaded the Council that Musiwa, if chosen, would wreak vengeance on all those who had helped drive out his brother.[6] For his part, Lubosi is said to have been considered a generous and popular young man, and, no less importantly, had the advantage of 'belonging' to both the southern and northern sections of the nation, since his mother had been born in Senanga and his father near Lealui.[7] In short, as one informant put it, Lubosi was 'really the only man of royal birth who had nothing against him',[8] and in August, 1878, the young prince—then about thirty years old—was formally installed as King.

If, as Lozi tradition suggests, the new King was an innocent at the moment of his succession, he acquired the proper posture of a monarch with remarkable rapidity. Serpa Pinto, a Portuguese army officer who reached Lealui, the capital which Lubosi was in the process of constructing, very shortly after his installation, was struck by his regal bearing and his regalia. Lubosi was wearing, he noted,

> a cashmere mantle over a coloured shirt . . . drawers of coloured cashmere, displaying Scotch thread stockings, perfectly white, and he had on a pair of low well polished shoes . . . and a soft gray hat adorned with two large and beautiful ostrich-feathers.[9]

Moreover, Lubosi was fully aware that he was the third King of Barotseland within a period of three years, and quickly took steps which he believed would preserve him from the fate of his two predecessors. The most immediate threat to his position came from Mwanawina, from whom an attack could be expected at any time; the King refused permission to François Coillard, a French missionary, to enter the country on the grounds of 'the civil war which was threatening it'.[10] To secure his position, Lubosi appointed his known supporters to the important offices in the kingdom. He had the Kuta agree to replace Mwanawina's Ngambela, Ngenda, with his own preference, Silumbu.[11] His sister Matauka was appointed Mulena Mukwae at Nalolo, several indunas were promoted to higher titles, and a number of commoners were made minor indunas.[12]

The King's next step, according to Gluckman, was to initiate the restoration of the *makolo* system. The Kololo had ignored the *makolo* system during their rule, and neither Sipopa nor Mwanawina had tried to revive it. Lubosi presumably believed that Sipopa and Mwanawina were the victims of ambitious indunas who, because the *makolo* system was not functioning, were able to raise an army of supporters in opposition to his predecessors. By reverting to the traditional Lozi system, Lubosi is said to have hoped to deprive potentially subversive councillors of a corporate group of followers. Gluckman also states that the King proposed to allow 'people' to reclaim land which had been controlled by their ancestors but which had been improperly claimed by some 'great councillors' after the Kololo had been overthrown;[13] 'people' presumably refers to minor indunas who were unable to resist the claims of the 'great councillors' but, if Gluckman is correct, it is not clear why Lubosi wished to ingratiate the former at the expense of the latter.

Lozi themselves speak of a different reform which the King attempted to institute. Lubosi is said to have been under the influence of Nalabutu, a very old and very conservative induna who supported him for the kingship in the hope of gaining influence over the young man. Apparently he was successful, for Lubosi apparently had much respect for Nalabutu's great age and experience,[14] but this may be because the old man offered the kind of advice the young King was anxious to have. Lubosi certainly may have learnt from Nalabutu the value to the reigning King of the *makolo* system, and Lozi informants agree that it was Nalabutu who inspired the King's plan to have indunas undertake physical labour. Nalabutu's argument was the indunas should not raid other tribes for slaves to till their fields; they should rather cultivate their own gardens in order to increase their self-respect while maintaining physical fitness. Lubosi apparently went so far as to demand that members of his personal bodyguard, which included a number of famed warriors, till some of the King's land.[15] We may assume, however, that the self-respect and physical condition of his indunas were not the King's primary motive for adopting Nalabutu's suggestion; more realistically, it may simply be considered a tactic for minimizing the number of legitimate occasions they had to collect as an armed band.

These, then, were the means by which the new King hoped to achieve his overriding objective, his own self-preservation. But inextricably connected to this goal was the preservation of his kingdom from another external invasion. To this end, a series of alliances, or at least agreements, with outside powers seemed necessary, even if they meant an end to the traditional

Lozi policy of isolationism. For in these early years of Lubosi's reign, no fewer than four alien sources—two European and two African—offered themselves as allies of the Lozi ruler. It soon became evident to him that although all of them could not be accepted, neither could all of them be rejected. Lubosi's decision would rest on his assessment of which power would provide the maximum protection from outside interference with the minimum infringement of the King's own sovereignty. Indeed, it was realistic for the King to assume that a foreign ally might support the King against internal as well as external attacks, and the question therefore became one of potential conflict between the faction of the ruling class supporting the King and the one which soon arose wishing to see his deposition.

It is probable that Lozi foreign policy at the time of Lubosi's accession was, in general, based on the assumption that the greatest external danger to the Lozi state emanated from Lobengula's Ndebele, and that the Ngwato of Khama (in modern Botswana) were potential allies. As we have seen, throughout the years of Kololo rule the Ndebele remained a serious threat to Barotseland. Serpa Pinto reported in 1878 that King Lubosi was 'not on the best of terms with the Matabele',[16] and if this was not because a direct Ndebele attack on the Barotse Valley was feared, it must at least have been based on Ndebele raids on the Ila, Tonga and Toka peoples whom the Lozi considered to be within their own sphere of influence. The Lozi found, therefore, that they shared with the Ngwato a common interest in containing Ndebele power. Although it is not clear which side initiated them, contacts between the Lozi and the Ngwato rulers apparently began shortly after Sipopa became King and continued under Lubosi.[17] The Lozi were therefore in a position to know that Khama had applied in 1876 for British protection against the Boers,[18] and that he wished as much as they to end the threat of Ndebele raids.[19]

Khama and Lobengula thus represented two diametrically opposed policies for dealing with the ever-increasing number of white men who were appearing in south-central Africa: the first was to find an accommodation with these men and, hopefully, manipulate them and harness the power they embodied in the interests of oneself and one's state; the second was to resist them on the grounds that their superior power could result only in the undermining of one's own power and of one's state. In fact, as the subsequent history of the Ndebele, the Ngwato and the Lozi all testify, neither resistance nor accommodation prevented the effective usurpation by white power of the sovereignty of their respective nations. But since this fact could hardly be foreseen at the time, the choice between the two conflicting policies appeared critical.

Given the traditional fear in Barotseland of the Ndebele, it was perhaps predictable that the Lozi would reject Lobengula and the policy he represented. Yet there is evidence that Lubosi briefly considered an alliance with the Ndebele. According to Frederick Arnot, a missionary who lived in Lealui between 1882 and 1884, during this period

> the chief of the Matabele sent a powerful emissary to Lubosi with presents of shields and spears, inviting him to become his blood brother and to join with the Matabele in resisting the invading white man. Lubosi was greatly delighted with the shields and inclined to accept Lobengula's advances. I was able to persuade Lubosi that ... Khama was a better man to make friends with than Lobengula .... Lubosi immediately decided to write to Khama asking for his friendship. ... I wrote the letter for him. ... Khama replied to Lubosi ... that he must join with him, not against the white man, but against the white man's drink if he wished to be Khama's friend.[20]

It was, of course, typical of the Europeans in Africa at this period to magnify their own influence on the peoples they encountered, and it is difficult to credit Arnot's assertion that he talked Lubosi out of one alliance into another. It is surely more reasonable that, in the first place, Lozi distrust of the Ndebele was too deep-rooted to allow them seriously to consider an alliance between the two nations, and, in the second, that Lubosi had already understood the futility of a direct conflict with white power. Indeed, there is evidence that, on the contrary, he was fully aware of the utility both to his own position and to the security of his nation could he gain access to white guns, white trading goods and white technology. To do so, however, was no simple task, for it seems that if his councillors shared his distrust of the Ndebele, some of them were equally suspicious of the white man, in part because they feared for the sovereignty of their nations, partly because they feared white power would buttress the King's own position. Moreover, there existed the problem of determining which white men to deal with. Both these reasons help explain the ambivalent attitude towards Europeans of which so many of them during these years complained.

The King, for example, wished to befriend and work closely with the first European to enter Barotseland after his accession, Serpa Pinto, a Portuguese army officer, but pressure from the Ngambela and Kuta forced him to expel Pinto from the kingdom. So far as the episode can be reconstructed, Lubosi was anxious to procure weapons and ammunition from the Portuguese, while the Lozi aristocracy feared he would monopolize these arms and thereby consolidate his personal position. Clearly the King was not, in this early stage of his reign, prepared to flaunt the wishes of his Kuta, and reluctantly acceded to the demand that Pinto leave Barotseland.[21]

The split within the Lozi ruling class was again revealed when its members attempted to decide whether to permit the entry into the kingdom of François Coillard, a zealous and earnest French Protestant missionary. Born in 1834, Coillard as a young man decided to join the Société des Missions Evangéliques, or, as the Lozi call it, the Paris Missionary Society. Coillard and his Scottish wife Christina Mackintosh were assigned to the PMS's mission station in Basutoland in 1858, where they remained until, nineteen years later, they left to lead a party of four Sotho evangelists to seek a new station in territory controlled by the Ndebele. Ejected by Lobengula from his sphere of influence, the tiny band made its way to Ngwato territory where Chief Khama strongly encouraged Coillard to proceed to Barotseland where Sesuto was understood. Khama himself sent an envoy to his friend Lubosi to inform him of the party's arrival. Although Coillard believed that Khama, as a Christian, was eager to further the spread of the Gospel, we may surely assume that the shrewd ruler saw this as an opportunity to establish a new link with the Lozi as against the threatening Ndebele.[22]

Coillard's party reached the Zambesi in July, 1878. Once permission was received from the senior indunas at Sesheke, the three Lozi representatives allowed them to cross the river and proceed north. But at Sesheke they had to stop. For reasons that are unknown, Khama's envoy failed to reach Lubosi, who was unaware of Coillard's arrival. A new message had therefore to be forwarded to the King and a reply awaited, for though the Sesheke indunas treated the mission with cordiality, they refused to allow it to continue to Lealui without Lubosi's permission.[23]

Serpa Pinto was still in the capital when the Kuta met to discuss Coillard's request. According to his account, a 'hot discussion' ensued, in which there was a considerable difference of opinion. He did not, however, suggest the composition of the opposing sides, though he specifically mentioned that induna Mataa was most vocal in opposing Coillard's admittance. The Kuta finally agreed to refuse Coillard's request, at least for the moment.[24] The missionary received two replies from Lubosi. In the first, the King 'politely refused to let me enter the country', Coillard reported, 'under pretext of the civil war [with Mwanawina] which was threatening it. He sent me a tusk of ivory at the same time, evidently mistaking me for a trader'. In the second, Coillard claimed, Lubosi 'expressed a great desire to receive us'. He suggested that if Coillard wished to leave the country before the rains began in December,

> it must only be on the condition that he returned before the beginning of winter in June. . . . He himself was building his town [Lealui] just now but by that time he would be in a position to receive me. He was already giving orders that, on our return, we should be brought before him without delay.[25]

Highly encouraged, Coillard returned to South Africa and left for Europe, where he attempted to raise funds to support his proposed Barotseland mission. He did not return to the Upper Zambesi until 1884.

Since Lubosi in fact warmly welcomed Coillard on his return six years later, it is probable that he was not exaggerating the enthusiasm contained in the King's letters. He was almost certainly wrong, however, in believing that the King was interested in him in his capacity as a missionary. Oral tradition is clear that the Lozi at this time were highly suspicious of any

European whose motives in coming among them were not absolutely clear. In practice, this encompassed traders such as Westbeech, and a few other whites who could directly serve the interests of the ruling class, as the Kololo believed Livingstone could do. Lubosi, as Coillard recognized, mistook the missionary for a trader, and an informant told me that 'All they wanted then from a white man was goods and gifts'.[26]

Yet the problem was in fact far more complex than this suggests. For ultimately the white man represented a powerful unknown factor to the Lozi. Contacts with a few whites, and above all with Khama, must have given the Lozi both respect and fear for white power. On the one hand, therefore, Coillard and Serpa Pinto alike represented a potential political threat; on the other, if the might they represented could be harnessed, it would obviously have great attraction. Moreover, Coillard in the first place had been sponsored by the famed Khama, and secondly, had among his party several Sotho evangelists who, he observed, were unfailingly treated with 'respect and esteem'.[27] And the Sotho, after all, were the people from whom the Kololo has sprung.

In short, both Coillard and Serpa Pinto embodied for the Lozi a whole new world of potential allies and potential enemies. It seems likely that Lubosi decided it was worth gambling that he could manipulate them, and their power, for his own ends. For this reason, indunas like Mataa—who soon emerged as the King's greatest enemy—wished to keep them out of the kingdom, although there apparently existed a group of traditionalist councillors, under old Nalabutu, who feared white power not because it might undermine its members' own political ambitions, but because it might destroy the Lozi nation. They were convinced, it is said, that the white man came 'only to steal their country' and to take their land.[28]

In determining which white men should be allowed into Barotseland, George Westbeech played a major role as a result of his influence on the King in these matters. Westbeech had already promised Coillard his support when the missionary returned from Europe. In 1882, he agreed to help Frederick Arnot, a Plymouth Brethren missionary, to enter Barotseland and to prevent a party of Jesuits from doing so; while the latter found themselves unable to rent boats or porters, an easy journey from Sesheke to Lealui was arranged for Arnot.[29] Westbeech acted as interpreter and warmly introduced the missionary to the King, who received Arnot warmly and with generous hospitality.[30]

The missionary remained at the Lozi capital for some eighteen months, and his account of the period makes relatively clear the reason why the King was prepared to allow him to remain. (It does not, however, reveal the attitudes to him of the Kuta members.) As Lubosi explicitly explained to Arnot, the missionary's function was to teach the children of the ruling class 'to read and write, and to know numbers'. For this purpose, he permitted Arnot to open a small school, which was attended by a small number of boys and young men, including the King's eldest son Litia (later King Yeta), one of his 'nephews', and Litia's close friend Mokamba, son of the late Ngambela Njekwa and later himself Lubosi's Ngambela. But only practical subjects could be taught at Arnot's school; Lubosi specifically forbade him to preach the Gospel, which he clearly considered irrelevant.[31]

It is possible that, however great were the constraints placed upon him, Arnot's presence at the capital served to exacerbate the tensions between the King and some of his indunas. We know that by October, 1883, Arnot was beginning to make brief allusions to the conflict within the ruling class. He implied that the capital was almost split between those who supported and those who opposed the King; the former virtually controlled the King, with the latter he quarrelled 'almost daily': 'they taunt each other, and I fear the end will be another king-killing'.[32] Arnot believed that it was Lubosi's fear of being overthrown which had briefly tempted him to accept Lobengula's offer of an alliance.

> Lubosi seemed at this time [Arnot had noted] to be in a very unsettled state of mind; he had many enemies . . . and some powerful rivals. My coming did not satisfy him, for I could not teach his people to make guns and powder, and it seemed [to him] a mockery to bring 'mere words' to a man who needed 'strong friends'.

The King had gone on to remind the missionary of the fate of his two unfortunate predecessors.[33]

Arnot was not exaggerating the amount of opposition which the King faced, and Lubosi was not overstating the precariousness of his position. Each step which he had taken to secure his own safety between 1878 and 1884 had resulted in the creation of a new set of enemies. He had been responsible, in the first three years of his reign, for the murder of Musiwa when he fled the King's wrath; three sons of Sipopa, as such potential rivals for the succession, etc.; and his own brother, whom the King believed was plotting against him.[34] Inevitably, the kin of those murdered desired vengeance, while at the same time were anxious to take steps to preclude their own deaths. Moreover, even those whose lives were not endangered are said to have resented the 'unconstitutional' way in which Lubosi took these measures, that is to say, without first seeking and following the advice of his indunas on the matter.[35]

Those indunas whom Lubosi had dismissed, but not killed, upon taking power, were naturally eager to recover their positions, which meant not merely political influence but status, land, dependants and cattle as well. Some indunas, like Mataa, desired promotions in the hierarchy of councillors' titles. Others, after the Kololo were overthrown, had taken possession of land not formerly attached to them, and naturally resented the proposal to allow such property to be reclaimed by its original owners. A number of the King's bodyguard, led by the renowned warrior Numwa, felt humiliated by Lubosi's demands that they do 'women's work' in the fields.[36] And many indunas must have feared the loss of their corporate group of dependants should the King succeed in re-establishing the ancient 'sector' or *makolo* system of administration.

Finally, the ruling class was divided on the question of its policy towards Europeans. In the cases of Serpa Pinto and Coillard, the Kuta seems to have forced the King to expel white men whom he was prepared to have in the Valley. Some indunas, like Nalabutu, are said to have opposed any and all whites remaining in Barotseland. But since Lubosi's usurpers were anxious to have Coillard settle among them, there must have been another basis for the split, and this, as has already been suggested, was probably the fear among the King's enemies that, with the support of white power, they would be unable to depose him.

For, as Serpa Pinto noted, it was induna Mataa who objected most forcibly to allowing Coillard to visit Lealui in 1878,[37] the same Mataa who in 1884 organized and led the coup against the King. Mataa seems to have been riddled by insecurity, fear and ambition. His resentment of Lubosi began early, although he apparently concealed this fact for some time. Although only a minor induna, he had probably supported Musiwa against Lubosi for the kingship with the expectation of being appointed Musiwa's Ngambela.[38] Thwarted in this ambition, he was not assuaged by the promotion which Lubosi gave him. At the same time, Mataa must have feared that Lubosi might some day take revenge on him, not only because he supported Musiwa, but because the King seems to have believed that it was Mataa's father who had encouraged the Kololo to murder his own father.[39]

Mataa's chief ally in organizing the coup was Numwa. He was one of the King's leading bodyguards, an induna of some seniority, and a warrier of renown. He apparently turned against Lubosi in protest against the new decree compelling indunas to till their own lands, and possibly feared losing some of the land he had controlled since the Kololo were overthrown. It is said too that he was alienated when the King had one of his close relatives at Nalolo murdered.[40]

Lubosi did not minimize the seriousness of the threat represented by Mataa, Numwa and their followers. Arnot referred ominously to the possibility of 'another king-killing' in October, 1883,[41] and in May of the following year, because of increasing rumours of an impending civil war, decided to quit Barotseland.

When I went to say good-bye [to the king, he wrote], he shook hands long and warmly, saying, 'You are my friend, come back very soon. But,' he added in a tone of sadness, 'you may not find me here.'[42]

Lubosi acknowledged that he desperately needed 'strong friends' to protect him from his enemies within the Valley,[43] and he must have been gratified when, in July, 1884, a messenger from Khama arrived in the capital to announce that Coillard was about to reach the Zambesi. Coillard was now seen as the representative not only of the distant white power structure; since the messenger came from Khama, who was supporting

the missionary, Lubosi probably believed that Coillard's presence might act as a deterrent to precipitate action by Mataa
and his followers. For the King sent instructions that Coillard
be brought to the capital 'at once' and canoes were sent to
Sesheke to expedite his passage. According to the missionary,
however, on the very date the canoes arrived,

> the rumour spread that the Matabele had crossed the
> Zambesi, and there was universal panic. . . . All prepared
> to flee. . . . The canoes which were to have brought us to
> the King were laden with ivory to buy powder and guns
> from Mr. Blockley (Westbeech's partner). . . . [44]

Although no invasion in fact took place, the King and much of
the kingdom were diverted from their other concerns, and
Mataa and Numwa might have chosen that propitious moment
to put their plot into effect.

Whatever the immediate cause, late in August, 1884, Mataa's
men surrounded the palace in Lealui, forcing the King to flee.
His supporters in exile included his son Litia, Ngambela
Silumbu, and Litia's friend Mokamba, who were soon followed
by Lubosi's sister Matauka, the Mulena Mukwae of Nalolo,
accompanied by a second group of loyalist indunas and headmen. 'Barotseland is divided,' Matauka informed her brother,
'many of the people, especially those of the south [i.e., the
southern half of the Flood plain], long for you. Let the chief
but return and we will fight for him and slay Mataa.'[45]

This assessment of the division in the country seems to have
been substantially accurate. Although Mataa's allies were
placed in all the offices controlled from Nalolo, he was unable
to subdue the considerable number of opponents of his régime
who remained in the area. That there was more general
hostility to the rebels in the south than in the Lealui area, the
north of the Valley, is not surprising given the traditional
competitive relationship between the two capitals.[46] As one
informant put it, 'The Nalolo people led the opposition to
Mataa because he had not consulted them before overthrowing
the King'.[47] Lubosi's father had been from the north and his
mother from the south, and another informant said that, unlike
his predecessor, he had been 'kind' to the people in both areas.[48]
Jalla's informants told him that, before the rebellion, Mataa

had urged the King to 'make war on the people of the south because they had stood by Mwanawina, but the chief had demurred, saying: "They are just as much my people as any others." This speech won the hearts of the people of the south.'[49]

Whatever their motive, southerners were the first overtly to challenge the legitimacy of the rebellion. A group from the Nalolo–Senanga area marched to Lealui to protest against Lubosi's deposition; threatened by Mataa, they returned to their homes, confirmed enemies of the new régime.[50] Mataa's strength rested on the shrewd and rapid steps which he took to consolidate his position. A rebel, not a revolutionary (following Gluckman's distinction[51]), he dared not antagonize his followers by making himself, a commoner, the King. Only a royal could aspire to the sancrosanct institution of the kingship, and Mataa therefore summoned Tatila Akafuna, grandson of Mulambwa and son of Imbua, from the Lukwakwa where Akafuna was ruler (unrecognized by Lealui) of a small community of Lozi refugees. Mataa, however, intended personally to rule; his King would merely reign. Akafuna, having lived outside the kingdom, lacked the land and the dependants which normally attached to princes, and had therefore no independent power base in Barotseland. He was totally dependent on, and in effect the puppet of, Mataa, who became his Ngambela. Mataa further protected his position by having Afakuna appoint Mataa's followers to the senior indunaships, while he hoped to control the south—the Nalolo–Senanga area —by having Lubosi's sister replaced as Mulena Mukwae of Nalolo by Afakuna's sister, Maibiba. At the same time, he is said to have murdered a large number of the deposed King's kinsmen and supporters,[52] though as we have seen, he did not liquidate all of Lubosi's followers in the south.

Once the machinery of government was in the control of his own people, Mataa urgently sent for Coillard, who was camped with his party at Leshoma.[53] Grasping the moment, Coillard departed immediately, reaching Lealui early in 1885, where, despite the 'desolation' of the ravaged capital,[54] he received a 'grand official reception'. Mataa welcomed the missionary warmly:

. . . it is with joy that we see your faces [the Ngambela

declared], and to hear you say that you have now come, not merely to visit us, but to live among us with your families. . . . The nation is weary; it sighs for peace, it languishes. Here it is; we place it before you; save it. You see, the king is only a child; be his father; uphold him with your counsels.[55]

Mataa then accompanied Coillard to Sefula village, about twenty miles south of Lealui, where he offered a site for a mission station which Coillard accepted. The latter then returned to fetch the rest of his party from Leshoma.[56]

Coillard's meeting with Mataa and Akafuna had been undertaken against the advice of Westbeech, who had warned him that the situation in the Valley was extremely unstable, and that if Lubosi succeeded in retrieving the throne he would obviously resent the fact that the missionary had negotiated with his usurpers.[57] As shall be seen, Coillard later paid for ignoring this prudent advice. Nor was he more sensitive to the real factors which surely led to his warm welcome by Mataa. He was convinced that 'the country is decidedly open to us' because the Lozi needed the word of the Gospel.[58] 'They know we speak of peace,' he wrote, 'and it is that which . . . opens their hearts to us.'[59]

It is true that Coillard consistently emphasized that the bringing of peace—the Lord's peace—was among the major purposes of his mission. Perhaps the Lozi indeed believed that this white man—with his cameras and magic lantern—possessed certain mystical powers by which peace and stability could be achieved. But it is more plausible that Mataa was merely adopting for his own ends Lubosi's tactic of using the missionary to secure his own position. Sponsored by Khama, again accompanied by Sotho evangelists who were once more treated with deference,[60] the representative, so it must have appeared, of the entire white power structure, Coillard must have seemed to Mataa, as he had to Lubosi, the man who was capable of helping him remain in power.

Certainly the stability of the new régime seemed uncertain. After only a short time in Lealui, and with the rebellion barely six months past, Coillard noted that

I cannot rid myself of the impression that a new revolution

is being prepared; it is impossible for Akafuna to remain on the throne for very long . . . . Discontent is already making itself felt. Some regret the expelled king; others think of a new chief.[61]

The missionary believed he understood the basis for the discontent. He described Mataa as being 'blinded by ambition', blatantly manipulating Akafuna, while

The King is a beardless boy, born and brought up in exile. He is a perfect stranger among the tribes who have called him to govern them, and does not yet speak the [local] language. . . . To him power means pleasure, and he occupies himself very little with business.[62]

Militant opposition now indeed became manifest. A band of Lubosi's supporters from the south—the Nalolo–Senanga area—mobilized in March, 1885, and advanced on Lealui but were forced to retreat.[63] In May they struck again but were once more driven off. Not until July, however, did the deposed King himself agree that an expedition of his supporters in exile should return to the Valley. According to an informant, Lubosi would not personally lead this force because he was 'still frightened',[64] and Ngambela Silumbu was instead placed in command.

Near Senanga, the exiles were joined by a contingent of 'southern people'. The combined forces seem to have taken Mataa's men entirely by surprise, for the latter fled north and Silumbu took the capital without a struggle.[65] By November, however, Mataa and Numwa returned to Lealui at the head of a reorganized army. At almost the same time, Lubosi and his sister and their supporters reached the capital to join Silumbu. So far as the very scanty evidence allows a judgment, it appears that the two sides were more or less evenly matched, although Lubosi's army at first seemed to be on the verge of defeat. Lubosi himself later admitted that he was saved only by the intervention of a band of armed Mambari traders, whom he wooed with the promise of special trading privileges in the future. By the end of the day, after seven hours of fierce fighting in which Silumbu, Mataa and Numwa all fell, the issue was resolved, and Lubosi reclaimed his throne.[66]

He now received the sobriquet 'Lewanika'—meaning 'to join, to add together'—but he seems to have been far from convinced that his kingdom was yet adequately 'joined together'. It is said that the bitterness of fifteen months in exile— and perhaps the guilt of having played such an equivocal personal role in the counter-rebellion—left Lewanika 'thirsty for vengeance'.[67] Even my informants who admire him as their greatest King believe that he now acted mercilessly in relentless pursuit of all the members of Mataa's family. They were hunted down, according to one informant, 'like animals', and even Mataa's mother was drowned.[68]

By January, 1885, the King succeeded in dislodging from their positions of power and influence in the Valley, as well as at Sesheke, all those who had supported his usurpers during the rebellion.

As we shall see, Lewanika was profoundly impressed by the traumatic events of the previous year and a half. They seemed to suggest that new circumstances had arisen in which a reign of fifty years, such as Mulambwa had enjoyed, was no longer possible for a Lozi king functioning independently within his personal empire. For isolationism itself was no longer feasible. The external threat from the Ndebele, the increased accessibility of arms, the penetration by white Portuguese from the north-west and white Englishmen and Frenchmen from the south—all tended to weaken those elements in the Lozi political structure which had once allowed Mulambwa to satisfy most of his subjects and to elimate as a threat those whose ambitions were not fulfilled. The successful re-establishment of the *makolo* system was a long-run project; in the short run, it merely alienated, as the King learned to his cost, those indunas who would lose by it their corporate body of followers. He could, therefore, not again attempt to reintroduce the system, even if failing to do so left possible rivals with a potentially dangerous number of dependants. Moreover, what was to prevent such rivals from, say, coming to terms with some white men and together attempting a new coup? Like all men of power, Lewanika's first priority was to safeguard his own position, and his experience had suggested to him a means by which he hoped to achieve this goal.

## REFERENCES

1. Adolph Jalla, *Lewanika–Roi des Ba-Rotsi* (Geneva, 1902), p. 3; Jalla, *History of the Barotse Nation*, pp. 40–1.

2. Ishee Kwandu, *The Origin of the Lozi Chieftainship*, ch. 15.

3. Unsigned note in *News from Barotseland*, No. 15, May, 1902, p. 3.

4. Mr. Mupatu.

5. Jalla, *History*, p. 41.

6. Ishee Kwandu, *op. cit.*, and Mr. N. Zaza.

7. Mr. Simalumba.

8. Mr. N. Zaza.

9. Serpa Pinto, *How I Crossed Africa from the Atlantic to the Indian Ocean through Unknown Countries* (2 Vols., London, 1881), Vol. II, p. 7.

10. Coillard, Journal, 14 Oct., 1878.

11. None of my informants was able to provide data about the backgrounds of these men.

12. Jalla, *op. cit.*, p. 41.

13. Gluckman, *Jurisprudence*, pp. 69–70. This critical point is not suggested in any other source, written or oral, and Gluckman unfortunately never elaborated upon it in his other works.

14. Mr. N. Zaza, who married into Nalabutu's family.

15. Messrs. Zaza, Simalumba and Mupatu; Ishee Kwandu, *op. cit.* Gluckman also heard the story; see his 'Barotse Civil Wars and the World War, 1939–43', in *Mutende*, undated typewritten mss. at Rhodes–Livingstone Institute (RLI), Lusaka.

16. Serpa Pinto, *op. cit.*, Vol. II, p. 28.

17. Mr. Zaza.

18. I. Schapera, *The Tswana* (London, 1953), p. 16, and Lord Hailey, *Native Administration in the British African Territories*, pt. 5. *The High Commission Territories* (London, 1953), p. 189.

19. Richard Brown, 'Aspects of the Scramble for Matabeleland', in Stokes and Brown (ed.), *The Zambesian Past*, p. 70.

20. Cited in E. Baker, *The Life and Explorations of F. S. Arnot* (London, 1921), p. 97.

21. Serpa Pinto, *op. cit.*, Vol. II, pp. 6, 9–11, 22–49, 52–71.

22. François Coillard, *On the Threshold of Central Africa* (2nd edition, London, 1902), pp. 31–57; C. W. Mackintosh, *Coillard of the Zambesi*, (London, 1907), pp. 3–31, 41–5, 140–3, 237–50, 254–65; Gann, *History of Northern Rhodesia*, pp, 42–4.

23. Coillard, *op. cit.*, pp. 53–61.

24. Serpa Pinto, *op. cit.*, p. 59 and 100.

25. Coillard, *op. cit.*, pp. 61–5.

26. Mr. Mupatu.

27. Coillard, *op. cit.*, p. 177.

28. Mr. Simalumba.

29. H. Depelchin and C. Croonenberghs, *Trois Ans dans l'Afrique Australe* (2 Vols., Brussels, 1882–83), Vol. II, pp. 431–3; Robert I. Rotberg,

*Christian Missionaries and the Creation of Northern Rhodesia, 1880–1924* (Princeton, 1965), p. 14; F. S. Arnot, *Garenqanze, or Seven Years Pioneer Mission Work in Central Africa* (London, 1889), pp. 50–1; Westbeech Diary, Folio 75, NAR. Hist. Mss. WE 1/2/1.

30. Arnot, *op. cit.*, p. 62.

31. Arnot, *op, cit.*, pp. 70, 72–4, 81, and Baker, *op. cit.*, p. 70.

32. Arnot, *op. cit.*, p. 91.

33. *Ibid.*, p. 97.

34. Ishee Kwandu, *op. cit.*, ch. 15; Jalla, *History*, p. 41; Jalla, *Lewanika*, p. 4; Mackintosh, *Lewanika*, p. 19; Messrs. Mupatu, Simalumba and Zaza.

35. Messrs. Zaza and Mupatu and former Ngambela Wina.

36. Mr. Zaza.

37. Serpa Pinto, *op. cit.*, p. 59.

38. Mr. Mupatu and Jalla, *History*, p. 41.

39. Jalla, *op. cit.*, p. 41, and Mr. Simalumba.

40. Mr. Zaza.

41. Arnot, *op. cit.*, p. 91.

42. *Ibid.*, p. 95.

43. *Ibid.*, p. 97.

44. Coillard, Journal, 9 Aug., 1884; also Coillard, *Threshold*, pp. 146–7.

45. *Ibid.*, pp. 45–9; Westbeech, 'Part of a Diary', p. 14.

46. Gluckman, *Seven Tribes*, p. 27.

47. Mr. Simalumba.

48. Mr. Zaza.

49. Jalla, *History*, p. 42.

50. *Ibid.*, p. 43, says the marchers were led by 'southern indunas', but Messrs. Simalumba, Mupatu and Zaza all independently claimed that the delegation consisted of ordinary Lozi under Muimui who is not mentioned by Jalla. It is difficult to believe that indunas supporting the exiled king were allowed to retain their positions.

51. Gluckman, *Seven Tribes*, p. 23.

52. Jalla, *op. cit.*, p. 43.

53. Coillard, Journal, 9 Dec., 1884.

54. *Ibid.*, 1 Jan., 1885.

55. *Ibid.*, 11 Jan., 1885; also Edouard Favre, *François Coillard, Missionaire au Zambèse, 1882–1904* (3 Vols. Paris, 1913), Vol. 3, p. 108.

56. Coillard, *Threshold*, pp. 176–7; Favre, *op. cit.*, p. 111.

57. Westbeech, 'Part of a Diary', p. 8.

58. Favre, *op. cit.*, p. 108.

59. *Ibid.*, p. 112.

60. Coillard, *Threshold*, p. 177.

61. Coillard, Journal, 19 Jan., 1885.

62. Coillard, *Threshold*, p. 179. Messrs. Mupatu, Simalumba and Zaza all agreed that Mataa was a 'treacherous' (Mr. Zaza) and 'autocratic' (Mr. Mupatu) ruler.

63. Westbeech, 'Part of a Diary', pp. 14–15; Jalla, *History*, p. 44; Messrs. Mupatu and Simalumba.

64. Mr. Simalumba.

65. Jalla, *op. cit.*, pp. 49–50; Westbeech, *op. cit.*, p. 15; Messrs. Mupatu, Zaza and Simalumba.

66. *Ibid.*, pp. 51–2; Westbeech, *op. cit.*, p. 16; Westbeech to J. Fairbairn, 9 May, 1886, NAR Hist. Mss. H. M. Hole Papers, HO 1/3/1, folios 5–6; Coillard, *Threshold*, p. 199; Mackintosh, *Coillard*, p. 324; Messrs. Mupatu, Simalumba and Zaza.

67. Jalla, *Lewanika*, p. 12; also Jalla, *History*, p. 52.

68. Mr. Simalumba; also Mr. Mupatu. It is true that both these men had read Jalla's *History*. But they are both amateur historians who have heard the tales of many older Lozi who could not have read Jalla, and as admirers of the King, they might have been expected to report accounts which conflicted with Jalla's. Westbeech informed J. Fairbairn, 9 May, 1886, *op. cit.*, that Mataa's supporters were being slaughtered, but he had not personally witnessed the events.

CHAPTER III

# THE SCRAMBLE FOR PROTECTION

I

Many African peoples during the imperialist scramble for Africa had white domination thrust upon them. Some asked for, and quickly received, European protection. A few, however, had to plead and importune before a white nation paid them heed. Lobengula was killed because he acceded to the demands of his warriors that he expel the unwanted white man from Matabeleland. Khama invited British protection, and tried to exploit it to secure his own position. Lewanika too requested British protection; this request very nearly led to his overthrow again, and because his 'protectors' took a decade to materialize, his position during that period remained extremely insecure.

During the first half of the 1880s, the two policies which would characterize Lewanika's kingship had begun to crystallize. The 'politics of survival'[1] which he adopted followed the pattern of the Ngwato and Ganda, rather than that of the Ndebele and Yao. Lewanika's chosen weapon by which to resist the military superiority of encroaching white power was accommodation rather than confrontation. He would seek the protection of a European nation to safeguard himself against internal opposition and his kingdom against an Ndebele invasion. And by attaining for his sons and the sons of his trusted councillors a European education, he hoped to create a loyal elite capable of preventing his white protectors from usurping his sovereignty and competent to develop in Barotseland an economically viable, self-sufficient nation.

It was perhaps in the nature of things that Lewanika's dynamic policy encountered a certain amount of internal opposition. In his capacity as king, he tended to be more concerned with the wider national interests of Barotseland than

38

were some of his councillors, as, for example, Lobengula was
*vis-à-vis* his indunas.[2] Neither written sources nor oral traditions
supply sufficient data to allow a precise analysis of this opposition. But it is clear that the conservative faction of the ruling
class feared the consequences of inviting powerful white men
to 'protect' the nation, while opponents of the King believed
that his white protectors would effectively eliminate the possibility of a new coup. Both these factions were, therefore, hostile
to the missionaries whom Lewanika used to educate his young
people, and who were also regarded as the advance guard of
white power. Despite this opposition, Lewanika eventually
succeeded in attaining his first objective. But he soon thereafter discovered that the white protecting power had no intention of allowing him to realize his second great objective of
developing on the Upper Zambesi a prosperous nation pat-
terned upon western lines.

Lewanika's first steps after recovering his throne were the
traditional ones for a new monarch: he uprooted his enemies
from positions of influence and replaced them with his own
supporters. The large majority of men who had been indunas
under the rebels were dismissed, some of them murdered. The
new National Council was filled entirely with those who had
refused to recognize Akafuna as king. In place of his late
Ngambela Silumbu, he appointed Mwauluka, who had led
one of his regiments in the decisive battle near Lealui in November, 1885.[3] Little is known of Mwauluka, and he does not
emerge as a prominent figure during these years. His sister
Matauka regained her title as Mukwae of Nalolo. Both Westbeech and Coillard observed that, by 1886, the Lealui Kuta
was virtually unrecognizable as compared with a year earlier.[4]
At the same time, Kabuku, the young son of Matauka, was
appointed senior induna of the Sesheke area. This appointment
seems to have served as public recognition of the prominent
role played in the counter-rebellion by Matauka, for Sesheke
thus fell under the responsibility of her capital at Nalolo.[5]
With Sesheke integrated into Barotseland proper for the first
time, the formal pacification of the kingdom was completed.

The King understood, however, that these traditional means
to consolidate his position were no longer adequate. He knew
an alliance with an external force was required, and was

immediately given the opportunity to reach an agreement with the Ndebele. Westbeech now informed Lewanika that, while he was in exile, Lobengula had extended an offer to assist the King in recapturing his throne. The offer seemed to imply an alliance between the two kings once Lewanika was restored to power, and he refused it. Westbeech wrote Lobengula that the King

> desires me to state that he is again in power and having done it without assistance will make him now more powerful than if he had received help from any other power.[6]

Indeed, Lozi mistrust of the Ndebele never wavered, and during the remainder of the decade their canoes were stationed on the Zambesi to defend against a possible Ndebele invasion.

Yet Lewanika's reply to Lobengula was not entirely honest. For he was anxious to receive help now from another power, but not from the Ndebele. He probably learned of the concept of a protectorate while he was in exile. A British Protectorate was declared over Khama's country in 1885. While in exile, Lewanika had despatched aides to visit the chief of the Lake Ngami region, who was in close contact with Khama, where they might well have learned the news. Coillard was told of Khama's Protectorate by Westbeech,[7] and the latter is likely to have informed Lewanika of it when he regained the throne.

By 1886, Lewanika was already determined to seek similar protectorate status for himself, but for a moment he was unable to decide who was best suited to forward such a request on his behalf. He appears never to have considered using Westbeech as his intermediary, perhaps because the trader refused to involve himself in negotiations of this kind.[8] The obvious alternative was Coillard. But the missionary, in the high-minded belief that political disputes were not his concern, had been prepared to accept the rule of Mataa and Akafuna.

There can be little doubt that Westbeech was correct in believing that this made the King both resentful and suspicious of Coillard. Consequently, Westbeech went to Lealui in February, 1886, and it is likely that his success in reassuring Lewanika that Coillard was not a supporter of Mataa was responsible for the King's decision to send canoes to Sesheke to fetch the missionary to the capital.[9]

The King welcomed Coillard warmly. 'Whatever his motives may be,' the missionary wrote, 'Lewanika has a great desire to see us in his Kingdom.'[10] These motives soon emerged in the frequent conversations which the two men held, though Coillard preferred not to see them. In the first place, the King took advantage of these sessions to learn as much as he could of the policies of Lobengula and Khama, Coillard observing that 'he seems to have a great wish to resemble Khama'. Secondly, Lewanika clearly did not yet grasp the distinction between a missionary and trader, and was palpably chagrined when Coillard told him that trading goods, not excluding guns, could only be bought from men such as Westbeech.[11] The King did seem to understand, however, that Coillard, like Arnot but unlike Westbeech, was willing to undertake teaching duties, and his third use for the missionary soon became manifest. 'Lewanika', Coillard observed, 'would gladly overwhelm us with apprentices, grown-up men, whom he would like to see learning in a couple of months or so to accomplish every possible handicraft of the whites.'[12]

Finally, and above all, Lewanika had decided that Coillard was the obvious agent through whom to make contact with the British government. The mission party immediately settled at their new station at Sefula, about twenty miles south of Lealui on the edge of the plain. According to William Waddell, the party's artisan, Lewanika shortly thereafter travelled to Sefula where he talked with Coillard

> about the future of Africa and the government of his country, and he wished to place his country under Queen Victoria's protection as Khama had done. . . . He did not trust his people and was also afraid of other nations such as the Portuguese and the Boers, the latter Khama was once affraid of [sic] but now he had nothing to fear being under the protection of the Queen[13]

The King wanted Coillard 'to sit down and write a letter to the Queen then and there',[14] but though Coillard wrote the letter, 'he said he would not send it untill [sic] the matter had been discussed and sanctioned by his [Lewanika's] people'.[15]

For the next two years the King continued to importune Coillard to write requesting 'the Queen's protection', which the latter consistently refused to do.[16] Yet he and his colleagues had, in private, become convinced by 1885 of the advantages— both to Barotseland and to themselves—which British protection would mean.[17] His reluctance now to assist in securing this goal was not due to his self-proclaimed reluctance to meddle in political affairs,[18] for as Richard Hall has commented, 'In fact the missionary was tireless when politics could advance his evangelical aims. . . .'[19] Coillard now adopted a policy of political neutrality because he did not wish to identify the mission too closely with the King, whose position he considered to be highly insecure.

The King, then, needed Coillard for several reasons, the most important being his desire to follow Khama's example in receiving British protection. Westbeech, however, warned that Lewanika's confidence was not yet adequate protection for the mission. For the King himself, Westbeech believed, was far from secure, while

> the people want to know what he [Coillard] wants there, as he wont [sic] trade with them and they want to know nothing about the white man's book, as by learning it they then can have only one wife, and where are they going to get beer?

'I expect , Westbeech concluded, 'it will go hard with him yet. . . .'[20] The King himself was obviously not prepared to allow the mission party to remain in the country without the consent of the Kuta, which assembled early in 1887 to debate the issue. Its members proved to be deeply divided between those who saw no use in having missionaries in the country, and those who considered that they were likely to bring future benefits. No one considered the value of the mission in spreading the word of its god. According to Coillard's artisan assistant Waddell, the mission's opponents argued that,

> No we do not need these teachers unless they know and teach us to make powder (for guns) and such like things. . . . They did not want to know how to pray they knew that already . . .

The main arguments in favour of the mission were that, if they stayed, 'we shall have a mine of stuffs and of waggons', and that in Khama's country, the missions had provided everyone with European clothing, breech-loading guns, and 'rifled cannon'. In the end, it was agreed the missionaries might remain, but only so long as they did not interfere in the affairs of state. They were to restrict themselves to teaching the women and children, and not to intervene in 'the business of men and the kuta'.[21]

Both Westbeech and Coillard believed that this compromise muffled a much deeper conflict. The trader claimed that Lewanika's position remained so insecure that he 'can be deposed and murdered at any time. . . .'[22] Coillard realized that the Kuta meeting had revealed the existence of opposition both to himself and to the King. 'Poor man!' he wrote of the King; 'he is not free from cares. . . . He is suspicious of everybody, even of those who have brought him to power.' He concluded, almost certainly accurately, that the faction in the Kuta which was 'hostile to strangers, which sees our presence in the country with an evil eye', was highly suspicious of the King's desire to keep the mission in Barotseland.[23]

Nevertheless, because he thought that British protection was only obtainable through Coillard's intercession, and because he believed such protection to be indispensable to the maintenance of his position, Lewanika continued to look to Coillard for assistance. Without the knowledge of the Kuta, he was still imploring Coillard to write to the Queen on his behalf. Moreover, he remained anxious for Coillard to begin a school. Through learning the white man's superior skills, his people would, he hoped, be better equipped to deal with the increased numbers of Europeans who were bound to appear. In March, 1887, therefore, with the King's approval, the first PMS school at the Sefula mission site was inaugurated. Like that of Arnot several years earlier, the new school was essentially the private domain of the elite. Among its students were two of the King's sons, including Litia, five of Lewanika's 'nephews', and the sons of several indunas.[24] By the end of the year, Coillard was complaining that, 'with one or two exceptions . . . we have found it impossible to make voluntary recruits among the surrounding villages. The school is still considered exclusively that of the young princes. . . .'[25]

It was, of course, precisely 'the young princes'—or anyone

else he could use for his own ends—for whom the King intended the school. Yet his very interest in it may well have served to increase the opposition to him. For many Lozi did not grasp the practical function which Lewanika assigned to the mission and its school. Many indunas believed the PMS was intent on establishing white domination over Barotseland. Three independent sources relate that great suspicion immediately greeted Coillard's instructions that worshippers must shut their eyes during prayers. One old Lozi recalled years later that 'I did not close my eyes. I peeped through my spread-out fingers in case the white man tried to murder or bewitch me. One could not be too sure in those days.'[26] The school was likewise seen by a certain faction as part of the strategy of a white take-over, and commoners even wrote songs accusing Lewanika of selling his children to the missionaries when he sent them to live in at the school.[27]

This divergence of interests between the King and a segment of the Kuta soon produced serious hostility between them. Coillard referred several times during 1887 to evidence of discontent against Lewanika. 'Sinister rumours of a new revolution are flying about the country,' he reported. 'In certain places they [are] talking to each other about a plot, which they assert . . . [is] to break out immediately.'[28] Such stories continued to circulate widely through the first half of the following year,[29] while the King grew increasingly desperate for British protection. Yet only Coillard could make such a request for him, but the missionary still insisted that he would not contact the British authorities until the agreement of the Kuta had been won. Lewanika therefore decided that the issue must be brought into the open at last. In this tense atmosphere, he summoned both his indunas and Coillard to a special assembly at Lealui. The Ngambela, Mwauluka, acted as the King's mouthpiece.

> Barotsi [he is reported to have said], we are threatened with enemies from without and from within. I have sought missionaries for you, so that you should not be behind other nations . . . . The chief Khama has missionaries, but he also has *masole* (soldiers). They go together. So if you like to have the missionaries, ask Satory [Victoria] to send us her soldiers.

The indunas were shocked, partly because they had not been consulted in the matter earlier, but above all at the extraordinary prospect of having foreign soldiers among them. Coillard informed the assembly that the mission was entirely neutral on this question, and tried to explain the little he understood about 'what a protectorate is, the liabilities it involves', and—we may surely guess—the benefits it would bring.

In response, according to the missionary's version, the Kuta expressed its general confidence in the mission, but nothing else.

> If you will have the *masole* [they declared], let them come, but not while we are here. We serve you because you are king and sovereign; but if you become the *motlanka* (the servant of rulers), the subject of a master and foreigner, that is a humiliation the Barotsi will never accept.

Later the same evening, the King met with his senior indunas in his private office. 'But discussion', Coillard reported, 'was no longer possible. The chiefs had laid their heads together and taken their stand . . . : "The missionaries—yes, them we understand . . . but we will not have foreigners to rule over us." ' Their meaning was clear: the mission could remain so long as it did not stray from its proper duties, but they were determined to preserve the sacrosanct nature of the Lozi kingship, if necessary against the King himself. Lewanika understood the implied threat. 'Why not ask me what I want them [soldiers] for myself?' he demanded. Then addressing Coillard and pointing to the indunas, he added: 'It is to protect myself against those Barotsi. You do not know them; they are plotting against my life.'[30]

At this point, it appears that the King decided upon a show of strength against the dissident faction of the Kuta. His stewards, according to Coillard, organized on the following day a public trial to 'unmask the schemes' of those said to be plotting against him. One induna seems to have been selected to be the scapegoat and publicly humiliated.[31] Coillard claimed that the remainder of the 'compromised' indunas now no longer 'dared oppose' the King's wishes, and seemed satisfied that Lewanika finally had 'the full assent of his principal chiefs' to open negotiations with the British government.[32] In fact, it seems more plausible that the opposition was merely momentarily intimidated by the King's power and that a large faction of the Kuta, by Coillard's own evidence, opposed British intervention. The change, surely, was in the position not of the Kuta but of the missionary. It is likely that Coillard had perceived, between 1886 and 1888, that it was the King alone who wished the mission to remain in Barotseland, and that only foreign protection could secure the position of the King and, by implication, of the mission.

He thereupon discarded the pretence of his political passivity, and wrote two letters on Lewanika's behalf. The first was to Khama:

> I understand [the King dictated] you are now under the protection of the great English queen. I do not know what it means. But they say there are soldiers living at your place, and some headmen sent by the Queen to take care of you and protect you against the Matabele . . . . Are you happy and quite satisfied. . . . I am anxious that you should tell me very plainly, your friend, because I have a great desire to be received like you under the protection of so great a ruler as the Queen of England.[33]

Shortly thereafter, on 18 January 1889, Coillard finally wrote to Sir Sydney Shippard, the Administrator of British Bechuanaland, informing him that the Lozi wished to be placed under British protection. At the same time, he added a 'second request', allegedly on behalf of the King, 'concerning a threatened invasion of the Matabele'. Lobengula's troops had raided Toka and Ila territory in 1888, 'and they have boastfully declared that their next war path would be this year, 1889, to invade Barotseland'. Since Lewanika had heard that Lobengula had come under British protection—a badly distorted interpretation of the Rudd Concession—he hoped the Queen's representative would 'do your utmost to prevent the Matabele invading his country and spreading terror and desolation among the tribes north of the Zambesi. . . .'[34]

For several months the Valley remained calm while replies from Khama and Shippard were awaited. In April, however, the latent tension became manifest once again. A calculated attempt was apparently being made in Lealui to convince the King that the missionaries and their newfangled ideas were responsible for the prevailing discontent. On several occasions Lewanika complained to Coillard that his people were saying he had gone mad. 'Since I began to learn to read, I am all alone, no one supports me, courage begins to fail me.'[35] Three months later the missionary recorded that 'the pagan conservative party has raised its head once again, and we were very nearly chased from the country'.[36]

The 'pagan conservative party' was that faction within the Kuta which Coillard believed to be most hostile to the King's policies. Indeed, it is possible that their 'paganism' was a reaction to Lewanika's support for the mission. With old induna Nalabutu as their chief spokesman, they voiced their alarm that the King's policies meant the surrender of Lozi autonomy to white men in order to secure his own position, and they resented the influence which they believed Coillard had won over Lewanika, It was, in short, a classic instance of a King attempting to increase his own power at the expense of his traditional advisers, and the latter were inevitably fearful that he would be successful.

Lewanika indeed seized the first opportunity that presented itself to consummate his plan. In June, 1889, Harry Ware arrived in Lealui, seeking on behalf of a South African mining syndicate a concession from Lewanika to prospect for gold in certain outlying districts of the Lozi kingdom. Coillard advised the King that there was only a dim prospect of receiving British protection in the near future, but suggested—with little pretext of impartiality—that an agreement with Ware would be 'the first step' in that direction. The Kuta was assembled, and Ware explained through Coillard that he wished to dig for *tsepa* (iron or metal) in Barotseland, but that he had not come to buy land which belonged to the Lozi; this assurance was warmly received. Moreover, he produced a number of rifles and pieces of cloth, which pleased several indunas who had declared that since Westbeech's death in 1888, 'what they wanted was a man like him to buy their ivory that they may get powder and blankets. . . .'[37]

The King and Kuta then agreed to concede to Ware the right to prospect for twenty years in that part of the Lozi kingdom extending east from the Machili River, south from 'the cattle path' leading to Ila country, and north from the Zambesi; no eastern boundary was delineated. In short, as Coillard pointed out, the concession covered 'the whole of the Batoka country (a tribe tributary to the Barotsi). . . . It is immense, and Mr. Ware has reason to congratulate himself on so great a success.'[38] In return, Ware agreed to pay Lewanika the sum of £200 annually plus 'a royalty of four per cent on the total output of any minerals or precious stones won by me in the said granted territory'.[39]

The Lozi had little to lose and much to gain by allowing Ware access to Toka territory. This, almost certainly, was the reason that not only the King but even Nalabutu's 'pagan conservative party' was prepared to accept the concession. For the Toka, once considered part of the Lozi sphere of influence, had in the previous few years seemed to fall increasingly under the sway of the Ndebele. The Toka had called for Ndebele assistance against a band of Lozi warriors, while in the same year, Coillard had informed Shippard, the Ndebele had raided Batokaland (it is possible that this 'raid' was in fact the Ndebele response to Toka appeals for aid). It was, therefore, far from clear that Lealui any longer possessed the authority to allow prospectors in Batokaland. Consequently, they would be surrendering nothing for something—Ware's £200 plus royalties. Moreover, the Lozi may even have considered that the presence of Ware and his colleagues in the area would deter any further Ndebele encroachment on it, and that Lozi influence over the Toka could be reasserted. In short, as one informant put it, the King and his indunas alike must have believed that they were getting the best of both worlds. [40]

Lewanika indeed must have considered the Ware Concession a great personal victory. He had managed to take, as Coillard assured him, 'the first step' towards receiving British protection without a clash with those who refused to agree to such protection. The victory, moreover, was closely followed by two further ones. Only weeks after Ware's departure, the King received Khama's reply to the letter which Coillard had earlier written to the Ngwato chief. Unknown to the Lozi, Khama was now co-operating closely with Cecil Rhodes against the Ndebele.[41] It was hardly surprising, therefore, that Khama expressed great satisfaction to have 'the People of the Great Queen' with him. 'I live', he wrote, 'in peace with them, and I have no fear of the Matabele or the Boers any longer attacking me', and he offered to have a British representative sent to meet with Lewanika in Lealui.[42]

Although doubtlessly encouraged by his reply, the King soon learned to his satisfaction that Khama's offer was superfluous. For in September, 1889, Shippard, the Administrator of British Bechuanaland, also replied to the letter which Coillard had written him on Lewanika's behalf. The King's request for British protection, Shippard wrote, was being considered by the Queen's government. In the meantime, Rhodes's new Chartered Company would

> be able to afford to Lewanika and his people the fullest protection. . . . Mr. Rhodes has written to his board to support Lewanika's petition, and has offered to take the pecuniary responsibility. . . . He is sending a Mission to you.[43]

This was, so far as we know, the first occasion on which either the Lozi or Coillard learned about Rhodes and his new Company. Shippard did not, in his letter, attempt to explain the nature of the Company, except for the obvious implication that it was closely tied to the British government. It soon became clear that Coillard understood no more about a chartered company than did Lewanika, and the introduction of this new factor seems to have heightened the suspicions of those who in any event objected to a British protectorate.

These suspicions were shrewdly played on by George Middleton, an Englishman who had joined Coillard's expedition to Barotseland as a lay member in 1883. Four years later, however, he quit the mission and returned to South Africa, apparently having decided that there were more profitable ventures on the Upper Zambesi than spreading the Gospel. For at the beginning of 1890 he reappeared in Sesheke as a representative of a business firm in Mafeking.[44] Middleton was sufficiently familiar with the political situation to know the kind of arguments which would impress the King's enemies in Sesheke and the Valley; these he was prepared to use in order to have the King abrogate the agreement with Ware, refuse to sign one with Rhodes's representative, and instead give a new concession to Middleton's company.

By signing the Ware Concession, Middleton claimed, Lewanika had 'sold the country' to white men, and it was the missionaries who had duped him into doing so.[45] Nor could Frank Lochner, Rhodes's agent who reached the Valley in April, 1890, be trusted. Lochner reported that Middleton told the Lozi that if they signed an agreement with him, Lochner, 'Your country will be sold, you will not have enough ground to sit upon, that white man (meaning myself [Lochner]) does not come from the Government, he is only for himself like Ware, and will buy your country etc.'[46] Since these accusations merely confirmed the existing prejudices of many Lozi, they naturally made a considerable impact. Soon 'messenger after messenger' was hurrying from Sesheke to Lealui 'to upset the minds of Lewanika and his ministers'.[47]

The King was certainly upset, partly fearing that perhaps he had in fact been deceived over the Ware Concession, partly because the messengers' stories must have strengthened the position of his opponents. For three months after Lochner's arrival Lewanika refused to summon the Kuta to discuss the issue; Coillard thought the King 'did not seem anxious to face the question of the so-called Protectorate', and the missionary, as ever noting the gloomiest aspects of a situation, did not rule out the possibility of another rebellion.[48] Nor did Lochner's open contempt for Africans help ingratiate him with those from whom he sought a concession.[49]

Yet several factors were operating to Lochner's advantage. He had been accompanied to the Valley by Makoatsa, Khama's regular messenger to Lewanika and the man who had earlier escorted Coillard from Ngwato country to Barotseland;[50] curiously, however, Makoatsa seems to have disappeared for some time after reaching Lealui, reappearing again dramatically only towards the end of the Council meeting which was considering the new concession. Lochner, moreover, received the full support and co-operation of Coillard and Adolph Jalla, the two missionaries closest to Lewanika. There were several reasons for this. Lochner possessed a letter of introduction from their friend J. D. Hepburn, one of Khama's missionaries, in which Hepburn stated that Rhodes's agent 'has full power to offer Lewanika protection against the Matabele' so that

'Lewanika would be safe and your wars done with. . . .'[51] Indeed, despite his personal unpleasantness, the missionaries were delighted to welcome a new white man with whom they could converse, and when Lochner initially reached Sefula quite ill from his voyage, Coillard and his wife offered him the hospitality of their home as a 'manifest duty',[52] thus seriously compromising in Lozi eyes Coillard's reputation for neutrality. That 'neutrality', as has been seen, had always been spurious, and the missionary himself now acknowledged that he had become 'more and more firmly convinced that . . . if the concession can give the country some sense of security, it will be a blessing hitherto unknown'.[53]

Above all, both Coillard and Jalla seriously misunderstood the relationship between the British government and the Chartered Company, with critical consequences for the future of Barotseland. Jalla referred to Lochner as 'the representative of the English government',[54] and Coillard believed that 'a treaty with the Company was the equivalent of a treaty with the Government itself'.[55] Indeed, for all of Coillard's 'neutrality', when Rhodes wrote inviting him to become Company Resident in Barotseland, the missionary replied:

> Well, I cannot serve two masters [the Church and the Company]. But if without any official title I can be to your Company of any service as a medium of communication until you get the proper man, I willingly place myself at your disposal.[56]

Lochner himself deliberately declined to clarify these misconceptions. He consistently misrepresented his own position and that of the Company. He claimed to be the special envoy of the Queen and implied that the Company was a department of the British government. He intimated that it was the Company which was protecting Khama,[57] although it of course had no status in Bechuanaland. The Colonial Office was moved to acknowledge that 'Mr. Lochner may have made too free a use of Her Majesty's name in communicating with Lewanika. . . .'[58] Even later writers sympathetic to Rhodes and the Company have agreed that Lochner consciously deceived the Lozi, but, one explained,

> Had he not adopted this course, Lewanika would have

C

refused to deal with him, and Barotseland might never have been added to the Empire – might even have become the prey of a foreign syndicate with no nice scruples as to how it acquired territory.[59]

Lochner used his 'nice scruples' first to convince the missionaries, then to have them convince the King, that Company protection was tantamount to the Queen's protectorate. Early in June, Lochner invited the King, the Mokwae of Nalolo, and several senior indunas and princes to Sefula, where they spent many hours discussing the Sesuto translation made by Coillard of the concession which Lochner brought with him.[60] The obvious technical difficulty was that certain words and concepts in the concession were virtually untranslatable. 'Chartered Company', for example, Coillard translated dubiously as *lekhotla* (Kuta), the King's council.[61] Further, according to a Lozi informant, for the word 'grant', implying perpetual right, which is *kufa*, Coillard used *kukalima*, meaning 'borrow'.[62] By thus obscuring the real nature of both the Company and the concession, Coillard significantly mitigated its unacceptability to many Lozi.

At the same time, the missionary insisted that the King's annual subsidy be not £800, as Lochner offered, but £2,000 per annum. Lochner cleverly observed that Coillard was by this means attempting to ingratiate himself with both King and Kuta.[63] For even the dissident indunas shared Lewanika's desire to obtain sufficient weapons to balance those which they knew Lobengula was receiving. When the King therefore demanded enough money to buy his own weapons, Lochner had little alternative but to agree.[64]

This financial arrangement seems to have given the King adequate confidence to believe he could now overcome the opposition of the dissident indunas. We may also assume that he shrewdly used to his own advantage the months during which the protection issue was being thrashed out, by wielding the powers that were uniquely attached to the kingship; we can imagine him threatening opponents with loss of their titles, while promising promotions, land, cattle and dependants in return for pledges of support. Thus prepared, he at last summoned not merely the Kuta, but the full National Council.

To decide this crucial question, all the members of the three mats, many headmen from throughout the Valley, and representative indunas stationed among the subject tribes, all crowded into Lealui.[65]

The assembly opened on 22 June, Coillard and Adolph Jalla acting as official interpreters. Through them, Lochner explained that many other tribes had accepted 'British protection for their own welfare', and that by accepting the concession they would 'grow rich, make progress, graze your flocks and cultivate your land with full security'. In return, Lochner received a volley of 'all sorts of questions about their slaves, wives, lands. . . .'[66] What the indunas were demanding to know, in short, was whether their own powers would be circumscribed while the position of the King was strengthened, and though the terms of the concession offered assurances on this point, a number of them remained unsatisfied.

Then, 'at the critical moment of the negotiations, when the . . . success of Mr. Lochner's mission was trembling in the balance, Khama's ambassador, Makoatsa, entered the *lekhotla* [Kuta] with his suite. . . .'[67] 'Barotsi', he declared, ostensibly in Khama's name,

> . . . Today I hear sinister rumours, you speak again of revolution. Take care! Lewanika is my friend, and if you dare to make attempts against his life or power, I am Khama! You will see me with your eyes and hear me.[68]

He apparently went on to support Lochner's mission, stating that the Company was comprised of the 'Queen's men' to whom she had assigned the task of spreading 'civilization' in the heart of Africa.[69]

Since the threat obviously implied in 'Khama's message' was believed by the missionaries to have been decisive in silencing the dissident indunas,[70] it is worth noting that Lochner had earlier promised Makoatsa that if the concession were signed, 'I would ask the Company to make him a good present; he stated that if the Company would give him a waggon, nothing would please him more.'[71] His vested interest helps explain both the vehement nature of his speech and why he had disappeared until 'the critical moment of the negotiations'.

The Lozi could not, however, have been aware that Makoatsa was compromised, and with his speech the opposition to Lochner collapsed. On 27 June, 1890, Lewanika, his son Litia, Ngambela Mwauluka, and thirty-eight indunas signed the concession, which 'shall be considered in the light of a treaty between my said Barotse nation and the Government of Her Britannic Majesty Queen Victoria'. Though the Company was granted no administrative rights, it received 'the sole, absolute, exclusive and perpetual right and power' to 'search for, dig, win and keep' any and all minerals in Barotseland.[72] Coillard later recorded what the King and Council considered to be the extent of their kingdom; they made the very dubious claim that Lozi authority was recognized by the Lunda and Luvale in the north, the Kaonde to the north-east, the Ila to the east, and the Tonga and Toka to the south-east.[73] In effect, then, through the Lochner Concession, the Company assumed the whole of what was to become North-Western Rhodesia; its authority over all the peoples named by Lewanika rested solely on its agreement with the Lozi; no independent agreements were ever signed by chiefs of the Lunda, Luvale, Ila, Tonga or Toka, who nevertheless had to submit to Company overrule.

In return for this vast accretion to Rhodes's empire—estimated by Coillard at some 200,000 square miles[74]—the Company undertook 'to protect the said King and nation from all outside interference and attack', but pledged not to 'interfere in any matter concerning the King's power and authority over any of his own subjects'. To King and councillors alike, the annual payment of £2,000 with which they could buy weapons against the Ndebele must have seemed fair compensation for mineral rights. For the King himself, two further clauses were of critical importance. By the first,

> The Company further agrees that it will aid in the education and civilization of the native subjects of the King, by the establishment, maintenance and endowment of schools and industrial establishments.

Here at last seemed to be the means by which his dynamic policy for the modernization of his nation could be implemented; he could not know that the same clause was written into the *pro forma* contracts which Company agents were having signed by the chiefs of other tribes in North-Eastern Rhodesia.[75]

Secondly, Lewanika's conviction that he could manipulate white power to buttress his own position seemed to be implied in the promise that the Company would 'appoint and maintain a British resident, with a suitable suite and escort, to reside permanently with the King.'[76]

In the years that followed, the Company managed to renege, temporarily or permanently, on nearly every commitment it made: the powers of both the King and the Kuta were severely circumscribed, no payment was made for the first seven years, no school or industrial establishment was ever maintained with Company money, and its resident arrived only in 1897, with a tiny and unimpressive suite and escort, and he soon moved his headquarters far from the Barotse Valley. In short, the worst fears of those who opposed the Concession were vindicated, while the brightest hopes of the King failed to materialize. One Lozi informant compared Barotseland's fate under Company 'protection' to the parable of the camel and the Arab:

> The camel first asked to put just his head in the Arab's tent, then his legs, and finally his entire body. The camel then saw there was not room enough for both of them in the tent, and threw the Arab out.[77]

None of this, however, altered the historical significance of the signing of the Lochner Concession. For better or worse, but in any event irrevocably, the Lozi had taken, in Stokes's words, an 'independent initiative . . . to open a window on to the modern world',[78] with results, in the opinion of L. H. Gann, which 'profoundly affected the subsequent course of history in Central Africa'.[79] There is no doubt that the responsibility for taking the original initiative belonged entirely to the King himself, who understood before any other Lozi that white power must one day be confronted, and that by making the initial overture himself, he might be able to harness that power both to secure his own position and to help develop his nation along European lines.

It was precisely when they grasped these motives that a faction among his indunas decided to oppose his policies. Yet their defeat was as inevitable as the Ndebele's. They themselves had no alternative policy for preventing an Ndebele invasion, a threat which united all Lozi. Khama's great satisfaction with

British protection was clearly of considerable influence, as was Coillard's role in convincing the Lozi that Lochner in fact represented 'the great Queen'.[80] But what Khama, Coillard, and Lochner all represented in the final analysis was a distant white power structure for which all Lozi had come to have a fearful respect. It is possible that Khama's envoy informed the Lozi of Rhodes's plan of 1889, in which Khama was deeply implicated, for a private force of European mercenaries to crush the Ndebele.[81] It is true that the Company was determined to build a settlement in Matabeleland, and was prepared to go to any lengths to achieve this end. But the Lozi could hardly have known that Rhodes was not interested in Barotseland for the same reason. Lewanika therefore decided that an accommodation with, rather than resistance to, white power could best preserve the integrity of the nation. Some of his indunas, less concerned with the long-run stability of Barotseland than with their own immediate self-interest, saw only that white power would strengthen the King's authority at the expense of their own. But in the end, their fear of the white power which stood behind Lewanika was great enough to silence their opposition, and the Lochner Concession was signed. Almost alone among the powerful kingdoms of Central Africa—the Bemba, the Ndebele, Mpezeni's Ngoni—colonial rule came to the Lozi peacefully and—for their King at least—with great relief. Whether this amicable settlement provided the Lozi with a more satisfactory future than was the case with say, the Ndebele or Bemba, had still to be seen.

## II

Lochner left Barotseland believing that the Lozi were fully reconciled to accepting the concession. In fact, the dissident indunas had merely been silenced, and their opposition rematerialized quickly enough. Moreover, the King himself profoundly feared any unforeseen development which might give his opponents their opportunity. This new development soon arose. Lewanika discovered that he had not been placed under the direct protection of Her Majesty's government, and one of the major themes of Lozi history during the succeeding thirty-four years[82] is the continuous attempt by both him and his successor to throw off Company rule. Nevertheless, his first priority was to receive the 'British Resident' promised in the Lochner Concession. A resident, even if he in fact was sent by the Company, would be seen as the physical manifestation of the King's unassailable position, and Lewanika was intent upon having him. His major political objective in the seven frustrating years which followed was, therefore, to secure his resident before his opponents were able to depose him.

Within weeks of Lochner's departure, Lewanika was prepared to tear up the entire Concession. In September, 1890, George Middleton arrived in Lealui and convinced the King that the missionaries had deceived him into surrendering his country to a mere commercial concern. At this information, Coillard reported, Lewanika became 'crazy with anger',[83] presumably fearing, as the latter informed Sir Henry Loch, High Commissioner at Cape Town, that it would 'not fail to cause much excitement and trouble in the country among my people'.[84] Apparently at the King's request, Middleton wrote a long, bitter letter direct to Lord Salisbury, stating that Lewanika 'repudiated' the Lochner Concession,[85] and a shorter one to Henry Loch requesting the protection of the British government.[86] So far as Lewanika was concerned, the Company had no rights in Barotseland, and early in 1891 two of its agents were refused permission to cross the Zambesi from Pandamatenga into his country.[87]

At the same time, relations between the King and the missionaries predictably were deteriorating, and by the middle of 1891 both were growing alarmed at the insecurity of their respective positions. Lewanika, Coillard wrote, 'is accusing everybody of having made a plot against him and wishing to kill him to put Sepopa [a son of the late King Sipopa] in his place'.[88] Moreover, fearing the mission would be victimized by the 'tempest' that was raging, Coillard angrily complained to the Company that Lochner's duplicity had 'unconsciously made [him] a dupe and accomplice in these transactions' and announced that 'he would no longer have anything to do with those affairs [between the King and the Company]'. This letter mollified Lewanika only mildly,[89] and the 'wildest excitment' continued in the capital.[90]

Towards the end of the year, Lewanika finally received a

reply from Loch in Cape Town. The High Commissioner assured him that 'you are under the protection of Her Majesty the Queen' and that 'the Company is recognized by Her Majesty as acting under a Royal Charter which she has given them. . . .' Loch promised that Harry Johnston, the Queen's Commissioner for Central Africa, would visit Lewanika as soon as he could to 'explain Her Majesty's wishes and feelings in regard to your country'.[91] Coillard reported that the King was 'very pleased', but had nothing to say until he spoke to Johnston. Middleton still held the King's ear, Coillard pointed out, and Johnston would have to work smartly to 'win back his confidence'.[92]

But it was not Harry Johnston who now—or ever—appeared in the Valley; it was Dr. James Johnston, an eccentric Scots doctor who had come to Africa from Jamaica with two Jamaican Negroes for 'Christianization and civilization of the African savage tribes. . . .'[93] Though Johnston was no more successful in converting the King to Christianity than Coillard was, the visitor became a personal admirer of Lewanika as well as his staunch ally against the Company.

Johnston revealed a penetrating insight into the King's vision of the future of his nation. Lewanika, he wrote,

> says he longs for light and knowledge and wonders why more missionaries do not come to teach him and his people. It must not be imagined by this, however, that he yearns for a knowledge of the gospel. By no means; he wants teachers to instruct his people how to read and write, but especially to train them as carpenters, cabinetmakers, blacksmiths and for other trades that they may make furniture and build houses for him. . . . He has a great idea of the ability of the Marotsi to learn the various arts and become wise like Europeans.[94]

In turn the King, having come to trust Johnston, poured out to him his bitterness against the Company, stressing repeatedly how he had been deceived into signing the Lochner Concession.[95] When Johnston finally departed, Lewanika handed him a letter, probably written by Middleton, entreating him to see that the Lozi grievances received maximum publicity in Britain.[96] Johnston published this letter, along with his own biting indictment of the Company's rule, in a book which spurred the Aborigines Protection Society to write to the Colonial Secretary demanding whether Lewanika's grievances had been met.[97] The Colonial Office issued a long reply stating, in essence, that Lewanika had never really had any grievances but had merely been deceived into so believing.[98]

Tension in the Valley remained acute and Middleton's position strong. Nevertheless, Coillard decided in February, 1892, to seek permission to establish a mission station at Lealui itself. The Kuta agreed to his request. 'We have seen great things,' he reported one induna saying:

> foreigners closeted with our king, overrunning our malapa (courts). . . . We heard them speaking of mines, of trades, and of presents without our being told of what it was all about. And we asked ourselves, 'Wither are we drifting? Are we at the mercy of foreigners?' Today our father comes amongst us; all these plots will end.[99]

It is indeed plausible that the Kuta would feel reassured by Coillard's closer propinquity, but hardly for the reasons the indunas openly presented. For in their eyes he was no longer simply a preacher and teacher; he had become a diplomat, a representative of the Company, and therefore a centre of power in his own right. Surely their motive now was to have him in Lealui in order to keep him under surveillance and above all to maintain a close scrutiny over the relationship between the missionary and the King.

This fact was recognized neither by Coillard nor by Middleton. So far as the latter was concerned, Coillard's move to Lealui could only decrease the likelihood that the King would grant a concession to Middleton's company. He therefore confidently demanded that the King expel the missionaries or else he himself would leave the country. Lewanika is said to have replied that he could not 'chase away my missionaries', and in April, 1892, Middleton returned to South Africa.[100] Coillard and his colleagues believed the King's choice was based on his personal affection for the missionaries and his respect for their integrity.[101] More realistically, as one of my informants emphasized, Lewanika still ardently desired British protection to stabilize his own position, and Coillard, not Middleton, contined to be his only link with the Queen's government.

But Middleton's departure did not end the crisis. Another vague reassurance from Loch that 'it will not be long' before a resident was appointed[102] was little consolation to either the King or the nervous Coillard. In September, 1892, the latter again wrote Loch informing him that 'the situation here is improving but very slowly if at all.' Remarkably accurate new rumours had begun to circulate of 'the Company's strange doings in other lands, and of their resolve of appropriating to themselves boundless rights over the land and people'; and where, the King demanded to know, were his resident and his £2,000 a year? Tales were being told as well that both white traders and Ndebele warriors were trying to enter Barotseland, and therefore 'a large village has been founded at Kazangula in order to watch the ford and to control the crossing of any stranger'.[103] In November, with reports of an imminent Ndebele raid becoming more urgent, Lewanika forbade the handful of white traders and hunters at Kazangula and Pandamantenga —whom he feared would aid the Ndebele—from crossing into Barotseland.[104]

The King was outraged that, despite the Concession and all the subsequent assurances of its validity, he should still have to fear Ndebele attacks. In a letter written on his behalf by Coillard in February, 1893, he bitterly complained to Loch that the threat from the Ndebele was seriously weakening his personal position. Accusations that he had been deceived by those wanting to 'steal' Barotseland were once again increasing.' The people are loud in their expressions of bitterness and distrust. . . . The Government have taken no notice of him, and they have left him to himself, exposed to the vexations of his enemies and the suspicions of his people.'[105]

Lewanika's personal position became even more tenuous as a result of a brutal Ndebele incursion into Batokaland in August, 1893. Rumours that the invaders had reached as far as Sesheke were given credence for some time, until in late November news arrived that war had broken out between the Ndebele and the Company south of the river. Lewanika was clearly relieved, and began renewing tentative overtures to the Company, meekly apologizing—perhaps for tactical reasons— for the distrust he had shown.[106] Coillard followed with a personal appeal to Rhodes to 'show some interest in the welfare of the people'.[107] Early in 1894, Loch wrote to the King from Cape Town announcing proudly that 'the Matabele have been conquered', and though Lobengula had escaped north towards the Zambesi with a band of warriors, they would 'be followed up' once the rains had stopped.[108] This news seemed to satisfy the King that British power was in fact ranged against the enemies of the Lozi and that his missionaries had not therefore betrayed him, and several times during 1894 he went out of his way publicly to support the mission and to castigate those indunas who refused to send their children to its schools.[109]

Yet the war against the Ndebele must have been viewed by the Lozi as a mixed blessing. In the first place, it meant that the Company would continue to be absorbed south of the Zambesi, to the consequent neglect of Barotseland. Secondly, the Company was demonstrating in Matabeleland in no un-certain terms how it dealt with recalcitrant African rulers. Almost certainly, the Lozi were highly intimidated by the power which Rhodes's men had unleashed against Lobengula, and much of their subsequent dealings with the Company in the years that followed can only be understood if considered in this light.[110]

To the opposition faction in the Kuta, then, the position remained that, on the one hand, the Ndebele threat had not yet been crushed, and, on the other, if Lewanika's 'protectors' ever did materialize, might they not attack the Lozi as they did the Ndebele? The King had staked everything on the gamble that the white men would support, not undermine, his position. He therefore was prompted to write again to Loch, declaring himself 'uncared-for and forlorn', and repeating his plea 'to be recognized as one of the Queen's children'. In-creasingly his opponents were claiming that he had been deceived, saying: 'You have sold your country and your liberty to a trading company.' His mind, the King declared, was 'greatly disturbed', and he had begun to doubt whether Harry Johnston was 'a real living man'.[111]

By the end of 1894, Lewanika's position seemed to be in real jeopardy. Several leading indunas, as has been seen, now be-lieved that his foreign policy could lead only to disaster— whether at the hands of Europeans or the Ndebele—and equally resented his intimate relationship with the missionaries.

It was mission influence, they believed, which not only kept him faithful to the Lochner Concession, but which appeared also to be convincing him of certain dangerously heretical Christian notions.

Now a number of conservative councillors, led by old Nalabutu, the Ngambela, and Kalonga, a senior induna, decided to put an end to these disruptive tendencies. They attacked the mission's African evangelists for showing disrespect for the King by accusing him of preventing his people from being converted. Curiously, the King supported the evangelists, claiming that their attackers merely feared that 'I will become a Christian, send away my wives, and that I will oblige you to do the same'. Why the King felt sufficiently confident at this juncture so to challenge the dissident faction in the Kuta is not at all clear, and his speech led, not surprisingly, to what Jalla called 'a recrudescence of discontent among the chiefs at Lealui, Sefula and everywhere'.[112] Coillard believed that Nalabutu and the Ngambela went so far as to threaten Lewanika that they would not tolerate having a Christian King.[113]

With relations within the ruling class thus seriously strained, a new external threat again provoked panic throughout the kingdom. This time the 'invaders' consisted of two parties of white prospectors which appeared on the southern and eastern frontiers of Barotseland in the first few months of 1895. In Lealui it was believed that the prospectors were 'bullying the natives and threatening to fight and burn their villages. . . .'[114] Lewanika immediately perceived the potential danger in the situation. Perhaps recalling the precedent in Matabeleland, he feared that his own people might afford the Company provocation to attack Barotseland. But, he desperately demanded of Dr. Jameson, 'how could I be held responsible for anything happening to any white people' if he had no white official living with him?[115]

Coillard also wrote to Jameson, elaborating upon the Lozi's very reasonable alarm: if prospectors were to continue to enter Barotseland and provoke the local people, he stated,

> there must certainly be before long serious trouble, in spite of the King's sincere and strenuous efforts to keep peace. Unfortunately, the impression has spread that it is exactly what is wanted, and these pioneering men are looked upon

as mere tools to foster disturbances and bring on war, so that the country may be wrested from the hands of the natives.

The entire episode, he concluded, had served to confirm yet again the general Lozi suspicion that the King 'has not been fairly and honestly dealt with' by the Company.[116]

Jameson replied offering the usual assurances,[117] but what Lewanika could not know was that the Company in fact now intended to act. The initiative came from London, where the Foreign Office had become concerned that the Lochner Concession did not adequately prove Britain's right to claim Barotseland as against the contrary claims of Portugal.[118] Rhodes responded with alacrity and announced that Hubert Hervey, a Company official in Mashonaland, would be sent as 'Resident Commissioner' to Barotseland early in 1896.[119]

But two problems remained. In the first place, the Colonial Office decided that the Lochner Concession did not confer any administrative rights on the Company, and that a new concession was accordingly necessary.[120] Secondly, Portugal and Britain had, in a series of agreements, defined the provisional frontier between their respective spheres of influence in west-central Africa as the line following the Upper Zambesi to its junction with the Kabompo River and thence up that river. The definitive boundary was to be subject to further negotiations between the two European powers. Lewanika had never been informed that about half the territory he claimed as part of his kingdom had tentatively been handed to Portugal by the government to whom he looked for protection, but Rhodes protested strongly against what he believed was an abject surrender of so vast an area by Britain.[121] Lord Salisbury, of course, had no means of knowing whether the western boundary of Barotseland was the Upper Zambesi, as the Portuguese claimed, or the twentieth meridian as Rhodes insisted. It was therefore decided that Major Goold-Adams, a Colonial Office official in Bechuanaland, be sent as 'Special Commissioner to inquire into the territorial claims of the Chief of Barotseland in the direction of Angola . . .', and Lewanika was duly informed of the Major's impending visit.[122]

This information reached Lealui at a propitious moment, for the Lozi had just discovered to their dismay that two Portuguese forts had been constructed on the western side of the Upper Zambesi. The King regarded the forts as the advance guard of an imminent Portuguese invasion of Barotseland, and protested by letter to the Portuguese commandant against this 'invasion' of his country.[123] Adolph Jalla communicated this protest to the British authorities in South Africa, adding his own firm opinion that not until the Resident actually appeared would the King 'know of a certainty that he is under the protection of the Great White Queen'.[124]

It was, however, not the desired Resident but Goold-Adams who became the first official English representative to arrive in Barotseland. He reached Lealui in October, 1896, preparatory to investigating the western limits of Barotseland, with instructions to 'Explain to Lewanika that you have been sent direct from the Queen'.[125] Six years of extreme insecurity had, however, left the King deeply suspicious of all white strangers. 'For some reason,' Goold-Adams reported ingenuously, 'he appeared to doubt my coming from the Government'. Lewanika explained that 'he could now not trust any white man, and that if he allowed me to go over his country, I would probably return to England and say that I had purchased the country as Mr. Lochner had done'.[126]

Fortunately for Goold-Adams, relations between Lewanika and the mission were now warmer than they had been at any time since Lochner's time.[127] Adolph Jalla, who was representing the PMS in Lealui with Coillard on holiday in Europe, successfully interceded on Goold-Adams's behalf, Lewanika finally declaring that 'he did believe I came from the Queen and that therefore I was free to go wherever in his country I wished'. Goold-Adams was highly impressed with the King, whom he described as 'an enlightened man . . . intelligent, industrious . . . [and with] a great idea of the capabilities of his people to learn the arts and trades. . . .'[128] Moreover, as an opponent of the slave trade, 'thoroughly loyal' and 'civil', he considered Lewanika 'a man to be made a friend of',[129] which Goold-Adams believed the future Resident could achieve without 'the slightest difficulty' so long as he showed more 'tact' than the openly racialist Lochner had done.[130]

Lewanika himself confirmed the accuracy of this assessment. After Goold-Adams explained to him the boundary controversy between Portugal and Britain, the King wrote to both the Queen and Robinson, the High Commissioner, that he would be

> very glad if the [British] government separates me from the Portuguese, because if the latter come into my land they will steal it. . . . I do not wish my country to be divided into two parts between Portugal and Germany; it must be in one part under England. . . . The government must carry me as a woman carries a child upon her back.[131]

This was the plea of a desperately frightened and insecure ruler of a threatened nation, and Lewanika was properly gratified when, in May, 1897, Milner, the new High Commissioner, wrote him to say that though Hubert Hervey had been killed, Robert Coryndon had now been appointed Resident and would be arriving in Lealui within a matter of months. Milner explained that Coryndon, though selected by the Company, had been approved by the government and was 'responsible for his actions, through the Company, to the Great Queen . . . [who] is always anxious for the welfare of yourself, your headmen, and your people.'[132]

There is reason to believe that certain of the King's 'headmen' were not impressed by the Queen's solicitude for their welfare. Several years later, Frank Worthington, one of Coryndon's officers, claimed to have discovered a 'plot', to be carried out 'a few months after we entered the Barotse country', to 'kill all the white men in the country'. Worthington acknowledged that 'It would have been very easy to have killed us all', for even including the missionaries the number of Europeans in Barotseland was tiny. But 'At the last moment, the King refused to sanction the scheme and remained firm against all arguments. . . .' The motive of the conspirators, of course, was to prevent the Company from taking over the country. According to Worthington's account, he presented this information to Litia, the King's son, who 'seemed surprised to hear that I knew about the little plot', but 'did not deny it'.[133]

So far as is known, there is no other written evidence concerning this alleged plot. But Lozi oral tradition tends to confirm its existence. One informant told me the plan was not to kill the whites, but simply to 'request' that they leave.[134] Three

others, however, agreed that all white males were to be murdered and their wives taken as brides by Lozi men, much as
happened, it was pointed out, when the Lozi defeated the
Kololo three decades earlier.[135] None of these informants was
able, or prepared, to name the particular indunas involved,
but all agreed that it was Lewanika himself who crushed the
plot. The King in fact is said to have decreed that any Lozi
who killed a European would himself be killed together with
seven of his relatives.[136] We may assume that the conspirators
were later grateful to Lewanika for his prudence, for Worthington flatly informed Litia that 'if they had made an end of us,
the people of England would have avenged us to such an extent
that today [1902] there would be no Barotse nation'.[137]

In October, 1897, Robert Coryndon arrived in Lealui, quite
unsuspecting the alleged intrigues which might have cost him
his life. A 'Company man', Coryndon had been one of Rhodes's
'twelve apostles' who led the Pioneer Column into Mashonaland. He then became private secretary to Rhodes for a year
before the latter selected him—despite his limited administrative experience—to be Lewanika's resident.[138] As in the case
of Goold-Adams, however, Lewanika initially refused to believe
that Coryndon genuinely represented the British government.
But once again Jalla successfully interceded,[139] and with the
King's doubts thus assuaged, he accorded Coryndon 'almost a
royal reception, and has ever since shown a strong desire to
maintain friendly relations between his nation and Her Majesty's
government'. On Milner's instructions, Coryndon presented
Lewanika with a portrait of the Queen, for which he was
'deeply gratified'; conspicuous by its absence, however, was
the sum of £14,000 which was now owed to the King by the
terms of the Lochner Concession, and which he in fact never
received.

In a major address to the Kuta, the new Resident declared
that Barotseland was officially a British Protectorate, and
implicitly assured the assembly that Portuguese advances,
about which Lewanika had immediately complained to him,
would be dealt with. Although Coryndon also discussed with
the King 'questions connected with the Lochner concession',[140]
he contrived in the beginning to keep his relationship with the
Company in the background.[141]

Above all, Coryndon endeavoured to obliterate the notion that his presence, and the Concession, meant any diminution of Lozi sovereignty. In London, Coillard had asked for clarification of the Company's right to make land grants in Barotseland. The Colonial Office pointed out that the concession of 1890 gave the Company rights in land solely for mining and trading purposes, and that no land could be granted by the Company to white settlers without a new concession from the King explicitly empowering it to do so.[142] Coryndon hastened to pass on these assurances. He promised the Kuta that he had not come to interfere in Lozi affairs or in relations between the King and his subjects. Indeed, the proof that his mission was a peaceful one was in the small escort of only six Europeans which he had brought with him.[143] He then wrote formally to the King, stressing the same point:

You are definitely under British protection. You gave a concession to the British South Africa Company. Afterwards you were afraid you had sold your country. Do not believe this: you have not sold your country.[144]

The struggle between the King and his opponents, then, appeared to have been resolved in favour of the former. The dynamic elite had defeated the static elite. The modernizers had won out against the conservatives. That faction of the ruling class, which believed that the King's policies for development could only be implemented at the expense of their own powers, had been unable to overthrow him before his protectors had arrived. By the same token, to Lewanika his seven frustrating years of waiting seemed not to have been in vain. The promised representative of the 'Great Queen' had at long last appeared, expressing all the proper sentiments. Now his own position would be secure. Now he could, with the co-operation of Britain and the new group of aristocratic young men whose education he had commenced, begin putting his modernizing schemes into effect. He informed Milner that he was finally satisfied; he declared himself to be 'Her Majesty's servant', and expressed the hope that 'there shall be nothing to disturb peace and to destroy the friendship' between himself and the Queen.[145] Rhodes's most recent biographers have claimed that, with Coillard's arrival, 'a new era of peaceful and progressive administration' began in Barotseland.[146] Such complacency is no doubt justified in so far as the interests of the Company were concerned. For Lewanika, disillusionment was quick to set in, for the worst fears of his opponents were soon realized.

## REFERENCES

1. Roland Oliver, 'After the Oxford History: Historical Research in East Africa', paper for African History Seminar, Institute of Commonwealth Studies (London), 27 Oct., 1965, p. 7.

2. Richard Brown, 'Aspects of the Scramble for Matabeleland', in Stokes and Brown (ed.), *The Zambesian Past*, ch. 4.

3. Jalla, *History of the Barotse Nation*, pp. 44, 50, 52.

4. Coillard, Journal, 8 April, 1886; Westbeech to Fairbairn, 9 May, 1886, NAR Hist. Mss. Hole Papers, folios 5–6.

5. Messrs. Muhali Mutemwa and M. Kawana; Coillard, Journal, 7 Aug., 1886; Westbeech Diary, folios 34 and 53, NAR.

6. Westbeech to Fairbairn, 9 May, 1886, *op. cit.*

7. Coillard, Journal, 11 July, 1885.

8. Although it is true that Westbeech transmitted messages between Lobengula and Lewanika.

9. Coillard, Journal, 23 March, 1886.

10. Coillard, *Threshold*, p. 226.

11. *Ibid.*, pp. 212–3.

12. *Ibid.*, p. 262.

13. Waddell's Diary, 14 Nov., 1886, NAR Hist. Mss. WA 1/1/3.

14. So Waddell later told Miss Mackintosh, cited in her *Coillard*, p. 381.

15. Waddell's Diary, 14 Nov., 1886. Also Coillard to Mrs. Coillard, 14 Oct., 1886, NAR Hist. Mss. Coillard Papers, Vol. 2, 1883–91. CO 5/1/1/1.

16. At no time did Lewanika apparently ever ask Westbeech to write on his behalf. The latter's diary in fact never mentions the protection issue.

17. Coillard, Journal, 24 June, 1885, and 22 Jan., 1887; L. Jalla to Boegner, 9 Sept., 1889, PMSP; Favre, *Coillard*, Vol. 3, p. 161.

18. Mackintosh, *Coillard*, pp. 372–3.

19. Richard Hall, *Zambia* (London, 1965), p. 63.

20. Westbeech Diary, folio 65, NAR.

21. Waddell's Diary, 6 Feb., 1887, *op. cit.*

22. Westbeech, 'Part of a Diary', p. 45, RLI.

23. Coillard, Journal, 20 Jan., 1887, and Coillard, *Threshold*, p. 281.

24. Coillard, Journal, 4 March and 5 March, 1887.

25. Coillard, *Threshold*, p. 291.

26. Cited in Peter Fraenkel, *Wayaleshi* (London, 1959), p. 110. Mr. Njekwa reported the same fears to me in almost identical words, and Coillard learned in 1895 that old induna Nalabutu had initially advised people never to shut their eyes during services; Coillard, *Threshold*, p. 599.

27. Mr. Mupatu, and Memorandum by A. Jalla, 26 Oct., 1928, NAZ. KDE 2/30/9.

28. Coillard to Boegner, ? Nov. 1887, PMSP.

29. Coillard, *Threshold*, pp. 208 and 320, and Coillard to L. Jalla and Goy, ? Dec., 1891, PSMP.

30. Coillard, *Threshold*, pp. 329–32; see also A. Jalla to Colin Harding, undated but after Lewanika's death in 1916, in NAR. Hist. Mss. Catherine Mackintosh Papers. MA 18/1/4, folios 2–3.

31. Coillard, *Threshold*, pp. 332–3.

32. Coillard to L. Jalla and Goy, ? Dec. 1891, PMSP.

33. Cited in Hall, *Zambia*, p. 63, and H. M. Hole, *The Making of Rhodesia* (London, 1926), p. 213.

34. Coillard to Shippard, 8 Jan. 1889, cited in T. W. Baxter, 'The Concessions of Northern Rhodesia', in National Archives of Rhodesia and Nyasaland, *Occasional Papers*, No. 1, June, 1963, p. 4. It is difficult to determine how much of this letter represented the opinions of Coillard rather than those of the king.

35. Coillard, Journal, 15 April, 1889.

36. Coillard to Boegner, 20 June, 1889, PMSP.

37. Waddell's Diary, July, 1889, NAR.

38. Coillard to Boegner, 28 June, 1889, PMSP.

39. The Ware Concession, 27 June, 1889, cited in Baxter, *op. cit.*, pp. 5–7.

40. Mr. Zaza, who also pointed out that most of his own Lozi informants were unable to distinguish between the Ware Concession and the more famous Lochner Concession of the following year.

41. Brown, 'Aspects of the Scramble for Matabeleland', *op. cit.*, p. 70.

42. Khama to Coillard and Lewanika, 17 July, 1889, NAR Hist. Mss. Mackintosh Papers. MA 18/4/1, folios 4–7.

43. Shippard to Coillard, 1 Sept, 1889, NAR Hist. Mss. Coillard Papers CO 5/5/1, folios 13–15.

44. E. W. Smith, *The Journal of Andrew Baldwin, Pioneer Missionary in Northern Rhodesia* (typewritten mss. 1953, Methodist Missionary Society Archives, London), p. 7.

45. Reported in Coillard to Mrs. Hart, 28 May, 1890, NAR Hist. Mss. Coillard Papers. CO 5/1/1/1, folios 984–5, and Waddell's Diary, 7 June, 1890, NAR.

46. Lochner to ?, undated NAR Hist. Mss. Mackintosh Papers. MA 18/4, folios 32–3.

47. Waddell's Diary, 7 June, 1890, NAR.

48. Coillard to Rev. Smith, 20 June, 1890, NAR Hist. Mss. Coillard Papers. CO 5/1/1/1, folio 991.

49. See A. Jalla, *Pionniers Parmi les Ma-Rotsi* (Florence, 1903), p. 36, and Coillard to Jameson, undated, cited in Hall, *Zambia*, p, 93.

50. Lochner to Company, 2 July, 1890, cited in Maxwell Stamp Associates, *History of the Mineral Rights of Northern Rhodesia*, Vol. 2, p. 21.

51. Hepburn to Coillard, 22 Nov., 1889, NAR Hist. Mss. Mackintosh Papers, MA 18/4, folios 8–9.

52. Coillard, *Threshold*, p. 385.

53. 'Of course,' he added, 'we too shall reap some advantages from these changes, for postal communications and perhaps also for our supplies'. Coillard to Hunter, 12 Aug., 1890, NAR Hist. Mss. Coillard Papers CO 5/2/1, folios 62–3.

54. A. Jalla to Boegner, 5 May 1890, PMSP.

55. Coillard to L. Jalla and Goy, ? 1891, PMSP. Louis Jalla commented that he had read this statement with 'great astonishment' and felt that Coillard 'had been deceived', for he himself had 'never believed this'. L. Jalla to Boegner, 18 Feb., 1891, PMSP.

56. Cited in Mackintosh, *Coillard*, p. 383.

57. James Johnston, *Reality vs Romance in South Central Africa* (London 1893), p. 148.

58. C.O. to F.O., in FO 403, Vol. 157, No. 169.

59. Hole, *Making of Rhodesia*, p. 217; also J. G. Lockhart and C. M. Woodhouse, *Rhodes* (London, 1963), p. 239.

60. Coillard to Boegner, 25 June, 1890, PMSP.

61. According to Andrew Baldwin, a Methodist missionary who saw the documents; see Smith, *Journal of Baldwin*, pp. 8–9. No copy of the original Sesuto of the concession seems to exist.

62. Mr. Simalumba.

63. Lochner to Harris, 23 April, 1890, NAR Hist. Mss. Mackintosh Papers, MA 18/4, folio 28.

64. Lochner to Company, 2 July, 1890, NAR HC 3/3/1, and Coillard to Rhodes, ? 1890, NAR Hist. Mss. Mackintosh Papers, MA 18/4, folio 28.

65. So A. Jalla recalled in a letter written in 1903, cited in *Balovale Commission Report*, 1939, p. 51.

66. Jalla, *Pionniers Parmi les Ma-Rotsi*, p. 39.

67. Mackintosh, *Coillard*, p. 385.

68. Cited in Coillard, *Threshold*, p. 388.

69. Cited in Hall, *Zambia*, p. 69, but no source is recorded.

70. And by Mr. N. Zaza, though it should be pointed out that he had read Miss Mackintosh's biography of Coillard.

71. Lochner to Company, 2 July, 1890, cited in Maxwell Stamp Associates, *op. cit.*, p. 21.

72. Cited in full in Baxter, 'Concessions of Northern Rhodesia', *op. cit.*, pp. 8–10.

73. The Frontiers of the Barotse Kingdom as defined in a Council by the King Lewanika, his Councillors and the principal Headmen of the Nation, held at Lealui, 25 June, 1890, and recorded by Coillard, cited in M. Stamp Associates, *op. cit.*, pp. 24–6.

74. ' "See how things grow", said Rhodes gleefully when the news of the treaty was brought to him".' Lockhart and Woodhouse, *Rhodes*, pp. 239–40.

75. See the Agreements with Kazembe of the Lunda and Nsama of the Itawa branch of the Bemba in Baxter, *op. cit.*, pp. 3–57.

76. *Ibid.*, p. 9.

77. Mr. Zaza.

78. Stokes, 'Barotseland', *op. cit.*, p. 261.

79. Gann, *op. cit.*, p. 21.

80. Lochner freely admitted that 'the Company owes as much, if not more, to M. Coillard than myself in having secured the Barotse Country—he is heart and soul with the Company'. Lochner to Company, 30 July, 1890, NAR Hist. Mss. Mackintosh Papers, MA 18/4, folio 34. Adolph Jalla agreed that 'Without Coillard, the King would never have agreed to the treaty'. Jalla to Boegner, 5 July, 1890, PMSP.

81. Brown, 'Aspects of the Scramble', *op. cit.*, pp. 88–90.

82. That is, until 1924, when the Colonial Office assumed the administration of Northern Rhodesia from the Company.

83. Coillard, Journal, 26 Oct., 1890, and 16 Nov., 1890.

84. Lewanika to Loch, FO 403, Vol. 157, No. 119.

85. Middleton to Salisbury, 27 Oct., 1890, FO 403, Vol. 157, No. 158.

86. Lewanika to Loch, FO 403, Vol. 157, No. 119.

87. L. Jalla to Boegner, 4 Feb., 1891, PMSP, and Lewanika to Bagley and Fraser, ? Jan., 1891, NAR. CT 1/4/1. This letter appears to be in Coillard's handwriting.

88. Coillard, Journal, 8 June, 1891.

89. *Ibid.*, 10 June, 1891. I have not been able to discover the original copy of this letter.

90. Coillard to Smith, 30 June, 1891. NAR Hist. Mss. Coillard Papers. CO 5/1/1/1, folios 1015–16.

91. Loch to Lewanika, 19 Sept., 1881, NAR. CT 1/4/4.

92. Coillard to Loch, 13 Nov., 1891. FO 403, Vol. 174, No. 50.

93. Johnstone, *Reality vs Romance in South Central Africa*, p. 7.

94. *Ibid.*, p. 142.

95. *Ibid.*, pp. 45–7.

96. *Ibid.*, pp. 149–51.

97. Society to Ripon, 25 Jan., 1894. FO 403, Vol. 197, No. 89.

98. CO to FO, 29 March, 1894, *ibid.*

99. Coillard, *Threshold*, pp.451–2. Coillard's account at the time was identical; see Coillard to Waddell, 22 Feb., 1892, cited in Waddell's Diary, *op. cit.*

100. A. Jalla, *Lewanika*, p. 10, and Waddell's Diary, 24 April, 1892, *op. cit.*

101. Waddell's Diary, *op. cit.*

102. Company to Coillard, 29 July 1892, NAR Microfilm. Royal-Coillard Papers, folio 2, file 2.

103. Coillard to Loch, 21 Sept., 1892, FO 403, Vol. 185, No. 26.

104. Mr. E. Fry, in an article on his journey to the Victoria Falls in the *Cape Times*, 12 Nov., 1892, cited in FO 403, Vol. 185, No. 26.

105. Coillard to Loch, 7 Feb., 1893, FO 403, Vol. 197, No. 91.

106. Lewanika to J. S. Moffat, 24 Nov., 1893, FO 403, Vol. 197, No. 91.

107. Coillard to Rhodes, 27 Nov., 1893, NAR CT 1/4/1.

108. Loch to Lewanika, 18 Jan., 1894, FO 403, Vol. 197, No. 91.

109. Coillard to Boegner, 21 March, 1894, PMSP.

110. Mr. N. Zaza placed great emphasis on this argument to explain the countless 'surrenders' by Lewanika to the Company.

111. Lewanika to Loch, 30 Oct., 1894, FO 403, Vol. 212, No. 74.

112. Jalla, *Pionniers*, pp. 122–7.

113. Coillard, *Threshold*, p. 579. Alone of my informants, Mr. Simalumba had a vague recollection of an attempt to depose Lewanika during this period on account of his Christian sympathies. As we shall see, there were several subsequent abortive coups against the King, and informants showed considerable difficulty in distinguishing accurately between them all.

114. Coillard to Jameson, 4 July, 1895, NAR Hist. Mss. Coillard Papers, CO 5/5/1, folios 51–4.

115. Lewanika to Jameson, undated, FO 413, Vol. 213.

116. Coillard to Jameson, 4 July, 1895, *op. cit.* The missionaries were also concerned that the advent of white immigrants would undermine their own unique status among the Lozi; see A. Jalla to Boegner, 3–12 June, 1895, PMSP. Their disillusionment with the Company must have increased, moreover, when J. S. Moffat wrote Coillard that he was 'much concerned at what you tell me about the doings of white men in Barotseland. Nowadays, might is right. The Charter Company controls everything, even the High Commission'. Moffat to Coillard, 1 Sept., 1895, cited in Hall, *Zambia*, pp. 91–2.

117. Jameson to Lewanika, 13 Aug., 1995, NAR CT 1/4/4, and Jameson to Coillard, 5 Sept., 1895, FO 403, Vol. 213, No. 128.

118. FO to Company, 1 Nov., 1895, FO 403, Vol. 213, No. 139, and Harris to Rhodes, 5 Nov. 1895, NAR CT 1/4/1.

119. Rhodes to Harris, 6 Nov., 1895, NAR CT 1/4/1; Company to FO, 15 Nov., 1895, FO 403, Vol. 213, No. 150.

120. Johnston to Roseberry, 19 Aug., 1893, FO 403, Vol. 185. No. 225; FO to Company, 1 Nov., 1895, FO 403, Vol. 213, No. 139; CO to FO 4 April, 1896, CO African South 517; CO to FO, 16 Jan., 1897, *ibid.*

121. Salisbury to Petrie, 22 Jan., 1892, FO 403, Vol. 174, No. 11; Rhodes to Kimberley, 7 Dec., 1894, FO 403, Vol. 212, No. 1; D'Avila to Machado, 17 April, 1895, FO 403, Vol. 212, No. 151; Milner to Chamberlain, FO 403, Vol. 246, No. 45; Robinson *et al*, *Africa and the Victorians*, pp. 246–7; Lockhart and Woodhouse, *Rhodes*, p. 389.

122. FO to CO, 18 Feb., 1896, FO 403, Vol. 229, No. 49, and FO to Treasury, 2 March, 1896, FO 403, Vol. 229, No. 63.

123. Lewanika to Portuguese Commandant, 20 March, 1896, CO, African South 517, enclosure.

124. Jalla to Rosemead, 15 May, 1896, *ibid.*; also Lewanika to Robinson, 15 May 1896, FO 403, Vol. 230, No. 107.

125. FO to Goold-Adams, 12 March, 1896, FO 403, Vol. 229, No. 77.

126. Goold-Adams to High Commissioner, 21 Oct., 1896, CO, African South 517.

127. Jalla, *Lewanika*, p. 9, and *Pionniers*, p. 195.

128. Goold-Adams to FO, 7 Feb., 1887, FO 403, Vol 245, No. 108.

129. Same to same, 24 Aug., 1897, FO 403, Vol. 246, No. 35.

130. Same to Rosmead, 21 Oct., 1896, FO 403, Vol. 245, No. 38.

131. Lewanika to Robinson and Lewanika to Victoria, 23 Oct., 1896, FO 403, Vol. 245, No. 96. Two years later Lewanika told another British soldier that he wanted 'no other' than Englishmen in his country. 'To the

Portuguese he took special exception . . . as they treat people with whom they come in contact as though they were beasts'. A. St. H. Gibbons, *Africa from South to North through Barotseland* (2 Vols., London, 1904), Vol. 1, pp. 126–7.

132. Milner to Lewanika, 18 May, 1897, CO, African South 552. The King expressed his pleasure in a letter written to Milner on his behalf by Jalla, 28 July, 1897, *ibid*.

133. Worthington's Journal, 1902, NAR Hist. Mss. Worthington Papers, WO 3/1/2, folios 2–5.

134. Mr. Simalumba.

135. Messrs. Arthur and Newo Zaza and Mr. Njewka. Arthur Zaza was given his information by 'a very old man' in Limulunga village, but I was unable to meet him.

136. Mr. N. Zaza.

137. Worthington's Journal, *op. cit.*

138. Coryndon remained in north-western Rhodesia until 1907. He later became, successively, Administrator of Swaziland and of Basutoland, and Governor of Uganda and of Kenya. He died in 1925. See Kenneth Bradley, 'Statesmen: Coryndon and Lewanika in North-Western Rhodesia', *African Observer*, Vol. 5, No. 5, Sept., 1936, pp. 48–9 and 54, and Gann, *History of Northern Rhodesia*, p. 79.

139. Jalla to Boegner, 22 Oct., 1897, PMSP.

140. Coryndon to FO, 25 Nov., 1897, CO, African South 559.

141. H. M. Hole, *The Passing of the Black Kings* (London, 1932), p. 297.

142. CO to FO, 29 Sept., 1897, FO 403, Vol. 246, No. 49.

143. As reported in Jalla, *Pionniers*, p. 236.

144. Coryndon to Secretary of State for Foreign Affairs, 25 Nov., 1897, CO, African South 686.

145. Lewanika to Milner, 1 Nov., 1897, FO 403, Vol. 264, No. 8.

146. Lockhart and Woodhouse, *Rhodes*, p. 240.

CHAPTER IV

# COMPANY RULE

Shortly after the arrival of Coryndon and his party in Lealui, Lewanika made the following pronouncement to the Kuta:

There are [he declared] three types of white men: (1) those of the government; (2) the traders; (3) the missionaries. Those of the government, fear them, they have the power; the traders, eat them, for they have come to eat you; the missionaries, they are ours, they are our family.[1]

This astute analysis was quickly substantiated. Three considerations governed the actions of the Company's representatives. In the first place, as Coryndon was specifically instructed, 'it is absolutely necessary to reduce expenditures of Company for Administration to a minimum. . . .'[2] Secondly, being orthodox Company men, they wholly accepted the South African tradition of direct intervention in the affairs of the people they governed.[3] Finally, with only minor exceptions, they regarded Africans as being inherently inferior to Europeans. Frank Worthington, who was typical of most Company officials, began his career believing that 'The Barotse had not learned to treat a white man with that respect his colour demands',[4] and was soon 'getting to hate niggers more and more. . . . I would shoot him [the African] to the last man if I had my way. . . . Slavery is much too good for the reptile.'[5]

These three premises had inestimable consequences for Barotseland's future. The Company had no intention of providing the revenues needed by Lewanika to modernize his nation along western lines. The philosophy of direct rule meant that its agents would do their utmost to establish their own control over the activities of the king and his Kuta,[6] while their racialist attitudes left them blind or indifferent to the

74

unquestionable resentment of those whose positions they were undermining.[7]

The 'protectors' for whom Lewanika had so impatiently awaited did their work swiftly and thoroughly. In his recent study, Eric Stokes has analysed the process by which, between 1898 and 1911, Lewanika 'had lost whatever governing powers he had possessed or could have exerted outside Barotseland proper, and even within his reserved powers he had no more than a limited subordinate jurisdiction'.[8] It is not necessary to reproduce here Stokes's entire essay, except in so far as sources which he did not use—above all, missionary records and oral tradition—allow us to set his findings in the perspective of a more detailed elaboration of internal Lozi politics in the period.

Not long after Coryndon's arrival, Lewanika, Litia, and several senior indunas were summoned to Victoria Falls to agree to a new concession conferring administrative powers in Barotseland on the Company.[9] This document differed from the Lochner Concession in three decisive ways. It gave the Company the right to 'deal with and adjudicate upon all cases between white men and between white men and natives . . .'; the Company could 'make grants of land for farming purposes' in Toka and Ila country 'to white men approved by the King'; and finally, as compensation for this extension of the Company's authority, the annual grant to the King of £2,000 set down in the 1890 concession, and never paid, was *reduced* to the sum of £850.[10]

Lawley reported that the Lozi negotiators 'expressed themselves perfectly satisfied with the terms'.[11] Yet Coillard refused to participate in the negotiations,[12] and the Lozi would not sign the document unless, Lewanika declared, a further clause was added: the Company must agree to exclude from prospecting or settlement an area consisting, in effect, of the Barotse Valley east of the Upper Zambesi and the Sesheke district.[13] In any event, the promulgation in 1899 of the Barotseland–North-western Rhodesia Order in Council superseded, so far as administrative powers were concerned, this concession.[14] The Order, one of two which divided Northern Rhodesia at the Kafue River into two distinct administrative units, necessitated the drawing up of yet another concession to legitimize the Company's administrative rights in Barotseland.[15]

Coryndon, now Administrator of North-Western Rhodesia based at Kalomo in Toka country, therefore travelled to Lealui where he met with Lewanika and twenty-seven senior indunas for the purpose of negotiating the new concession.[16] Unlike the Uganda Agreement of 1900, which 'for many years . . . [gave] no compelling reason . . . for fundamental reconsideration',[17] the Coryndon Concession of the same year, and those which followed it, produced serious conflict between the Administration and the Lozi ruling class. Coryndon's document contained the three clauses which distinguished the Lawley from the Lochner Concession, but included the proviso demanded by Lewanika excluding the Valley and Sesheke from prospecting. According to Coryndon, this inclusion met the King's most important demand, since, he thought, the reserved area was the richest part of Barotseland in terms of tribute paid, available manpower, and good grazing lands,[18] and the concession was duly signed.[19]

Why had the King and his indunas agreed to grant the Company so much freedom of action outside Barotseland proper? Coillard, after all, refused to witness the new concession, considering it highly unfavourable to the Lozi,[20] although it is true that he was probably resentful that his own influence was declining. Colin Harding, who was one of the witnesses for the Company, later intimated that Coryndon had not revealed to the Lozi the full contents of the document. He believed that the Lozi representatives signed the concession only with 'some hesitation and misgiving', and after some subtle threats by Coryndon.[21] This may well have been one of the occasions alluded to by Lewanika when he complained in 1907 that whenever he raised a grievance against the Company, its officials replied: 'Do you want to be conquered?'[22]

Moreover, Lewanika, the Mokwae of Nalolo, and at least some indunas had learnt of the outbreak of the Anglo-Boer War.[23] They professed to the missionaries their shock at the thought of two groups of white Christians slaughtering each other,[24] but it is quite likely that the war illustrated to them a crucial truth. Englishmen had destroyed Lobengula when he stood in their way; now they were prepared to destroy white antagonists. According to one informant, Lewanika knew of Rhodes's deep involvement in the war. The King therefore reasonably concluded that opposition from Barotseland would hardly be tolerated for very long. This informant claimed indeed that the Lozi had discovered how the Ndebele had been manoeuvred into an aggressive stance, giving the Company an apparently legitimate excuse to attack them. In this knowledge, the King reconciled himself to the need to accept the Company's demands: he would reluctantly relinquish much of his sovereignty over the far reaches of his kingdom, so long as he could safeguard his position at least in Barotseland proper.[25]

It appears that the King's decision not to forcibly resist Company demands brought into the open once again the earlier conflict within the ruling class. This split was reflected in the competition to select a new Ngambela after Mwauluka's death in 1898. The Kutas of Lealui, Nalolo and Sesheke submitted to the King the names of Mubita, then induna Kalonga, and Mokamba from whom to appoint Mwauluka's successor.[26] Kalonga was much the older man, a contemporary and close personal friend of Lewanika, renowned as a great Lozi warrior, powerful by virtue of his holding one of the senior titles in the council hierarchy. He was the choice of those Lozi aristocrats who had grown to manhood before the advent of missionaries and Company officials, and who had opposed the concessions fearing that white power would undermine their own authority as well as the integrity of the nation.[27]

Mokamba represented the modern generation of the ruling class. Although only in his middle thirties, he was already a man of considerable experience. The son of Njekwa, Sipopa's Ngambela, Mokamba remained close to the throne through his intimate friendship with Prince Litia. He fled with Lewanika into exile in 1884, and fought with him in the decisive battle against Mataa's forces in the following year. Mokamba and Litia were among the first students at the PMS school in Sefula, where they shared an enthusiasm for learning and a sympathy for Christian ideas. Like his father, Mokamba married one of the King's daughters, and soon found himself appointed to an important indunaship.[28]

The King recognized the significance of the choice he now had to make. Kalonga had a powerful and influential position, and even Adolph Jalla, when asked his opinion by the King, supported Kalonga on the grounds that Mokamba was too young to become the senior commoner in the nation. Lewanika replied, however, that Kalonga would do 'all in his power to favour paganism, while Mokamba was a Christian with a mind open to every sort of progress'.[29] Lozi informants agreed that to Lewanika, Mokamba's Christianity was important not in a religious sense, but because it reflected—as it did, for example, among the Ganda[30]—an attitude of receptivity to modern techniques and development. Because, unlike Kalonga, he was literate and educated, Mokamba would be able to meet with the white man on terms more approaching equality; because he shared with Lewanika and Litia a proper respect for white power, he would not provoke the Company to crush the Lozi nation. He was the man who could best achieve a balance in the relationship between the Lozi ruling class and the Company, and it was already clear to the King that that relationship would henceforth be the critical one in the survival of his nation. When therefore, the traditionalists in the Kuta wished to reject the concessions with Lawley and Coryndon, it was the more realistic Mokamba who supported the compromise measure of making 'Barotseland proper' a reserve area in which the King's power would not be circumscribed.[31]

Mokamba's appointment was naturally resented by Kalonga's supporters. Nevertheless, his twenty years in office earned for him among the Lozi the reputation of being the best Ngambela since his father,[32] while his intelligence, tact, administrative ability and popularity were remarked upon by missionaries and Company officials alike.[33]

Moreover, shortly after the turn of the century, as Lewanika grew perceptibly more tired with advancing age and under the increased strain of Company rule, the actual governing of the country fell increasingly upon the shoulders of his Ngambela.[34] This was of great significance, for Mokamba naturally turned for advice and assistance to younger men who, like himself and Litia, had been educated at mission schools. In this way, the supreme status of the Lozi kingship and government was upheld. For, as Pratt has observed in connection with the Buganda, 'many of the abler "westernized" young men whose equivalents in West Africa were active and open opponents of the tribal authorities either joined the ruling hierarchy or aspired to it'.[35] The prestige of the 'old order' was, therefore, not merely untarnished but enhanced. At the same time, Lewanika received, through his payment from the Concession and, as shall be seen, his share of the hut tax, far greater revenues than were allowed to any other Paramount Chief in the Zambesi region. This money served as an adequate substitute for the goods and tribute with which Lozi kings had formerly been able to win the attachment of their subjects. It also saved the Lozi elite from the humiliation of their counterparts among, for example, the Fort Jameson Ngoni, who were materially outclassed by returning labourers from the south.[36]

But if these developments buttressed Lewanika's position, they simultaneously created new tensions which endangered it. Paradoxically, the absorption into the centres of power of the new mission-educated elite led to a decline in the influence of the missionaries themselves, as their former students began to handle tasks such as corresponding with the white officials. Even more important, the influence of the young men was equally resented by the older indunas and the white administrators alike. Coryndon, for example, could not abide the 'cheekiness' and 'arrogance' of 'so-called educated natives',[37] and was determined that he, not they, should have most control over the King. And his ability to achieve this was facilitated by the role of the traditionalist faction within the Kuta. The hostility of its members towards the King's younger advisers was inevitably directed against Lewanika himself. He therefore felt that his position was once again tenuous, and looked to Coryndon and his officials to reinforce it. This they were gladly prepared to do, in return for gaining even greater control over the King and for his abject acceptance of every Company demand which served to circumscribe his own powers and severely limit the extent of his authority.

Many of these cross-currents manifested themselves early in the new century when the King welcomed an 'Ethiopian' church to Barotseland. This fascinating episode in Lozi history has been perceptively examined by Ranger, although he failed to see that the traditionalist indunas did not share the enthusiasm of Lewanika and Ngambela Mokamba for the Ethiopians. For the latter were welcomed, as Ranger accurately pointed out, 'not because they offered an indigenous form of Christianity but because they promised to provide a relevant education and

to assist in the "modernization" of Lozi society'.[38] Mission
teaching was weighted towards learning Lozi and the Gospel;
as the missionaries themselves realized, the new elite wanted
far more teaching of English and other 'practical' subjects.[39]
As a result, Lewanika had already in 1901 sent his son Imwiko
and one of his nephews to a private school in England.[40]

When, therefore, Willie Mokalapa, a Sotho evangelist who
had worked with the PMS, turned against the mission and
offered to provide the kind of education the King desired, the
latter accepted with alacrity. By 1903, the Ethiopians' schools
had succeeded in drawing away a majority of former PMS
students. By late 1905, however, the Ethiopian movement had
virtually collapsed, largely because Mokalapa, entrusted by
Lewanika with a large sum of money to purchase wagons,
carriages and boats in South Africa, was swindled out of the
cash by a firm of South African merchants.[41] In any event, it
is unlikely that the Administration would have long tolerated
the Ethiopian presence, Coryndon, for example, believing they
preached 'dangerous doctrines . . . nor the least pernicious
being the practical equality of white and black races. . . .'[42]

Nevertheless, the mark left by Mokalapa's activities was a
very tangible one, 'more through the stimulus which his presence gave to government than through his own direct action'.[43]
For the local Company officials were fully aware of the King's
motivation in welcoming Mokalapa's schools, and recognized
that only an extension of educational opportunities, particularly in the teaching of English and 'useful technical knowledge', could prevent a resurgence of Ethiopianism.[44] No steps
had been taken to fulfil that clause in the Concession of 1900
promising to promote African education. The Company now
realized it could meet its obligations by spending only those
revenues which Lewanika was receiving as his share of the hut
tax. This fact doubtless made more palatable its sanctioning,
in 1906, of the Barotse National School, 'which was for a very
long time the only school in Northern Rhodesia not run and
financed by a mission society, and one with significantly
superior resources and offering a more advanced standard of
education than any other in the territory.'[45] The BNS was to
play a substantial role in Lozi life, and indeed in the life of
Northern Rhodesia, and it owed its existence directly to the

initiative of the King, supported by the emerging educated
new elite, in welcoming the Ethiopians to Barotseland.

Essentially, Mokalapa and his assistants were considered by
Lewanika to be the instrument by which Lozi independence
could be safeguarded: with a properly trained elite loyal to the
King, his reliance on both missionaries and Company officials
could be significantly reduced. Yet during the same period, a
conflict in the north with Kakenge, a Luvale chief, was
forcing him into an even closer dependence on white power.

Kakenge had made an alliance with the Portuguese who
were continuing to build forts in his region, and forbade any
other Luvale from sending tribute to Lewanika. The latter
wished to send an expedition against Kakenge, but Harding
vetoed the plan.[46] A number of Lozi indunas felt that Lewanika's
submission to Harding's veto was a humiliation to Lozi national
pride: 'Not only is the King getting anxious about it,' Coryndon
reported, 'but his headmen are talking among themselves much
more than I care to see.'[47] Lozi resentment of Britain's failure
to support their case was shared by the Company. The extent
of its mineral rights was co-terminous with the extent of Lewanika's empire. Moreover, Company officials were anxious to
have access to as much territory as possible from which labour
could be recruited for Southern Rhodesia. For these reasons
they all supported the Lozi claim to a vast area north and west
of the northern extremities of the Barotse Valley.[48] Chamberlain was no less concerned about 'the serious danger to British
interests' on the Upper Zambesi, but preferred an amicable
settlement of the question with Portugal.[49] Lewanika wrote
Chamberlain expressing his anxiety for a swift and satisfactory
settlement.[50] In reply, the latter informed the Lozi King that
the Kings of England and Portugal 'have asked the King of
Italy, who is the good friend of both, to hear all that each has
to say [on the matter], and then to decide between them'.[51]

Lewanika and the Kuta were obviously disappointed at this
outcome. The affair had been taken entirely out of their hands;
the future extent of their kingdom rested solely with the British
government, on which they were thus dependent. The Company
regarded this state of affairs ambivalently: they feared the loss
of desired territory, but were pleased with any development
which further increased the dependence of Lewanika on its

officials. For the Company's greatest asset in Barotseland was the King's need for its protection against both his internal opponents and the Portuguese at his frontiers. And the greater Lewanika's reliance on Company support, the easier it would be to gain his consent to further Company limitations on his sovereignty.

It was for this reason that Lewanika was allowed to attend the coronation of Edward VII in 1902. He had yearned to visit England for many years, probably since he had learned of Khama's successful trip in 1895. It would conclusively demonstrate that there was a special relationship between the monarchs of England and Barotseland. Specifically, it would give Lewanika the opportunity personally to entreat Edward 'to shift the Government of his country from the BSAC to the Crown'.[52] The Company's motive in sanctioning the trip was as clear as Lewanika's, if diametrically opposite. '. . . It would,' Coryndon pointed out, 'increase his reliance upon us. . . .'[53] And it did. Although Lewanika was given the British grand tour, he 'had not got', Jalla reported, 'the main thing he had gone for. . . .'[54] Although he had earlier assured Coillard that 'When kings are seated together, there is never a lack of things to discuss',[55] in fact their interview was confined to non-political pleasantries. And from Chamberlain Lewanika received only vague assurances that Lozi interests would be safeguarded.[56] The overriding impact of the visit was clear: having seen British might at first hand, the King and Ngambela understood once and for all that their country's destiny had effectively been removed from their hands.[57] The obvious futility of resistance begat Lozi submission.

Lewanika returned home, then, with none of his doubts and insecurities laid to rest. Indeed, they were exacerbated when he was welcomed back with tales of a coup which was said to have been attempted in his absence. It was claimed that his first cousin Muimui, aided by the unsuccessful candidate for Ngambela, Kalonga, had considered seizing the throne with the support of the anti-white faction of the Kuta. No evidence was ever uncovered to confirm that such a plot had ever existed, [58] but Lewanika acted as if he believed his enemies were capable of such a move.

Late in 1903, the King became mildly ill; the malady was

not grave, but Company officials began considering the question of the succession, for they had already decided that,
whoever else might be nominated, Litia would follow his
father. Hole, the Acting Administrator, believed that Litia
was 'not at all *persona grata* with many of the influential chiefs',
probably the older traditionalist ones. But this weakness made
him even more attractive, for, Hole pointed out, 'he would be
more likely to lean on the British for support if he became king
without a unanimous following'.[59] Accordingly, Aitkens, DC
for Lealui district, broached the subject with the King in 1904,
and reported that Lewanika 'informed me that he and the
Barotse were all of one mind, and that Litia, his first born,
would succeed him', although the King acknowledged that the
final choice lay with the Kuta.[60] It was happening, then, the
way many of his indunas had feared: the King and the white
men colluding to maximize their own authority at the expense
of the Kuta, for Coryndon soon 'let it be known unobtrusively'
that the Administration intended Litia 'naturally' to succeed
his father.[61] This removed from indunas one of their most
powerful sanctions on a king, the right to claim that since they
had appointed him, they had the equal right to remove him if
they considered that he was ruling unjustly or without seeking
their advice.

At about the same time, indunas' freedom of action was
physically curtailed. Coryndon was administering North-
Western Rhodesian through five districts, each under a District Commissioner with control over most facets of law and
order.[62] In 1903, Lewanika was informed that no headman or
induna was to leave or enter a district without reporting to its
DC.[63] In a further move, a Lozi induna was attached to each
DC, in an explicitly subordinate status, to represent continuing
Lozi dominance over all of North-Western Rhodesia. In fact,
Lozi control over much of Ila, Toka and Luvale country had
evaporated years earlier.[64] But the advantage to the Administration of propping up the disintegrating representative induna
system was clear: as the Secretary for Native Affairs acknowledged in 1905, the Lozi elite would be grateful believing their
former authority would be recovered, while 'the entire Administration of Natives [would be placed] in the hands of officials of
this Department.'[65] For in fact the purpose of this move was to

D

legitimize Company authority over tribes with whom it had no concessions. But the charade was not prolonged. In 1907, the Lozi indunas stationed among the Ila and Toka were ordered back to the Valley.[66] Lewanika finally understood that he was to have no influence outside the reserved area, and complained angrily to Selborne, the High Commissioner in South Africa:

> Now I also ask Your Excellency what is the meaning of the expulsion of all my representatives from the Mashukulubwe [Ila] and Makota districts? Does the Company intend to take away those districts quite out of my power? I have always done all in my power to keep the peace in all my country and to have all my people submissive to the Company. I am sorry to see they have so little confidence in me. . . . I feel it very keenly. Oh! that we were granted to pass directly under the Government of King Edward![67]

Selborne, however, refused to intervene.[68] The British government clearly had no intention of halting the Company's increasing encroachment on Lozi sovereignty, although it was felt that Lewanika's formal consent should be gained for each prerogative he was forced to surrender.[69] In 1904, for example, Coryndon had got the King to agree to a new proclamation to extend Administration jurisdiction in Barotseland to encompass all 'serious cases' between Africans, such as murder and witchcraft. Coryndon promised that white magistrates would not 'interfere in the small matters which concern only native custom and tradition',[70] but the King and Ngambela only agreed to relinquish their right to try cases of murder and witchcraft; all other cases in the reserved area they wished to retain.[71] In the end, however, the Courts of Justice Proclamation of 1905 left to the King and Kuta in the reserved area only 'civil and criminal cases between natives of a minor kind in which native custom is not repugnant to English law'.[72]

By a steady process of attrition, then, Lozi sovereignty was being forced back into the relatively narrow confines of the Valley and Sesheke, and even there it was being emasculated. The next step in this process has been described by Stokes as constituting Lewanika's 'greatest surrender'.[73] The Concession of 1900 gave the Company the right to grant land in Toka and Ila country only to white men approved by the King. Coryndon now asked for 'the authority to issue land over all your territory [save the usual reserved portion] to whoever I consider to be a good and *bona fide* farmer or settler'.[74] Lewanika replied giving his consent,[75] but at the insistence of the Secretary of State, the agreement was ratified by him in a more formal deed of cession in 1906.[76]

The Colonial Office recognized that the concession amounted to 'a land grant of the whole of North-Western Rhodesia, except Lewanika's own reserve'.[77] There are two possible explanations for the King's agreeing to sign the agreement. He may not, in the first place, fully have understood its implications. In later years, as we shall see, he and his successor repeatedly insisted that they never intended to allow the Company to sell land, for, as one informant argued, the Lozi naturally saw farming and settlement in their own terms; the King placed blocks of land under the control of others, but all land remained, ultimately, the King's, in his capacity as *litunga*, 'owner of the land'.[78]

In the second place, the King and Ngambela probably accepted Coryndon's demands without seeking the consent of the Kuta. Aitkens, the DC at Lealui, had discussed the Courts of Justice Proclamation only with the King and Ngambela.[79] It was true that the King's powers had been circumscribed no less than those of his indunas. But he nevertheless remained king, and most of the privileges left to Lozi by virtue of the Concession of 1900 accrued to him. It was he who conferred with the representatives of the Company, he who had travelled to England, he to whom the £850 a year was given. And this position was safeguarded, as he fully grasped, so long as he co-operated with the Administration. He had seen the consequences of resistance in the case of the Ndebele and the Boers. He surely had not forgotten Worthington's threat to Litia in 1902 that, had the alleged plot of 1897 to kill all Europeans succeeded, 'today there would be no Barotse nation'.[80] No doubt the indunas shared the King's fear of white power. The fact that they seemed more willing to resist it, as we shall see, is likely due to the simple fact that they had less to lose by so doing than Lewanika did. For that reason, he was prepared to capitulate on virtually every issue, so long as the Company allowed him to remain King of Barotseland proper. For, as one informant emphasized, if the Company was not given what it demanded, there was good reason to fear that it would simply take by force everything—including the kingship itself.[81]

Lewanika therefore submitted time after time. In 1902, for example, he agreed with alacrity to Coryndon's suggestion that tax collection begin in Toka country.[82] Lewanika wished his representative indunas to collect the tax, in order 'to show the people he is still their king', though agreeing that all receipts be handed over to the Administration.[83] Coryndon, however, intransigently opposed any scheme to augment the King's status outside the Valley. He would only allow a Lozi induna to instruct people in Lewanika's name to pay the tax to a European collector,[84] and Lewanika reluctantly conceded.[85]

Similarly, Lewanika refused to accept Coryndon's suggestion that his share of the tax be 5 per cent; the King demanded 50 per cent, then 30, then 20.[86] Since it was agreed that the King's share was to be distributed among the royal family, all indunas and senior headmen, the entire Lozi elite supported his demand for the largest percentage he could win.[87] Milner and Lyttleton acknowledged that the Lozi could hardly receive less than the 10 per cent share given in Basutoland and Bechuanaland. As a compromise, the Colonial Office decided that Lewanika's formal share of the hut tax be 10 per cent, of which, however, no more than £1,200 would be given directly to him; this sum was to be on top of the £850 per annum he was receiving from the Concession of 1900. If his percentage totalled more than £1,200, as it was expected to do, the difference would be paid into a fund for public works in Barotseland. This decision was final; it was announced to the King and the Kuta and imposed upon them, and for decades they and their successors complained bitterly about its inadequacy.[88]

For the Company, the hut tax proved a great success. Set at ten shillings per hut per annum, by 1907, with collection taking place in all districts, over £33,000 was brought in.[89] Coryndon proudly reported that the number of 'defaulters' was minimal, which he attributed to the efficiency of his organization.[90] But the consequences of not paying could hardly have been a negligible factor in its success. Initially, defaulters had their huts and even their crops burned,[91] but the government, ignoring the destruction of crops, believed such punishment to be excessively lenient in view of the 'flimsy and temporary manner in which they [huts] were built'.[92] Instead, defaulters were either to be fined or imprisoned.[93] This policy was followed rigidly, defaulters being arrested and 'dealt with severely'[94] as many Lozi still remember.

A large number of informants singled out the imposition of the hut tax as the most despicable feature of Company rule. The power struggle between the Lozi ruling class and the Company's officials barely impinged upon the lives of the mass of Lozi. The hut tax hit them directly and powerfully. They had of course never been consulted about the Concessions, probably did not understand their purpose, and certainly derived no perceptible benefits from Company rule. Yet they suddenly found themselves obliged to pay money they often did not have and for reasons they did not comprehend. Informants talked vividly of arrests, handcuffs, miserable prison food, ticks in the blankets, men often enchained, sometimes being forced to carry buckets of excreta on their heads. If the King and even the Kuta had reason to regard the Administration with a certain ambivalence, to the mass of Lozi the Bomas increasingly became symbols of fear and oppression at the hands of the white men.[95]

It was true that many among the elite were similarly antagonized by the outcome, since the largest group of minor indunas and headmen received no more than a few shillings per head as their share of the tax. Nevertheless, this share, combined with the greater opportunity of even the most subordinate member of the ruling class to exchange his cattle for cash with white traders in the Valley, allowed every Lozi aristocrat to find the money to pay his own tax.[96]

But for the great majority of Lozi, there was only one way to earn the cash to pay the tax. The Company s policy was already set: Barotseland was to remain undeveloped, its primary function being the supply of cheap labour to Company and other white enterprises south of the Zambesi. The imposition of the hut tax assured the success of this objective. Lozi began streaming south in the tens of thousands,[97] many on their own, many others recruited by the (Southern) Rhodesian Native Labour Bureau which the Administration had authorized to seek labourers in Barotseland 'for the purpose of bene-

fiting the industries of [Southern] Rhodesia'.[98] By the end of
the decade, the magnitude of labour migration had become
one of the chief concerns of the King and Kuta. When Ngambela Mokamba implored Wallace, the Acting Administrator,
to find work for more people in the Valley, he was unceremoni-
ously rebuffed; Lozi 'boys', Wallace informed him, must
continue to seek work on the line of rail or south of the Zambesi.[99] This was the position in 1909, and it remained unaltered
during the entire life of Northern Rhodesia.

On every occasion, then, the interests of the Company took
precedence over those of the Lozi. This truth was illustrated
vividly in 1905 when, at the demands of the Company, the
boundary between North-Western and North-Eastern Rhodesia
was shifted from the Kafue River eastwards to the narrow
waist of the territory between Katonga and Moçambique.
Copper had already been assessed as of great potential importance in what was to become the Copperbelt, and the Company
felt that its mines in that area were more secure under the
Concession of 1900 with Lewanika than under those 'made
with personages [in North-Eastern Rhodesia] whose existence
today are somewhat mythical. . . .'[100] By this simple administrative device, the line of rail and the Copperbelt now fell
under the jurisdiction of the Barotseland–North-Western
Rhodesia Order in Council of 1899, but in no sense under the
jurisdiction of Lewanika himself.

The King had never asserted any claim to authority over
territory so far east of his kingdom, yet formally he received it. He
consistently made claims upon a large area west of the Upper
Zambesi, yet in the same year, much of it was denied to him.
In July 1905, the King of Italy handed down his judgment on
Lewanika's disputed western boundary. It was, in a word, a
simple compromise between the claims of Portugal and Britain.
The former argued that the Upper Zambesi was the legitimate
western boundary of Barotseland; the latter, in support of both
Lewanika and the Company, claimed the twentieth meridian
east of Greenwich. The King of Italy decided, roughly, to
divide the disputed area evenly, making the twenty-second
parallel Barotseland's western frontier.[101] This settlement
reduced Barotseland to about 180,000 square miles, just
larger than the size of France.

London had no illusions about Lewanika's reaction to the award. The High Commissioner, Selborne, quickly wrote him admitting the decision was disappointing, but warning that he must nevertheless 'respect and loyally abide by the decision arrived at. . . '.[102] Lewanika was hardly mollified; through his Lozi secretary Kambai, he wrote sharply to Coryndon:

> . . . It is not quite a good boundary, is only to make us much disappointed; how a boundary can go like zig-zag, to cut Imilangu tribe in half, Mazengo tribe in half, Ba-Mokowa tribe half, Mambunda tribe half . . . is not a boundary only a joke indeed. . . .
> How shall we do, all Barotse indunas, their villages and cattle will be outside, also my sons, nephews and cattle will be outside. . . .
> How shall we do, Sir, to be cutted half and half.[103]

The boundary decision was merely another in the long series of humiliations and defeats that the Lozi aristocracy, and, in the case of the hut tax, the Lozi peasantry, had suffered at the hands of the Company since 1897. There can be little doubt that a large faction among the indunas blamed the King for this wholly unsatisfactory outcome. It was true that much of his own authority had been circumscribed, but their own powers, as they believed, had been almost entirely emasculated. All the worst fears of the 'pagan conservative party' between 1888 and 1897 had been confirmed, and although their King had often complained, never once did he attempt to resist a Company demand.

Not surprisingly, then, even before the King of Italy's award was announced, the DC at Lealui felt that Lewanika had become unpopular among both the people and the indunas in the Valley. He was convinced that an opposition 'party' had once again sprung up, under induna Kalonga and Imoana (Muimui?), with, as its main grievance, the tiny percentage of the King's share of the hut tax which he distributed to his indunas. The compliancy of the King had convinced the Company that he was their greatest single ally in Barotseland, and Coryndon reacted to this report by ordering to Lealui a patrol of forty police and a Maxim gun, under two European officers, 'as a moral support to the constituted authority and to Lewanika himself. . . .'[104] Lewanika's personal response to the appearance of the patrol was, as Stokes has said, 'to throw himself into unreserved dependence on the Administration', agreeing finally to the extension of the hut tax in the entire kingdom, including the Barotse Valley.[105] As for his putative conspirators they quickly muffled all signs of open protest in the face of white power, and within weeks the patrol was able to leave the capital.[106]

Several months later, however, after the news of the boundary award had been received, Coryndon and Harding again discovered that the 'political atmosphere' was 'not as clear as it should be.'[107] Both Worthington and Aitken, Coryndon reported, agreed that there was an 'atmosphere of constraint' at the Kuta, that few indunas regularly attended its sessions, and that the King was taking unusually frequent hunting and fishing trips away from Lealui. '. . . Perhaps', Coryndon speculated, 'Lewanika is largely blamed for many of the irritating restrictions which come with a white administration', such as the hut tax. 'I do not think,' the Administrator concluded, 'he would be Paramount Chief today had it not been for the establishment of a white government which has consistently supported his authority.'[108]

This may well have been true. More important, the Kuta, the King, and the Administration all probably believed that it was true. The armed patrol which Coryndon despatched to Lealui early in 1905 may be seen as the decisive event in determining the respective positions of all the parties involved in Barotseland during the remainder of Lewanika's reign. The Company was determined that he should reign, even if its own officials now ruled. The King realistically decided that this unsatisfactory status was better than no status whatever, and he remained, as the Company clearly grasped, at its mercy. Those indunas to whom the new situation was intolerable were equally aware that, with the King wholly dependent upon the Company and the Company wholly determined to support the King against his opponents, any chance of their deposing him, or of his leading them in resisting further Company encroachments on their authority, had disappeared. Only the 'new men' had confidence that they could appeal over the heads of the Company officials to the British government itself to save their country.

Lewanika's victory, then, in winning 'British protection', proved to be a pyrrhic one: he succeeded in remaining King only by forfeiting a large proportion of the traditional authority of the kingship. His second major policy, to build a modern nation on the Upper Zambesi, was an even more abject failure. This too became undeniably apparent in 1905. Ironically, this second 'betrayal'—as he saw it—took the form of an event that did *not* transpire: the railway line from Victoria Falls completely by-passed the 'severely truncated and attenuated'[109] Lozi 'kingdom' as it wended its way to the Copperbelt. Lewanika and the Ngambela, together with the missionaries, had cherished a dream that the line would follow the Upper Zambesi, and that the Barotse Valley would become the hub of a developing, prosperous Northern Rhodesia.[110] The realization that the railway would run east of the Kafue River was a rude awakening, and with it the dream crumbled. Lealui, as a later writer pointed out,

> was no longer the centre on which the successful development of the north depended. Lewanika was no longer the all-important factor in the situation. He was king of only part – a great part – but an increasingly unimportant part, of the much greater territory of North-Western Rhodesia. From now on, Barotseland was bound to sink more and more into the political and economic background.[111]

## II

All Lozi were highly dissatisfied with the results of Company rule. But, so far as the limited evidence of both oral and written sources allow us to judge, because they feared the consequences of open rebellion, no Lozi actively resisted the burdens and humiliations which Company domination meant. Lewanika himself was forced to collaborate with the Administration as the price of his remaining King. The traditionalist faction in the Kuta probably wished to depose him in the hope that his successor might provide more militant leadership, but its members were realistically intimidated by white power. Failing this objective, they continued to apply pressure on the King to be less docile in his reactions to Company demands. In this, they had the support of the small but increasing number

of educated young aristocrats who, though resented by the
traditionalists, shared the desire of the latter to revive their
proud heritage of a powerful kingdom. These young elitists,
moreover, had considerable influence on the King and Ngambela Mokamba, who remained receptive to new techniques in
their desire to preserve Lozi sovereignty. Eschewing to a large
extent the advice and assistance of missionaries—who, after
all, were white—they adopted the tactics of fellow black men,
above all those of South Africa, convincing the King that success was achievable if only more sophisticated methods of
protest were utilized; this meant, primarily, the use of literate
well-documented and reasoned petitions setting forth Lozi
grievances and presenting more desirable and equitable alternatives. Secondly, such petitions, were, if possible, to be directed
to representatives of Her Majesty's government rather than
to those of the Company.[112] Lewanika accepted these tactics
and, during the remaining decade of his life, submitted a
number of petitions to the High Commissioner if possible, the
Company Administrator when necessary. Without exception,
the requests incorporated in these petitions were rejected,
while the British government refused in any way to interfere
as the Company continued to fulfil its insatiable demands
leading to ever greater diminution of the Lozi 'empire' and
the authority of its traditional rulers.

The commencement of the 'era of petitions' began in 1906
with the arrival in Lealui of F. Z. S. Peregrino. Peregrino was
a Gold Coaster who had gone to South Africa, where he had
become editor of the *South African Spectator* and head of the
Coloured Peoples' Vigilance Committee of South Africa, and
therefore was familiar with the techniques being used by non-
whites in that country of submitting petitions of grievances to
the British government.[113] Lozi contact with Peregrino may
have been made through Prince Imwiko, when he returned to
Barotseland from his private school in Kent via South Africa,
or possibly by two other sons of Lewanika whom he sent to
Lovedale College in South Africa. Peregrino offered himself
to the Lozi as 'the agent of natives in making complaints to the
Government'. 'The path of the native is difficult', he wrote.
'I am a black man and have acted for years between the black
man and the government in Cape Colony with much success.'

Here, it appeared, was precisely the man the Lozi needed to combat Company domination, and Litia invited Peregrino to Barotseland.[114]

Shortly after his arrival, he prepared for the King a petition to be submitted to Selborne, the High Commissioner for South Africa. These set out the major Lozi grievances. The boundary award of 1905 was, of course, one; the problem of many Lozi in raising money to pay the hut tax was a second; and finally, the Company had not fulfilled its agreement to 'establish and maintain' schools, while its payment of Lewanika's share of the hut tax had been made 'but in part'.[115]

Two months later, in October, 1906, Lewanika and the Ngambela travelled to Bulawayo, where they had a brief personal interview with the High Commissioner. The complaints raised in the Peregrino petition were raised, Selborne rejecting all but one of them. He was convinced that most of the issues had been invented by Peregrino, and that the Lozi were unaware of the contents of the petition. In fact, he modestly reported, whatever Lewanika's anxieties might be, they 'will perhaps be forgotten for a time in his pleasure at having seen me and at my promise . . . to visit his country before long'.[116]

Selborne's complacency reflected the failure of white officialdom to recognize the extent to which its intrusions had wounded the sensibilities of a proud people, as well as the cherished colonial fiction that Africans protested only at the instigation of a handful of unrepresentative agitators. But it reflected, as well, Administration pride in at last having a concrete contribution to point to: the establishment during 1906 of the Barotse National School. The Company's promise to support schools in Barotseland was only implemented now that a school could be financed from that part of Lewanika's percentage of the hut tax exceeding £1,200. The purpose of the school was to produce English-speaking interpreters, skilled artisans and clerks. This, explained Worthington, was the kind of education desired by the King, and he believed that the BNS 'would go a long way towards giving the Barotse occupation and would satisfy the headmen that the Government is at last doing something for them. . . .'[117]

Within a few years the new school was functioning successfully, many of its students being the sons of headmen and indunas, and even some of Lewanika's younger sons attended.[118] Moreover, the existence of the BNS prodded the mission into expanding its own school system.[119] Even so the King was not quite satisfied, and sent several of his elder sons and a number of the sons of senior indunas and court favourites to Lovedale College in South Africa and to the more advanced PMS school in Basutoland.[120]

This upsurge of educational zeal had far-reaching political consequences for the Lozi. At home, it meant the creation of a generation of young men with new ideas and new aspirations who were already influencing the old King and who would become the main advisers of his successor. Moreover, although fewer than a thousand Lozi out of an estimated population in the reserved area of some 125,000 people were at schools,[121] this was a far greater proportion than obtained elsewhere in Northern Rhodesia. The consequences of this were already perceptible in the rest of the territory by the beginning of the war, when educated Africans from Nyasaland and Barotseland had a virtual monopoly on the few semi-skilled jobs then open to black men.[122] Living outside their homeland had a curiously ambivalent impact upon those Lozi, still relatively few, who thus found suitable employment: on the one hand, it heightened their ethnic consciousness and sense of superiority; on the other, it gave them a sense of identity with other Africans vis-à-vis the expanding European community. These experiences, too, would influence political developments both within and outside Barotseland proper.

These wider ramifications of Lewanika's desire for educational opportunities were not, of course, foreseen at the time, and for the moment, the establishment of the BNS by no means assuaged the King's grievances. In 1907, at a meeting with Selborne, the High Commissioner, he and his delegation 'insisted' that they wished to pass from Company to direct British overrule. Selborne replied that the King of England was 'perfectly satisfied' with the Company's Administration, and that Lewanika had 'every reason to be friendly to the Company and trust the Company which had been a loyal friend to him'.

The Lozi delegation sharply repudiated this assertion. Company rule was not only unwanted, it was also harsh.

Above all, the financial arrangement was quite iniquitous. Lewanika's annual payment of £1,200 was wholly inadequate: that sum had been 'imposed upon us against our will, and we vainly protested against it'. Why, asked the Ngambela, was the BNS being financed from the 10 per cent of the hut tax promised to the King instead of by the Company as pledged in the various concessions? How was the remaining 90 per cent of the tax total spent? Since it was a commercial concern, the Company wished only 'to draw money from us. This the Imperial Government would not do.'

Selborne remained unmoved. He was certain that there was little likelihood that the King's subsidy would be increased since, as he accurately pointed out, Lewanika's revenue was in fact far greater than £1,200.[123] In 1905, for example, Worthington had compiled the following estimate of the King's total revenues for the year.[124]

|                                               | £      |
| --------------------------------------------- | ------ |
| Annual subsidy from Company                   | 850    |
| Share of hut tax                              | 1,200  |
| Sale of King's cattle (7,000 sold in 1904)    | 1,500  |
| King's curio shop in Livingstone              | 200    |
| Half receipts of game licences                | 150    |
| Hire of canoes, Livingstone to Lealui         | 200    |
| Toll collected at Gonye Falls                 | 50     |
| Half receipts of ferry licences               | 10     |
| TOTAL                                         | £4,160 |

'In money matters,' Selborne noted, the King 'is said to be not easily satisfied.'[125] On the other hand, Lewanika's revenues were divided among a large number of members of the Lozi ruling class, a majority of whom received only a few shillings a year, and we may assume that it was partly under pressure from this faction that the King consistently attempted to have his subsidy increased.

Moreover, the harshness of Company rule did not manifest itself only in financial hardship. Lewanika asserted, and Adolph Jalla confirmed, that many Lozi, including members of the ruling class, had been beaten up by both Company officials and private traders, often for failing to give 'proper respect' to white people by kneeling and clapping in their presence.

We sometimes are caused to feel as if we are a conquered nation, while we have made an agreement which was said to be just like an alliance between our nation and the Imperial Government. When we say so, those of the British South Africa Company ask: 'Do you want to be conquered?'

In reply, the High Commissioner did not even deign to refer to these complaints. He simply laid down the rules that, in future, the 'royal salute'—kneeling and clapping—must be given to himself and the Administrator exclusively, that 'a suitable salute of lower degree such as the clapping of hands' be accorded to all other Administration officials, and that 'all other whites should be treated with scrupulous courtesy and respect'. 'It is always polite', added Codrington, the new Administrator, 'to take off hats to white men. . . . It is right that they [Africans] should . . . treat all white men with respect.'[126]

The petition, then, was utterly rejected, a decision Lewanika and the Kuta had little alternative but to accept.[127] Clearly, though, they were sorely disappointed, and the King remained openly antagonistic to the Company which Selborne continued warmly to defend.[128] Lewanika was still bitter that Lozi tax money was not resulting in any benefits to Barotseland: 'No public work, nothing felt to promote the progress of the country.' Moreover, all the senior Company officials lived far from Lealui. They were seen 'hardly a few days' each year, he complained; 'their great interest, we feel, is somewhere else'.[129]

Codrington and Selborne both agreed that the King and the Kuta were not in close enough contact with the Administration. Their concern, however, was that Lewanika's relative isolation prevented the Company from firmly establishing its authority over the Lozi elite. As a result, they incorrectly believed, 'Lewanika was more or less in the hands of the missionaries who, since Coillard's death [in 1904], are antagonistic to the Company and took advantage of the High Commissioner's visit [to Sesheke] to submit, in Lewanika's name, several petty, and for the most part unfounded, grievances which they themselves cherished towards the Administration'. Their solution was to appoint a special officer, to be called the Resident Magistrate, to represent the Administration in the Barotse Valley.[130]

This assessment of the political situation in Barotseland was almost entirely inaccurate. As far as the Lozi were concerned, their grievances were neither petty nor unfounded. The ruling class needed no missionary to convince them that Company rule was detrimental to their interests. Indeed, to suggest it was to ignore the major theme of Lozi politics ever since 1890. And although it was true that the advent of the Administration meant a diminution in missionary influence on the King, there existed in the Valley manifest social harmony between missionaries, officials and traders.[131]

In any event, although the mission still had a certain role to play in helping to draft petitions in proper language, even this function was increasingly being usurped by members of the new educated elite. The 'new men', moreover, were highly suspicious of the missionaries because of their close relations with the other white men in the Valley. This suspicion served to bind the new elite with the traditionalists in the Kuta, who in many other ways were mutually hostile. The latter had always feared that the King's relationship with the missionaries would limit their own traditional role as his advisers. The young educated men suspected the missionaries of racialist attitudes. Together the two factions acted to reduce the King's need for missionary advice and assistance, and in tacit recognition of its diminished role, the mission increasingly turned its attention to non-political interests, to such problems as beer-drinking and divorce, the minute number of conversions, and 'heathenism' in general.[132]

Young educated Lozi, then, were increasingly able to take over the missionaries' role of helping the King deal with the Company on an equal basis, and it is probable that Lewanika hoped that, with their assistance, his dream of modernizing his nation might yet be realized. Frederick Arnot, Lewanika's first missionary in the early 1880s, passed through Lealui in 1910, and though he thought the King 'old-looking', nevertheless found him 'still full of plans for the development of his country'.[133] And these plans were fully shared by Ngambela Mokamba, upon whom the great proportion of the nation's business had now fallen.[134] Mokamba, with Prince Litia, were seen by the new educated elite as their chief allies in the ruling class. Together they influenced Lewanika to become the spokesman for an entire generation of newly-educated young Africans, when they had him write to the High Commissioner asking that 'those who understood the notion of progress' should be allowed to advance, and that there should be no discrimination on grounds of colour in the Administration's employment policy.[135]

Blatant discrimination, however, continued. In this, as in most other areas, Lozi wishes were ignored. Indeed, as Stokes has pointed out, by 1907

> the unequal contest [between the Lozi ruling class and the Company] had been decided. Outside the reserved area, Lewanika had given up his rights of tribute and jurisdiction, and his substantial rights over the land. All that he retained was his percentage of the hut tax receipts and the shadowy influence possessed by the representative indunas sitting as assessors in 'native cases'.[136]

And, as we have seen, the King and Kuta believed their share of the tax to be wholly inadequate, while by 1908 the representative induna system had been effectively dismantled.

Similarly, in the reserved area itself, though the ruling class was allowed considerably greater powers and privileges than any other tribe in Northern Rhodesia, its status as compared with the period prior to 1897 was greatly undermined. Yet this attrition of Lozi power continued, the interests of the Company as always taking precedence over those of the people they were 'protecting'. Among the major objectives of the Administration were the raising of revenues through the hut tax and the maintenance of a free flow of labour to the south. Its officials realized that one major obstacle in fully realizing these objectives was what they enjoyed calling the Lozi system of 'domestic slavery'. Like the missionaries, Company officials failed to distinguish between slaves, serfs, servants, and simply humble peasants, nor did they recognize the King's customary right to demand free labour from his subjects in return for his fulfilling his proper duties as King.[137]

In any event, such distinctions were hardly relevant in terms of the Company's needs. A man who was obligated to provide free labour could not pay his hut tax; a man who was tied to another man—whatever the nature of the bond—could not become a labour migrant. The system, therefore, must be abolished.[138] Worthington imposed upon the King and Kuta his own terms, and on 16 July, 1906, on his demand, the 'Proclamation of the Abolition of Slavery' was read aloud in Lealui by the Ngambela to a large crowd of some 'several thousand natives'.[139]

The Company was very pleased with its work. Not only had a 'degrading' institution been abolished, but also, as the High Commissioner did not fail to point out, many more Africans would now be in a position to pay their tax.[140] At the same time, a large pool of potential labour migrants was thus freed to supply the Company's enterprises south of the Zambesi.

The Kuta, on the other hand, considered that they had once again been betrayed. On a political level, it had been another test of strength between the Administration and the Lozi ruling class, and the latter had been decisively defeated. But this was not wholly accurate: the indunas had lost, but the King after all was not asked to make any major sacrifices. He could still demand free labour, if only for twelve days a year, for any purpose he saw fit. They, however, could demand it only for work 'rendered for the exclusive benefit of the community'. To have their gardens tilled, for example, they would have to pay labourers, yet where, from their tiny share of Lewanika's percentage of the hut tax, would they find money for such payments? Some headmen and minor indunas in fact were forced to undertake their own labour, while all members of the ruling class considered their status diminished by the loss of so many traditional dependants.[141] Few of these repercussions, however, would affect the position of the King, and the resentment aroused by the new Proclamation was directed as much against the Ngambela as against the Company, Mokamba, as Lewanika's mouthpiece and the first man openly to capitulate to Worthington's demands, being accused of sacrificing Lozi rights to the Administration.[142]

To the indunas, then, this episode must have seemed yet another vindication of their original fear of collusion between the King and the white men at the expense of the Kuta. Yet they could hardly argue that the King himself was not being severely humiliated by the actions of the Administration, actions which could serve only to unite the ruling class against the white intruders. Robert Codrington, who in 1907 replaced Coryndon as Administrator of North-Western Rhodesia,[143] succeeded in the eighteen months of life remaining to him importantly to influence Lozi politics in at least one critical way. Codrington abruptly decided that Lewanika must in the future be designated merely as 'Paramount Chief' of the Lozi: 'The title of "King" as applied to Lewanika and that of "Prince" to Letia,' he announced, 'are to be discontinued and discountenanced.'[144] This unilateral decree was a powerful blow to the prestige and status of the Lozi ruler, formally reducing his position to a level with those of other tribal heads in Northern Rhodesia, even though all the latter had been either minor figures or had been defeated by Company agents. Lozi themselves never ceased calling him *Litunga* ('earth'), their nearest equivalent to 'King' and the highest symbol of the unity of the nation. But the bitterness engendered by Codrington's decision lasted into the reign of Lewanika's successor, who, as we shall see, with the full support of the educated elite struggled fruitlessly to have his proper title restored.

Clearly Peregrino's faith in petitions praying for the intervention of the British government was proving illusory, as the Company continued, through the means of both formal concessions and practical encroachments, to eat away at the remaining vestiges of Lozi sovereignty. Company officials considered, for example, that even the severely circumscribed jurisdiction of the Kuta as against their own Magistrates' Courts, as laid down in the Proclamation of 1905, was too extensive. The Proclamation had deprived the Kuta of the right to try any serious criminal case, even one between Africans. Now the Administration refused to allow it to judge even minor civil cases such as those involving tax evasion, breaches of labour contracts, and the like.[145] Informally and swiftly, all such cases were handed over to the Magistrates' Courts, as persistent demands by the King and Kuta to be allowed wider jurisdiction met with complete failure. By the beginning of World War I, as one senior local official acknowledged, 'Lewanika [had] ceded all judicial rights to the BSA Company with the exception of very minor items and of civil cases between natives'.[146] In fact, what these amounted to were beer-drinking, and above all, divorce and adultery cases.

Indeed, until the end of the colonial era, divorce and adultery constituted some two-thirds to three-quarters of all the cases handled by Lozi courts.[147]

Nor was the Company yet satisfied. Only months later, in November, 1909, Lewanika was presented with the last important formal concession of this era. The Concession of 1906 had given the Company the right to dispose of land outside the reserved area for purposes of settlement. Wallace now asked the King to extend that right, in effect to turn over the ownership of that area to the Company. As a *quid pro quo*, he offered to extend the Barotse Reserve to that territory west of the Upper Zambesi which had been returned to the Lozi as a result of the King of Italy's boundary decision in 1905. Yet that area had in fact automatically reverted to Barotseland at the moment of the boundary award, since, at Lewanika's request, the Colonial Office had made this arrangement the condition of its confirmation of the Concession of 1900. In short, as Stokes has said, the Concession of 1909 was 'something of a sleight of hand', the Company giving nothing for something.[148]

According to Wallace, not only did Lewanika agree to this Concession, but did so with a speed which took the Acting Administrator aback.[149] There are two possible explanations for this. The first is that the King in fact did *not* agree, and Wallace simply ignored his objections. We know, for example, that this is what happened in connection with negotiations over the Order in Council of 1911.

The second explanation is that Lewanika agreed to something other than what the Concession actually contained. The records of the meetings between Wallace and the King and Kuta in 1909 do not suggest how the Lozi, particularly some of the English-speaking indunas, could have so completely misconceived its terms. But this was what Lewanika, the Ngambela and three educated young indunas claimed at an interview with Wallace in 1911. The crux of their argument was simple. The two Concessions of 1906 and 1909 had given the Company the right to 'dispose' of land outside the reserved area to Europeans. But 'disposing', the Ngambela emphasized, was a totally different matter from 'selling'. Indeed, the Lozi had no concept of the perpetual alienation of land, all of which belonged in perpetuity to the kingship, each reigning King being entitled to lend some of it if he so desired. What they had agreed, then, was that the Company could allow settlers to plough, but never purchase, land belonging to the King outside of the reserved area. In reply, Wallace and McKinnon, the Resident Magistrate, pointed out with equal simplicity that 'when a white man ploughs land he is not like a native': Europeans bought land, they did not borrow it.[150]

The question of 'disposing' of land outside Barotseland proper had become of such significance to the Lozi since it also arose out of the Order in Council of 1911 for the amalgamation of North-Eastern and North-Western Rhodesia, for which the Company had long pressed. Selborne, the High Commissioner, convinced the Colonial Office that Lewanika would accept the Order so long as his rights in the reserved area were safeguarded.[151] Once the decision to amalgamate had been taken, Lewanika's acquiescence was actively sought, though it is quite clear that the Order was to be promulgated with or without his agreement. His equivocal position was thus clearly illustrated: to no other chief in Northern Rhodesia was an attempt even made to explain the new arrangement, and no other chief or tribe was explicitly referred to in the Order, yet in the last analysis, were Lewanika to refuse to co-operate, amalgamation would take place all the same. This pattern was to be repeated on many occasions over the following decades.

The Order in Council of 1911 marked the final encapsulation of Barotseland within the larger colonial entity of Northern Rhodesia. The Lozi ruling class did not understand that, in effect, its separate treaty relationship with Britain was thus shattered, and that to all intents and purposes the Barotse Reserve became merely one of the seven provinces of Northern Rhodesia, albeit in certain minor ways *primus inter pares*. For this reason, the amalgamation proposal as such was not opposed. At Livingstone, Fair, Resident Commissioner of Southern Rhodesia, and Wallace met with Lewanika and his delegation and emphasized the two clauses—out of forty-eight —in the Order which explicitly safeguarded Lozi rights. The first provided for the non-alienation of land in the reserved area and confirmed Lozi rights and obligations under the Concessions of 1900 and 1909; the second stated that the provisions giving the Company power to remove Africans to make way for white settlement should not be deemed to 'limit or affect the exercise by the Chief of the Barotse of his authority in tribal matters'.

These provisions, however, did not meet the major source of Lozi dissatisfaction with the Order.[152] They disagreed, as the Ngambela declared, with the clause allowing the Company to sell land outside the reserved area to Europeans. Fair, however, could 'hold out no hope' that the clause would be changed to meet this objection,[153] and after the interview, he wrote an official letter to Lewanika referring to

> the long discussion we had today on the subject of the sale of land by the Company. As I said this morning, I listened carefully to your words and I cannot understand the words you said because I have also read the words which you had written. I cannot believe that you, being a wise man, signed the agreements [of 1906 and 1909] the words of which you did not know, and I feel sure that you will keep to the words of your agreement.
>
> I am now sending all your words to the High Commissioner and am informing him that you have told me that you well understand the order in Council.[154]

One wonders how many of the earlier 'agreements' between the King and the Administration were arrived at in a similar manner.

The Lozi were now certain that the Order in Council would include a clause permitting Europeans to purchase land outside of the reserved area. Three months after the interview with Fair, Lewanika sought Administration aid to protect him against alleged plotters. An administration show of police strength[155] was followed by the trial of Mboo (Fwabi), a son of the late King Sipopa, and Ikasia, a headman. The case against Mboo was non-existent. A poor man, deprived by Lewanika of all influence and recognition, he had manifested his resentment by refusing to give the King the royal salute. It was a reflection of Lewanika's own sense of insecurity that he misconstrued an act of disobedience for one of sedition.

It appeared, however, that Ikasia, who seems to have cherished certain grievances which were not brought out at the trial, might have been attempting to overthrow the King, using Mboo as his figurehead. Witnesses claimed Ikasia had spoken to several other headmen and minor indunas against the King, falsely claiming the Mboo 'had put these idea into his head'.[156]

The Administration officials were convinced that more intrigue existed than the trial revealed, since many indunas 'shun any exposure of the causes which have kept alive a widespread spirit of discontent' in the Valley. This was a reference to their belief that former 'slaves' and peasants were suffering due to the harsh exactions of the ruling class, freed slaves being forced to work without payment, poor peasants being obligated to pay their hut tax while continuing to give tribute to indunas in the form of unpaid labour and crops. At the same time, officials saw this episode as a dispute within the ruling class, Ikasia representing an undetermined number of indunas who considered that Lewanika was betraying the nation to the Company. Some indunas, Worthington reported, 'regret lost freedom, others that a larger measure of it has not come to them. Both parties [indunas and peasants] blame Lewanika, both imagine that a new chief would introduce a new order of things more to their liking.'[157] The officials were, in short, uncertain whether there had been conscious co-operation between the exploited lower classes and the dissaffected indunas against the King, or whether it was the latter alone for whom Ikasia spoke.

It is hardly likely, and no evidence was introduced, that the first interpretation was valid, although it is likely that Lozi subsistence farmers were discontented with their lot. Moreover, Lewanika's gross over-reaction to Mboo's disobedience strongly suggests that he at least believed that he was seriously threatened by a faction within the Kuta, presumably the same indunas who had from the first been unreconciled to 'British protection'. Nevertheless, the trial produced no concrete evidence of an actual plot against the King. Instead of asking that Mboo and Ikasia be imprisoned, therefore, Lewanika merely suggested to the Resident Magistrate that 'They should be sent out of the country, and I look to the Government to protect me inside and out'.[158]

Because he felt his position to be so insecure and his enemies to potentially dangerous, Lewanika had abjectly thrown himself upon the Company for support. Wallace, the Administrator, could not resist the opportunity thus presented to him further to undermine the powers of the King and Kuta alike. He acted in two areas. He first decided that since the Administration needed 'some guarantee' that the elite it was supporting did not abuse its powers, right of appeal must be granted from Kuta decisions to the Resident Magistrate's Court.

> I am aware [he acknowledged] that such a measure would be a serious change and could not be brought about, except for very weighty reasons, without previous agreement with the Chief and Council. It would certainly in time bring about a great diminution in the Chief's authority, but I think it is the only means to check abuse and discontent and it should be the price of our support and protection.[159]

Gladstone quickly agreed that the means to achieve stability in the Barotse Reserve was 'the gradual transfer of authority from the Chief and his headmen to the Administration', and the unilateral decision became law.[160]

In the second place, Wallace believed that 'the question as to who shall succeed Lewanika lies at the bottom of all these occasional periods of excitment'. He therefore decided that the Administration must categorically reaffirm its absolute support of Litia as Lewanika's successor, thereby closing this question as a potential arena for intrigue.[161] At the insistence of McKinnon, the Resident Magistrate, the Ngambela assembled 'all the principal indunas', but, McKinnon reported, 'No discussion was necessary as they all assured me they unanimously agreed that Litia be appointed Heir and Successor. . . .'[162] But a later missionary source claimed that there had initially been considerable opposition to this move within the Kuta, a number of indunas insisting, quite properly, that it was an infringement of their own prerogative to select a successor *after* the death or deposition of the reigning king.[163] According to a Lozi informant, their consent was now won only because Lewanika agreed, under pressure, that each of their sons should similarly succeed them as indunas.[164] This probably explains the Kuta's acceptance of McKinnon's proposition. He thereupon read a formal proclamation announcing that Litia would succeed his father, adding that 'should any other claimant arise attempting to oppose this decision, he will be looked upon as a usurper by the Government and dealt with accordingly'. At Lewanika's request, copies of the Proclamation were signed by himself and some forty indunas.[165]

Yet the ruling class had agreed to repudiate the ancient Lozi tradition of selecting a king and indunas in order to leave its successors little more than a tribal labour reserve. This was the ironic outcome of the initiative Lewanika had taken in having a treaty signed between himself and, as he was deceived into believing, 'Her Britannic Majesty'. Moreover, even the size of the reserved area had been further reduced. In 1909, the Caprivi Strip, which the Lozi claimed and which had not been dealt with in the boundary award of 1905, had been handed by Britain to Germany.[166] In 1914, a boundary commission concluded that the actual border between Angola and Northern Rhodesia was 'much further east' than had previously been thought, and the frontier finally agreed upon placed 'a considerable portion' of the Barotse Reserve west of the Zambesi in Portuguese hands.[167]

In 1914, too, serious controversy arose between Lealui and the Administration on the question of the extent of the jurisdiction properly belonging to their respective courts. This dispute, however, was far more serious than the many which had preceded it; indeed, it was the sole occasion on which Lewanika actively attempted to resist an Administration judgment. On this issue, the King, the traditionalist indunas, and the new educated elite were in full accord, for the Administration's demands impinged on the interests of all of them. The young educated aristocrats, 'possessing a novel awareness of legal rights and convinced that trickery had been practised on the illiterate Lewanika in the past',[168] now united with the older indunas to put pressure on the King finally to take an unequivocal stand against any further encroachments on the authority of the ruling class. The incident is no less significant for the light it throws, once again, on the manner in which Administration officials reacted to manifestations of Lozi dissatisfaction with Company rule.

The conflict arose out of a trivial enough incident, a cattle theft in the Sesheke district. The culprits were apprehended, brought before Litia and the Sesheke Kuta, found guilty and fined. Local Administration officials, however, argued that cattle theft was a criminal offence and therefore to be tried in a Magistrate's Court.[169] At a meeting with Willis, the Acting Resident Magistrate in Mongu, the Ngambela rejected this interpretation,[170] and in a letter written by the royal secretary Kambai, Lewanika added his protest:

> It is seeming that the Company is trying as much as it can to take all matters in its hands [despite our agreements]. . . . I will be objectioned to these matters always. . . . My son Litia what he did at Sesheke it is alright.[171]

Willis was infuriated, and forwarded to the King a letter written in 1912 by Gladstone implicitly supporting the Magistrate's argument.[172] Willis then met again with the King and Kuta.

> I pointed out [he later reported] that their [last] letter . . . was tantamount to saying that they refused to accept the High Commissioner's decision, and . . . contained certain insinuations against the Company to which I strongly objected. . . . Were they tired of the white Government and intercourse with the white people? . . . I [gave] them the opportunity of withdrawing their letter.

Properly intimidated by these implied threats, Lewanika apologized for the harsh tone of his letter, but nevertheless repeated that he had never agreed to surrender the Kutas' right to try criminal cases.[173] He then wrote direct to the High Commissioner, protesting that the decision to remove such cases from the jurisdiction of the Lozi courts was 'very grievous to us and contrary to what we had expected from the British Government', and requesting a personal interview with Gladstone to discuss the matter.[174]

Gladstone did not see the Lozi. Instead, McKinnon, the Resident Magistrate, Mongu, having returned from his holiday, met the Kuta and laid down the law, once for all. He drew up a list of those cases to be tried by the Magistrates, and had it signed by Lewanika, the Ngambela, and the seven senior indunas.[175] The Lozi defeat was total. Besides all cases between 'natives and Whitemen', murder, witchcraft, and slave-buying or -selling, the Magistrate would also try those involving cattle theft and 'serious assault'. The jurisdiction of the Kuta was restricted to cases of petty theft, property disputes, divorce and adultery.[176] The ruling class had taken its stand on the right of its courts to try cattle thefts, and it had lost. Clearly, the new elite especially must have recognized that, if the glory that was once Barotseland was to be revived, a new strategy must be devised.

But equally clearly, Lewanika was no longer the man to lead them in their counter-offensive against the Company. The King was now about seventy years old, sick and disillusioned. His dreams of a powerful alliance between the King of England and the King of Barotseland had failed to materialize. Only once, during his visit to the coronation a dozen years earlier, had he actually lived as his romantic imagination had long pictured. He had since moved very far from the glittering world of foreign royalty and politicians and professional soldiers.

World War I gave him his opportunity, as he must have believed, to re-establish that old link. Suppressing the bitterness built up in more than a decade of frustration and humiliation, he grasped the chance to recreate a role of importance for himself and his nation in the British Empire. He immediately informed McKinnon that

the Indunas and myself we want to call in all our people and . . . tell them to make ready for the war to help the Government . . .
We shall stand always to be under the English flag.[177]

The Administration, however, refused to use Africans as soldiers and were initially able to recruit enough porters from North-Eastern Rhodesia. Not even this disappointment was sufficient to dampen Lewanika's enthusiasm, and again he wrote to McKinnon:

Seeing my men cannot render service in a European warfare, I pray the Government to accept my service in a Two Hundred Pounds Sterling as a material support.[178]

The money was accepted willingly, and Lewanika received the reward he sought: messages of gratitude poured in from the

King, the Secretary of State, the High Commissioner, and the Administrator.[179]

Finally, in 1916, with their regular supply of porters dwindling, Administration officials called for 2,000 Lozi to fill the need. Lewanika had the required men collected quickly, and his son Mwanawina accompanied them on their march to the east.[180] According to one of my informants, Mwanawina was the only one of the King's sons to respond to his appeal that they volunteer to lead this mission.[181] Indeed, it seems that, aside from Mwanawina and Litia, the heir-apparent, Lewanika alone among the ruling class felt any genuine sense of duty to assist the war effort. As we have seen, no one but he would have had the psychological need to be actively working for the Empire. Except for Litia, the great majority of Lozi—royals, indunas, headmen, young peasants conscripted as porters—are said to have accepted their obligations as obligations, nothing more.[182]

This was one telling reflection of general Lozi hostility—save for the King and his two sons—towards Company rule. Another emerged during 1915–6, when a pleuro-pneumonia epidemic wiped out a large proportion of Lozi cattle, leaving the remainder unsaleable. Indunas and royals were the largest cattle owners, from which most of their income was derived.[183] Nevertheless, so profound was the Kuta's distrust of any Administration suggestion that most indunas initially refused to co-operate in an Administration project to inoculate all surviving cattle. Some frank words from McKinnon soon convinced them of the futility of further resistance, and the inoculation campaign was begun.[184] It was, however, already too late to save most of the cattle, a fact which confirmed the original suspicions of many indunas and led to their reluctance to co-operate during another epidemic in the 1930s.

It was somehow fitting that Lewanika should die at this moment. He had wanted his people to fight for the Empire; the Administration allowed them to be used as porters for white troops. The Administration wished to institute a scheme to save Lozi cattle; the indunas had agreed with the greatest reluctance, and in the end most of the cattle died anyway. Both these situations may be taken as telling symbols of a reign that had lasted for just under four decades. Barotseland had witnessed more changes in those thirty-eight years than in the two centuries since the Lozi first moved into the valley of the Upper Zambesi.

No Lozi changed more with the years than did Lewanika himself, but in the end he was faced with a world he had not made and which he could not control. Europeans outdid each other in their eulogies after his death.[185] This was in part, no doubt, a result of the unfailing politeness and respect which he showed all white men, and partly because ultimately he had surrendered to them most of his effective power. But there was more to it than this. So far as it was possible for racialists to have respect for Africans, most white men respected Lewanika. They respected his natural dignity, his astuteness, his admiration for and receptivity to the new and the modern; Goold-Adams, a British officer, spoke for many Europeans when he described Lewanika as 'far and away the most intelligent native I have ever met. . . .'[186]

From the beginning of his long reign, Lewanika followed two overriding policies. The first was to consolidate his own position and preclude for himself the fate of his two immediate predecessors. But the traditional tactics for achieving this end—promoting friends and eliminating enemies—proved inadequate in a new age. Consequently, upon recovering his throne in 1885, he turned for support to an outside power, a white power, and he took the famous initiative which resulted in the Lochner Concession of 1890.

His second major objective was to secure the safety and assure the progress of his nation. Here again the white man was to be utilized. White power would be invoked to protect the nation from outside attack, while white knowledge would, on the one hand, allow a select group of trained young Lozi aristocrats to be able to meet the white man on his own terms, and, on the other, enable them to co-operate with a benevolent white administration in developing a modernized, hierarchically-structured state on European lines.

It is reasonable to conclude that those indunas who, from the first, had feared that white power would diminish their authority as well as undermine the integrity of the nation, had proved more prescient than the King. It is true that he, unlike either of his predecessors, died in office at an old age, but he was able to do so only by forfeiting to his white 'protectors' much of his traditional authority. How much he gained by accepting, rather than resisting, Company overrule is a hypothetical question. While his formal status was considerably superior to that of other chiefs in Northern Rhodesia, his actual power was greater only in degree, not in kind. Presumably he himself believed in the end that it had been on balance worth securing the form, if not the substance, of kingly sovereignty.

In his second aim, his success was similarly equivocal. If the security of the nation was assured, it was at the expense of a drastic diminution of the size of his kingdom. It is arguable that Ndebele warriors could hardly have won more Lozi territory than Company officials were able to do.[187] In the same way, though Lewanika succeeded in creating an educated Lozi aristocracy, he failed to create the intrastructure of a modern state for them to take over. The new elite, whose influence over Lewanika's successor was very great, were by no means convinced that the bargain Lewanika had struck with the Company was an adequate one, and the history of the first half of the succeeding reign is the account of the relentless determination with which the new class struggled to win back some of the rights which Lewanika had been forced to surrender in return for remaining in power.

## REFERENCES

1. A. Jalla, *Lewanika, Roi des Barotsis*, p. 14.
2. Millar, Assistant Secretary of the Company, to Coryndon (Telegram), 4 Mar., 1905, NAZ A 1/2/5.
3. 'Editors' Introduction', Stokes and Brown (ed.), *The Zambesian Past*, p. xxxiv.
4. Worthington, 'Journal of my Kaloma-Lebebe Trip, 1902', NAR Hist. Mss. Worthington Papers. WO 3/1/1, Vol. 1, Folio 51.
5. *Ibid.*, WO 3/1/2, Vol. 2, Folio 7. For Coryndon's opinions see Coillard to Mrs. J. Mackintosh, 20 July, 1899, NAR Hist. Mss. Coillard Papers. CO 5/1/1/1, and *Journal of Stevenson-Hamilton*, pp. 93–4. For Frank Macauley, one of Coryndon's police escorts in 1897, see Colin Harding, *In Remotest Barotseland*, p. 260. Harding himself proved to be the sole white official to place the interests of the Lozi above those of the Company, in consequence of which he was dismissed from his post in 1906; see Harding, *Far Bugles*, pp. 140–1; Coryndon to Milner, 9 March, 1905, CO, African South 763, No. 102, and same to same, 30 May, 1905, CO, African South, 763, No. 178.

6. As contrasted, for example, with the greater degree of automony granted to the rulers of Buganda; see D. A. Low and R. C. Pratt, *Buganda and British Overrule* (London, 1960).

7. See, e.g., Coryndon to High Commissioner, 12 July, 1900, NAR HC 3/3/3; Hole to Milton, 23 Nov. 1903, NAR A 11/2/14/2; C. J. Hazard, 'Recollections of NWR in the early 1900s', *Northern Rhodesia Journal*, Vol. 3, No. 6, 1958, p. 525; R. H. Palmer, *Lewanika's Country: Reminiscences of a Pioneer* (private printing, no city, no date), pp. 14–16.

8. Stokes, 'Barotseland; the Survival of an African State', in Stokes and Brown, *op. cit.*, p. 296.

9. Lawley, 'From Bulawayo to Victoria Falls: A Mission to King Lewanika', *Blackwood's Magazine*, Dec., 1898, p. 369.

10. Cited in Baxter, 'Concessions of Northern Rhodesia', *op. cit.*, pp. 13–15.

11. Lawley, *op. cit.*

12. Coillard to C. Mackintosh, 20 Oct., 1900, NAR Hist. Mss. Coillard Papers, CO 5/1/1/1.

13. Lewanika to Lawley, 25 June, 1898, CO, African South 559.

14. Barotziland-North-Western Rhodesia Order in Council, 28 Nov., 1899, in CO, African South 574.

15. Chamberlain to Milner, 19 April, 1900, CO, African South 656, CO to Company, 8 May, 1900, *ibid.*

16. Coryndon to Milner, 29 Dec., 1900, CO 417, Vol. 319.

17. Low and Pratt, *op. cit.*, pp. 158–9.

18. Coryndon to Company, 28 June, 1901, CO, African South 659.

19. Coryndon to Milner, 29 Dec., 1900, CO 417, Vol. 319; for the actual concession, see Baxter, *op, cit.*, pp. 13–19.

20. Coillard to Mrs. J. Mackintosh, 23 Oct., 1900, NAR Hist. Mss. Coillard Papers, CO 5/1/1/1, folio 1823.

21. Harding, *Far Bugles*, p. 97. Harding's comment suggests that of Low describing Harry Johnston's negotiations with the Ganda in 1900: '. . . his arguments contained that nice balance of impeccability and threat that were characteristic of the time and the occasion'. Low and Pratt, op. cit., p. 82.

22. Lewanika to High Commissioner for South Africa, 1 Oct., 1907, CO, African South 872, No. 186.

23. Lewanika to Milner, 6 Aug., 1901, CO 417, Vol. 321.

24. Coillard, Journal, 26 April, 1900, and Coillard to Miss Mackintosh, 26 May, 1900, NAR Hist. Mss. CO 5/1/1/1, folio 1754.

25. Mr. Newo Zaza. It is now of course well established that the Ndebele were in fact provoked into a war. I cannot see, however, how Mr. Zaza might have become acquainted with the facts of the case given the books I know him to have read. So far as I can gather, he can only have learned them from his own Lozi informants of an earlier generation.

26. A. Jalla to Boegner, 21 Feb., 1899, PMSP.

27. Messrs. Mupatu and Simalumba.

28. Mr. Simalumba and A. Jalla, *Mokamba, Un Premier Ministre Chretien* (Paris, 1910), pp. 9–21.

29. Jalla to Boegner, 21 Feb., 1899, PMSP.

30. Low and Pratt, *op. cit.*, p. 6.

31. Messrs. Mupatu, Simalumba and N. Zaza.

32. *Ibid.*

33. D. W. Stirke, *Barotseland: Eight Years Among the Barotse* (London, 1922), p. 51; Memorandum by Worthington, 18 July, 1929, in Maxwell Stamp Associates, op. cit., Vol. 2, p. 374; A. Jalla to Boegner, 11 July, 1905, PMSP.

34. Annual Report, Barotse District, 1905, by F. Aitkens, 30 April, 1906, NAZ 1/5/2; A. Jalla to Boegner, 11 July, 1905.

35. Low and Pratt, *op. cit.*, p. 259.

36. J. A. Barnes, *Politics in a Changing Society* (London, 1954), pp. 108–9.

37. Cited in *Journal of Stevenson-Hamilton*, pp. 93–4; also Gann, *History of Northern Rhodesia*, pp. 82, 152–3.

38. Terence Ranger, 'The "Ethiopian" Episode in Barotseland, 1900–05', *Rhodes–Livingstone Journal: Human Problems in Central Africa*, No. 37, June, 1965, pp. 26–41. My own research led me independently to most of the conclusions reached by Professor Ranger.

39. Mann to Boegner, ? May, 1899, PMSP; Coillard to Boegner, 10 May, 1900, *ibid*; Coisson to Boegner, 15 March 1905, *ibid*.

40. Kitchener to CO, 28 June, 1901, CO 417, Vol. 320; Harding to Resident Commissioner, Southern Rhodesia, 15 Aug., 1901, CO 417, Vol. 321; Coryndon to same, 9 Dec., 1901, CO, African South 702.

41. Worthington to Native Commissioner, Matabeleland, 10 April, 1906, NAZ IN 1/7.

42. Coryndon to Milner, 24 Oct., 1904, CO, African South 763.

43. Ranger, *op. cit.*, p. 37.

44. Annual Report, Barotse District, 1904, by F. Aitkens, 6 May, 1905, NAZ 1/5/2; Worthington to Coryndon, 7 April, 1905, CO, African South 763.

45. Ranger, *op. cit.*, p. 38.

46. Harding to FO, 5 Feb., 1901, CO 417, Vol. 320.

47. Coryndon to Milner, 10 Oct., 1900, *ibid*.

48. Harding to Administrator, Southern Rhodesia, 21 Jan., 1901, FO 2, Vol. 527; Coryndon to Milner, 10 Oct., 1900, CO 417, Vol. 320; Goold-Adams to Milner, ? Sept., 1901, CO, African South 694.

49. CO to FO, 1 March, 1901, CO, African South 659.

50. Lewanika to Chamberlain, 12 Feb., 1903, CO, African South 717.

51. Chamberlain to Lewanika, 7 April, 1903, *ibid*.

52. Jalla to Harding, undated, NAR Hist. Mss. Mackintosh Papers, MA 18/4, folio 46; Harding, *Far Bugles*, p. 123.

53. Coryndon to Milner, 1 Dec., 1901, CO 417, Vol. 321.

54. Jalla to Harding, undated, NAR, *op. cit.*

55. Favre, *Coillard*, vol. 3, pp. 510–2.

56. Harding, *Far Bugles*, p. 123.

57. Messrs. Simalumba and Zaza.

58. Coryndon to Company, 18 Oct., 1902, NAR HC 1/2/11.

59. Hole to Milton, 11 Oct., 1903, NAR A 11/2/14/2.

60. Aitkens to Company, 29 Oct., 1904, CO, African South 763.

61. Coryndon to CO, 15 Oct., 1904, CO, African South 746.

62. 'Report on the Administration of Rhodesia, 1900–02', by Coryndon, pp. 448–50, CO 468, Vol. 3.

63. Hole to Lewanika, 5 Aug., 1903, NAZ A 3/24/4.

64. See, e.g., Jalla, *La Mission du Zambèze*, pp. 71–2; Harding *In Remotest Barotseland*, p. 277.

65. S.N.A. to DC, Hook of the Kafue District, 8 April, 1905, NAZ IN 1/5/4.

66. For a detailed account, see Stokes, *op. cit.*, pp. 284–9.

67. Lewanika to High Commissioner, 11 Dec., 1907, CO, African South 899, No. 45.

68. Selborne to Elgin, 17 June, 1907, NAR HC 1/2/6.

69. Lyttleton to Milner, 1 July, 1904, CO, African South 746.

70. Coryndon to Lewanika, 10 Oct., 1904, NAZ B 1/2/301.

71. Lewanika to Coryndon, 15 Nov., 1904, *ibid.*

72. Minute by Rodwell, Imperial Secretary, 8 July, 1905, NAR HC 1/2/4.

73. Stokes, *op. cit.*, p. 283.

74. Corydon to Lewanika, 19 Aug., 1904, NAR A 11/2/14/3.

75. Lewanika to Corydon, 24 Aug., 1904, *ibid.*

76. Declaration by Lewanika, 23 Jan., 1906, NAR HC 1/2/5.

77. Cited in Stokes, *op. cit.*, p. 283.

78. Mr. Simalumba.

79. As noted by the King in his letter to Coryndon, 15 Nov., 1904, NAZ B 1/2/301.

80. Worthington's Journal, 1902, NAR Hist. Mss. Worthington Papers, WO 3/1/2, folio 5.

81. Mr. Zaza.

82. For a more detailed account of the hut-tax controversy, see Stokes, *op. cit.*, pp. 275–82.

83. Lewanika to Company, 10 July, 1902, CO, African South 702, No. 337.

84. Coryndon to Company, 9 Jan., 1903, CO, African South 717, No. 76.

85. Company to CO, 8 May, 1903, CO, African South 717, No. 144.

86. Macauley to Hole, 12 March, 1904, CO, African South 746.

87. Coryndon to Selborne, 22 Nov., 1905, NAZ A 3/5.

88. See Stokes, *op. cit.*, p. 281.

89. Administrator to Company, 4 Feb., 1907, CO, African South 872.

90. Corydon to Milner, 23 Nov., 1904, CO, African South 763; same to same, 30 May, 1905, *ibid.*

91. Milner to Lyttleton, 23 Mar., 1905, *ibid*; Harding to Milner, 14 April 1905, *ibid.*

92. O'Keefe to Milner, 25 Apr., 1905, *ibid.*

93. Secretary of State to Milner, 15 July, 1905, *ibid.*

94. Report by McKinnon, Resident Magistrate, Lealui, Sept., 1908, CO, African South 932.

95. Messrs. Zaza, Njekwa, M. Kawana, and Simalumba, and Mupatu, *Bulozi Sapili*, ch. 12.

96. Coryndon to Selborne, 6 Dec., 1905, CO, African South 802, and Gelfand, *Northern Rhodesia in the Days of the Charter*, p. 127.

97. Beguin to Boegner, 27 April, 1905, PMSP; also *News from Barotsiland*, May, 1905, p. 8, and Oct., 1905, p. 7.

98. Gielgud to Coryndon, 19 Sept., 1903, NAZ KDE 2/23/1.

99. Wallace's Address to the Kuta, 11 Aug., 1909, and Wallace's interview with Lewanika, 2 Aug., 1909, NAZ B 1/2/292. For a parallel situation in Uganda, see P. Powesland, *Economic Policy and Labour*, East African Studies No. 10 (Kampala, 1957).

100. H. W. Fox to Codrington, 11 March, 1904, cited in Maxwell Stamp Associates, *op. cit.*, p. 233.

101. 'Award of His Majesty the King of Italy respecting the Western Boundary of the Barotse Kingdom (with attached Map), July, 1905', Parliamentary papers, 1905, Vol. 4, Cd. 2584.

102. Selborne to Lewanika, 24 July, 1905, CO, African South 763.

103. Lewanika to Coryndon, 19 July, 1905, *ibid.*

104. Coryndon to Milner, 9 March, 1905, NAR HC 1/2/4.

105. Stokes, *op. cit.*, p. 281.

106. Coryndon to Milner, 4 April, 1905, NAR HC 1/2/4.

107. Same to same, 9 March, 1905, *ibid*; Harding to Imperial Secretary, 19 Sept., 1905, CO, African South 763.

108. Coryndon to Milner, 19 Dec., 1905, CO, African South 802.

109. Stokes, *op. cit.*, p. 261.

110. Hunter to Coillard, 20 May, 1902, NAR Hist. Mss. Coillard Papers, CO 5/1/1/1, folio 2036.

111. Bradley, 'Statesmen Coryndon and Lewanika in North-Western Rhodesia', *African Observer*, Vol. 5, No. 5, Sept., 1936, pp. 53–4.

112. This reflected the commonplace belief that the metropolitan government would prove more humane than local officials, particularly if the latter represented a commercial company; see, e.g., J. Van Velsen, 'Some Early Pressure Groups in Malawi', in Stokes and Brown, *op. cit.*, pp. 410–11.

113. Mary Benson, *South Africa: The Struggle for a Birthright* (London, 1966), p. 19.

114. For Peregrino, see NAZ IN 1/7; KDE 1/5/2; and KDE 2/15/1–3. My own notes on Peregrino, taken from these sources, have unfortunately been lost. I am indebted to Prof. T. Ranger for the above quotations and references. I am fairly certain, however, that the archival sources did not suggest precisely how contact between Peregrino and Litia was initially established. Not a single one of my Lozi informants had ever heard of Peregrino.

115. Peregrino to Imperial Secretary, 20 Aug., 1906, CO, African South 802.

116. Selborne to Elgin, 19 Nov., 1906, *ibid.*

117. 'Memorandum on Technical and General Education in the Barotse Valley', by Worthington, 26 Feb., 1905, NAZ A 3/5.

118. Reports by the Principal, 16 Oct., 1907, 31 Jan., 1908, 31 Dec., 1909, 30 Sept., 1901, NAZ A 3/13/1.

119. A. Jalla to Director, 25 June, 1907, PMSP; Report on the Zambesi Mission Schools, by Williams, Principal of BNS, NAZ A 3/13/1.

E

120. List of Lewanika's sons, their educational training and employment, submitted by Yeta to Resident Magistrate, 18 Oct., 1916, NAZ KDE 2/34/20.

121. Acting Secretary, NWR, to Imperial Secretary, 19 May, 1901, African South 948.

122. Hall, *Zambia*, p. 112.

123. Minutes of the Proceedings at a Meeting with Lewanika at Sesheke, 30 Sept., 1907, CO, African South 872, Enclosure 6 in No. 186.

124. Cited in O'Keefe to Imperial Secretary, 10 April, 1905. CO, African South 763.

125. Selborne to Elgin, 11 Nov., 1907, CO, African South 872.

126. Minutes of . . . Meeting, 30 Sept., 1907, *op. cit.*

127. Selborne to Lewanika, 3 March, 1908, CO, African South 899; Lewanika to Selborne, 5 May 1908, *ibid.*

128. Selborne to Lewanika, 5 Oct., 1907, CO, African South 872.

129. Lewanika to Selborne, 11 Oct., 1907, *ibid.*

130. Selborne to Elgin, 11 Nov., 1907, *ibid*; Codrington to Company, 1 Jan., 1908, CO, African South 899.

131. As acknowledged in Ellenberger to Director, undated (c. Jan. 1913), PMSP.

132. See, e.g., Report from Lealui Mission Station, *News from Barotsiland*, June 1909, p. 9.

133. Arnot to Director, 6 Aug., 1910, PMSP.

134. Ellenberger to Director, 17 Jan., 1912, and A. Jalla to Director, 28 Feb., 1912, *ibid.*

135. Lewanika to High Commissioner, 17 Sept., 1911, NAR A 2/2/1. No reply to this letter has been unearthed.

136. Stokes, *op. cit.*, p. 287.

137. For the distortions of Europeans, see Coillard, *Threshold*, p. 152, 382, 401; Jalla, *History*, pp. 61, 63-4; Memorandum on Barotse Slavery, by Worthington, 22 Nov., 1906, NAR HC 1/2/6. For a more considered assessment of the subject, see Gluckman, *Seven Tribes*, pp. 6 and 13; Yeta to Administrator, 10 Aug., 1920, personally held: Y. Mupatu, *Bulozi Sapili*, ch. 7; Messrs. Simalumba and Zaza.

138. Worthington to Coryndon, 23 March, 1905, CO, African South 763; Coryndon to High Commissioner, 8 April, 1905, *ibid.* 'Certainly', said Mr. N. Zaza, 'we cannot think that the Company freed the so-called slaves for philanthropic reasons.'

139. Worthington to Secretary, Kalomo, 17 July, 1906, *ibid*; 'Proclamation of the Abolition of Slavery, 1906', in CO, Africa South 802.

140. Selborne to Elgin, 10 Sept., 1906, *ibid.*

141. Messrs. Simalumba and Zaza; Gann, *History of Northern Rhodesia*, pp. 109-10.

142. A. Jalla, *Mokamba, Un Premier Ministre Chretien*, p. 27.

143. R. Summers and L. H. Gann, 'Robert Edward Codrington, 1869-1908', *Northern Rhodesian Journal*, Vol. 3, No. 1, 1956, pp. 44-8.

144. S.N.A. to DC, Mongu, 3 Oct., 1907, NAZ Kde 2/34/17.

145. Gann, *op. cit.*, pp. 164-5.

146. Stirke, *Barotseland*, pp. 42-3.

147. See Gluckman, 'Kinship and Marriage among the Lozi of Northern Rhodesia and the Zulu of Natal', in A. R. Radcliffe-Brown and D. Forde (ed.), *African Systems of Kinship and Marriage* (London, 1950), p. 181.

148. Stokes, *op. cit.*, pp. 291–2. For the Concession, see L. H. Gann, *The Birth of a Plural Society: The Development of Northern Rhodesia under the British South Africa Company* (Manchester, 1958), pp. 223–5.

149. Wallace to High Commissioner, 12 Nov., 1909, CO, African South 932, No. 242.

150. Minutes of Proceedings at a Meeting. . . . Between the Administrator and Lewanika, 29 Sept., 1911, NAZ B 1/2/292.

151. Selborne to Imperial Secretary, 39 Nov., 1909, NAR HC 1/2/9; CO to Company, 14 July, 1910, NAR A 3/19/5.

152. Translation of a memorandum handed to Colonel Fair by the Ngambela, 28 Nov., 1901, NAZ A 2/1/4.

153. Proceedings at the Meeting of Colonel Fair with Lewanika at Livingstone 28 Nov., 1910, NAR HC 1/2/10.

154. Fair to Lewanika, 28 Nov., 1910, NAZ A 2/1/4.

155. Lewanika to Thwaits, 6 March, 1911, NAR HC 1/2/11, and Secretary of Administration to Imperial Secretary, 25 March, 1911, *ibid.*

156. 'Review of Evidence', prepared by Worthington, 20 April, 1911, *ibid;* transcript of 'Rex vs. Mboo, alias Fwabi, Ikasia and others, 16 March, 1911', *ibid.*

157. Memorandum by Worthington, 20 April, 1911, *ibid.*

158. McKinnon to Wallace, 23 March, 1911, *ibid.*

159. Wallace to Gladstone, 21 April, 1911, NAR HC 1/2/11.

160. Gladstone to Wallace, 8 May, 1911, NAZ B 1/2/301.

161. Wallace to Gladstone, 31 March, 1911, NAR HC 1/2/11.

162. McKinnon to Wallace, 4 May, 1911, *ibid.*

163. Macintosh, *Yeta III*, p. 43. None of the documents in the Paris archives of the PMS allude to this episode.

164. Mr. N. Zaza.

165. McKinnon to Wallace, 4 May, 1911, NAR HC 1/2/11.

166. Jalla, *History of the Barotse Nation*, p. 71.

167. BSA Company Annual Report on Northern Rhodesian Administration, 1914–15, NAR.

168. Stokes, *op. cit.*, p. 292.

169. Venning to Willis, 10 Feb., 1914, NAR RC 3/9/5/3.

170. Report by Willis on meeting with Ngambela, 16 March, 1915, *ibid.*

171. Lewanika to Willis, 19 March, 1915, *ibid.*

172. Gladstone to Lewanika, 18 Dec., 1912, *ibid.*

173. Report by Willis on his interview with Lewanika and the Council, 30 March, 1915, *ibid.*

174. Lewanika to Gladstone, 8 May, 1914, *ibid.*

175. Lewanika to Wallace, 29 July, 1915, *ibid.*

176. 'List of Cases to be tried by the Magistrate', undated, *ibid.*

177. Lewanika to McKinnon, 26 Aug., 1914, NAZ KDE 2/31/1.

178. Same to same, 9 Oct., 1914, *ibid.*

179. High Commissioner to Wallace, 15 Sept., 1914, *ibid;* Wallace to

Lewanika, 12 Sept., 1914, *ibid.*; Secretary of State to High Commissioner, 6 Nov., 1914, *ibid.*

180. J. H. Venning, 'Mwanawina III and the First World War', *Northern Rhodesian Journal*, Vol. 4, No. 1, 1959, pp. 83–6.

181. Mr. N. Zaza; Mwanawina became king in 1948.

182. Messrs. Zaza, Simalumba and Mupatu, and confirmed in 'Report on Effects of War in Barotseland', by Resident Magistrate, 6 March, 1919, NAZ KDE 2/21/3.

183. Report from Barotse District, 30 Sept., 1915, NAR HC 1/3/9; Report from Lealui Sub-District, 1915, *ibid.*; Report from Lukona Sub-District, 1915, *ibid.*

184. McKinnon's Speech to Ngambela and Indunas, 12 Feb., 1916, NAZ KDE 2/34/13.

185. Hole, *The Passing of the Black Kings*, p. 302; Stirke, *Barotseland*, pp. vi–vii; Palmer, *Lewanika's Country*, p. 14; Balovale Commission Report, 1939, pp. 98–9; James T. Addison, *François Coillard* (Hartford, Conn., 1929), p. 49.

186. Goold-Adams to Milner, ? Sept., 1901, CO, African South 694.

187. 'Truly the pen is mightier than the sword, and in the hands of experts . . . achieved more in Barotseland than the most potent lethal weapons in many of our less fortunate dependencies.' Harding, *Far Bugles*, cited in Stokes, *op. cit.*, p. 261.

# CHAPTER V

# YETA VERSUS THE COMPANY

King Lewanika died in February, 1916. So far as the Administration was concerned, the question of the succession had been definitively settled in 1911, and no written record suggests that the National Council attempted to challenge the accession of his eldest son, Litia. Yet no fewer than five Lozi informants independently testified that many indunas in fact favoured either Sikufele or Imwiko. The former, chief of the Lukwakwa area to the north, was supported by a number of traditionalist indunas who believed he would turn to them for advice, whereas Litia would look to his educated brothers.[1] He died, however, before his challenge became serious.[2]

A second group of indunas are said to have opposed Litia in favour of his younger brother Imwiko, who had been educated in England. As the most highly educated and worldly of Lewanika's sons, Imwiko could be expected most adequately to stand up to the Administration.[3] In the end the opposition to Litia melted away. There was good reason to believe he would resist Company encroachments. The traditionalists, in any event, remembered their arrangement of 1912 with Lewanika: their own sons would automatically succeed them if Litia became King, a bargain which was honoured for the first fifteen years of the latter's reign.[4] Moreover, no induna was prepared to challenge the Administration's threat to crush any man who opposed its choice.[5] When, therefore, the Resident Magistrate met the National Council on 8 March, 1916, he found that its members unanimously agreed that 'It is Litia we want, no one else'.[6]

Five days later, Litia officially became King (or, as the Administration insisted, Paramount Chief) Yeta III. Then about forty-two years old, he had been among the first Lozi to attend a mission school, and had taken quickly to western habits and ideas, not excluding Christianity. In 1890 he had accompanied Adolph Jalla to Bechuanaland, where he had been much impressed by Khama and became close friends of a young Bechuana Christian. On his return to Barotseland, he was publicly baptized—one of the first Lozi to be so. In 1891, his father appointed him chief of Sesheke, a post he retained until he became King. Although his English was inadequate for conversation, his intelligence, breadth of interest and knowledge were widely acknowledged.[7]

The Company on the whole welcomed Yeta's accession. It was true that he had been responsible for the serious jurisdiction dispute of 1914 by insisting that his own court try a case of cattle theft, and that his relations with the new elite were very warm. On the other hand, save for Mwanawina, he stood out among his brothers for unswerving loyalty to the British throne. Both as chief of Sesheke and as King, his support in recruiting porters for the war effort was as enthusiastic as his father's had been.[8] On the wall of his palace in Lealui, portraits of Edward VII and George V hung beside that of Lewanika.[9] After an interview in July, 1916, with Viscount Buxton, the High Commissioner, the latter felt reassured that the Lozi 'not only acquiesce in their control [by Administration officials] but welcome their advice and assistance. This was markedly the case in regard to Lewanika . . . and will be, I think, still more the case in regard to his son Letia. . . .'[10]

George Lyons, who became Resident Magistrate of Barotseland in 1916, wrote in the same vein in his first annual report. He was highly gratified by the co-operation which Yeta had demonstrated over the previous year, and considered—ironically, as it emerged—that the only serious problem was that, although the King's 'own ideas are all for the advance and improvement of his people, he is tremendously hampered by the conservative ideas held by some of the older and more influential indunas. . . .'[11]

It did not take long to recognize how wholly misconceived this was. The older conservative indunas were in no position to influence Yeta. On the contrary, the new educated elite soon achieved the ascendancy among his closest advisers, and they had as their primary objective the total repudiation of Company rule. The success of Lewanika's initiative in creating a group of trained aristocrats to buttress the traditional ruling class became manifest with Yeta's succession. Lewanika's own sons and those of senior indunas and his court favourites had begun to return to Barotseland from their advanced schools abroad. By 1916, no fewer than seven of Lewanika's sons had been to schools in England, South Africa or Basutoland.[12] Yeta selected two private secretaries: his brother Akashambatwa, who had studied at Lovedale and Zonnebloem, the Anglican College at Cape Town, and Mubukwanu Mataa (now Induna Imandi), who had been educated in Basutoland and at Zonnebloem, and whose father became Yeta's Ngambela in 1920.[13] Three other sons of the late King who were educated in Southern Africa—Mwanawina, Lubinda and Muanayanda—took their proper seats on the royals' mat in the Kuta, as did Yeta's own sons, Daniel Akafuna and Edward Kalue. Both the latter had received their schooling in South Africa, where they had mixed with politically-minded South African Africans, Akafuna finally being expelled for 'open rebellion'.[14] About the same time, sons of indunas who had been educated in southern Africa or in Barotseland were beginning to replace their fathers in the Kuta.[15]

George Lyons quickly came to loathe these young men, whom he described as 'half-educated schoolboys'.[16] No view could have been more inaccurate. Their grasp of legal complexities, their familiarity with the early concessions, their astute and logical reasoning as well as their political shrewdness, were all soon enough illustrated. The days of picturesque figures of speech, hand-written, were gone for ever, to be replaced by typewritten correspondence in 'concise, businesslike English'.[17] Indeed, as Gann has recognized, they were sufficiently competent and sophisticated to 'hold their own in a European assembly' and participate in a legislative debate.[18]

Given the close contanct of some, and the familiarity of all, of the young men who had been educated in South Africa with African political developments in that country, it was inevitable that they should return with new ideas and new aspirations. Because they were aristocrats by birth, and because they had as a heritage a formerly great empire, these young Lozis' aspirations centred on resurrecting Barotseland's lost glory, on resuscitating a powerful kingdom which they would rule as their ancestors had once done. Moreover, because the new King was himself virtually a member of the new educated elite, he welcomed these younger men into his Council. In their attempts to realize the hopes they shared, the new educated Lozi elite and their natural leader, Yeta himself, joined in an alliance against white rule with the traditional ruling class, much as their counterparts among the Ndebele and Zulu were doing at the same time.[19] This upsurge of nationalism, or tribalism, among the ruling classes of formerly powerful kingdoms, contrasted with the means by which the 'new men' of smaller tribes were attempting to acquire for themselves positions and privileges commensurate with their status as members of an educated elite. In Nyasaland and parts of eastern Northern Rhodesia, for example, where the past allowed no romantic illusions of restoring great empires, the new men turned to Native Welfare Associations based on a wider nationalism, that of Northern Rhodesia or Nyasaland as a whole rather than Barotseland or Matabeleland.[20] Lozi nationalism was, therefore, essentially reactionary, at attempt to restore the lost privileges of the past; Nyasa nationalism was progressive, in the sense that the new elite was concerned with upward mobility, with expanding opportunities in the larger colonial set-up by winning, for example, jobs hitherto reserved for white men.

There was, then, a fundamental divergence between the objectives of Lozi and the other new elites of Nyasaland and Northern Rhodesia. Yet for a short period their interests happened to coincide. It is true that at no time was the Lozi ruling class, led by Yeta and his 'new men', concerned with any interests but its own. But because it believed that its interests could be satisfied only by a direct frontal attack on the entire institution of Company rule, because it fought for increased powers for Africans as against the white Administration, the Lozi elite briefly represented the aspirations and interests of all black elitists in Northern Rhodesia.[21]

Yeta's young men were fully aware of the futile protests against Company encroachments on Lozi sovereignty during the last decade of Lewanika's reign. Although petitions to the High Commissioner had proved no more fruitful than those to Company officials, the new elite continued to cherish the belief that only under direct British protection could they hope to see the traditional rights and powers of the Lozi ruling class restored. The first eight years of Yeta's kingship witnessed, therefore, a veritable flood of long and well-argued petitions and supporting memoranda calling for an end to Company rule and the restoration of proper Lozi rights.

By 1917 the impact of the new men began to be felt. Rumours were spreading that the Company intended to hand over the administration of Northern Rhodesia to the British government. Yeta reminded the High Commissioner that his father had agreed to give the Company commercial rights in its capacity as the administering agent of Northern Rhodesia. The implication was clear: if it shed its administrative responsibilities, the Company automatically lost its commercial rights.[22]

By the end of the year, Yeta was asserting his right to be called 'King' of Barotseland, as his father originally had been called; his proposal was rejected harshly and unequivocally.[23] Nor was the Administration pleased with Lozi 'inter-meddling' outside the reserved area. District officers were reporting Lozi attempts to 'boss up' Ila and Sala chiefs in the Kafue District and to interfere in the succession to the Mumbwa chieftaincy. Wallace, the Administrator, revealed some understanding of the new mood of the ruling class.

They feel [he recognized] . . . a waning influence over the people and are unwilling to lose their power or diminish the state in which they live. There is a movement, originating I think with the English speaking sons, to renew their influence outside the Barotse District and so incidentally to receive tribute.

In short, as Wallace did not say, the invigorated Lozi patriotism of the new elite was creating conflict with the Administration. He was not greatly worried that the attempts to revive Lozi imperial pretensions would succeed, but he was not prepared to challenge the Lozi on a question of abstract right. To force Yeta formally to renounce his authority outside the reserved area might undermine the Company's mineral rights, since, as has been seen, the boundaries between North-Eastern and North-Western Rhodesia had been shifted in 1905 in order to have the Copperbelt fall under the concessions with Lewanika, rather than the more dubious ones which Company

agents had had signed with 'chiefs' in the north-east. Therefore, Wallance advised, 'it is better to encourage this natural
diminution of [Lozi] influence [outside the reserved area] than
by any drastic action to bring on a serious dispute as to our
rights and theirs'.[2][4]

Although Wallace was prepared to use subtle means to
thwart the renewed Lozi assertions of their rights over their
old domains, Administration attitudes towards the new
régime, had, by 1918, perceptibly hardened. Lyons's early
sympathy for Yeta was quickly waning. The King was too
frequently taking a 'wrong attitude', Lyons reported, due to
'the influence of the educated or semi-educated natives by
whom he is surrounded'.[25] Yeta's 'younger educated brothers',
he later added, had virtually taken over the Kuta from the
older indunas: 'It is an exception rather than the rule for any
of the older Indunas, except the Ngambela, to be present now
even when matters of great importance are being discussed.'[26]

At this point, early in 1919, Ngambela Mokamba died in his
twentieth year as the senior commoner in the land. Remembered
by his people as one of their greatest Ngambelas,[27] his last
years had been difficult ones, for he was demoralized by the
death of Lewanika and probably too weary after his years of
fruitless struggle against the Company to regard the renewed
counter-offensive with enthusiasm.[28]

Yeta immediately named as his new Ngambela Kueleka
Tawila, who had been educated in South Africa and with
whom he was said to have been 'of one mind' on most issues.
This quintessential 'new man' died only months later, however,[29] and the grieving Yeta appointed in his stead Induna
Mukulwakashiko, who took office as Ngambela Mataa. Mataa
fits less obviously into the 'new Lozi' pattern. An older man
with no especial reputation as a progressive, his great attraction to Yeta, several informants suggested, may well have been
their common hatred of beer-drinking. Informants agreed, too,
that the choice was unpopular among many in the Kuta,
partly because they favoured other candidates, in part because,
as a member of the royal family, Mataa was considered to be
constitutionally barred from the Ngambelaship. Yeta replied,
however, that the constitutional prohibition was inapplicable
since Mataa's connection with the royal family was through

his mother's side.[30] Nor did Lyons or the missionaries approve the appointment, the latter because Mataa was not a Christian, the former probably because he was Yeta's choice. With Lyons's encouragement, Adolph Jalla attempted to dissuade the King, but to no avail.[31]

The new Ngambela was quickly given opportunities to demonstrate that he intended to bridge the generation barrier between himself and the new elite and to co-operate with them fully in their ongoing dispute with the Administration. Despite the disruptions inevitably attendant on the deaths of two chief councillors, Yeta had never ceased pressing his demands. Late in 1919, he announced that he wished to visit England. Lyons strongly opposed such a trip 'on account of the unsettled state of his district and the dissatisfied condition of the natives with him'.[32] This was the first time Lyons raised these charges, to which he was to return again and again in the succeeding four years.

There were, he claimed, 'a number of existing evils' which Yeta must redress before he 'earned the right' to an interview with the King of England. He accused the ruling class of forcibly and illegally collecting tribute from outlying tribes and of compelling men to work for more than the prescribed twelve days of unpaid labour. He believed Yeta was ignoring the advice of his older indunas and, despite repeated warnings, continued to heed the advice of his 'semi-educated younger brothers'. On the other hand, though the severe penalties and rigorous enforcement of the new adultery and beer laws which the King had laid down soon after his accession had given rise to considerable discontent, Lyons considered that 'in the application of both these laws . . . he is in the right and should be upheld'.[33] Finally, Lyons told a group of Kalabo people that, by the terms of the Abolition of Slavery Proclamation of 1906, they no longer need assist indunas and headmen to cultivate their lands or build their homes. The ruling class had no right to demand free labour save for community projects such as digging wells, cleaning villages or cattle kraals, and the like.[34]

This interpretation of the 1906 Proclamation was correct, and it is undoubtedly true that many indunas were disregarding its provisions. Nevertheless, Lealui strongly protested on two grounds. It was angrily pointed out to Lyons that 'it was not good' for the Resident Magistrate to go around the country, without consulting the King and Kuta, undermining the people's respect for the authority of the ruling class.[35] Secondly, the Lozi denied that they were ruling harshly and unjustly. To make the position clear, Yeta had his secretaries send to Wallace, the Administrator, a long letter, skilfully and eloquently setting out the Lozi position. Demands by the ruling class that Lozi peasants provide them with free labour involved 'the subject of land tenure according to our law'. The Lozi had no concept of private property. All land belonged to the King and National Council, but they assigned land to those who asked for it. In return, they had the right to demand unpaid labour from the holders of such land. If Barotseland was in an unsettled state, this was the responsibility not of the ruling class but of Lyons, 'who has been declaring to the people that they can go anywhere they like and do whatever they like because they are free'. The position of the King and Kuta, in short, was simple and reasonable:

> As we are the rulers of this country we should have the power and authority to govern our people and to control their rights to land and to control their movements thereon.[36]

This impressive document failed to move the Administration. Coxhead, the Secretary of Native Affairs, informed Yeta that he would not be allowed to visit England because of the discontent in Barotseland which had arisen as a result of the ruling class's excessive demands for unpaid labour, although he acknowledged that he was unable to cite 'specific instances' of such demands.[37] Coxhead did realize that Lealui felt considerable mistrust not only for local officials but for the Administration as a whole, but he blamed this on Yeta's 'unfortunate' choice of advisers and on the new Ngambela, whom he considered 'most unsatisfactory'. Under their influence, he believed, 'Yeta thinks more of money now than anything else. . . .'[38]

This was considerably less than a half-truth. It was true that the King's demands for an increase in his share of the poll tax had not abated; after all, for the fiscal year 1917–18, taxation of Africans in North-Western Rhodesia had yielded the Company some £82,000.[39] The King's direct share of this amount continued to be £1,300, most of which was distributed among the royal family, indunas and headmen, obviously giving most recipients an insignificant percentage. On the other hand, the King personally received about £1,400 from such other sources as the Company's subsidy from the Concession of 1900 and his share of game licences and of ivory collected in the reserved area. Nevertheless, the income of the Lozi ruling class was in no way commensurate with the aspirations of an aristocracy striving to reassert its primacy, a fact the Administrator tacitly recognized when he noted that the King was 'being pressed by his headmen and particularly by his relations to pay them more'.[40] Moreover, these aspirations encompassed more than merely financial demands. Their fulfilment involved greater Lozi control over their own land, Imperial status, and the repudiation of the Company's right to hand over the administration of Northern Rhodesia either to a 'Responsible Government' of local Europeans, or to a government formed by the amalgamation of the two Rhodesias, or to a government formed by the union of the two Rhodesias with South Africa—all alternatives then being discussed by the tiny European community in Northern Rhodesia.[41] It was in this sense that the Lozi ruling class, though concerned solely with its own interests and privileges, inadvertently and unconsciously came to share the interests of all Africans in the territory.

This role became clear in Cape Town in March, 1921, when Yeta personally handed to Prince Arthur of Connaught, the new High Commissioner, a petition which Ranger has described as 'the only coherent African view presented to the debate on the governmental future of Northern Rhodesia'.[42] It contained five major points. The first request was for 'the direct rule of the Imperial Government as a protected native state' not merely over the reserved area but over the entire territory earlier known as 'Barotseland-North-Western Rhodesia'. The second was a demand that all concessions granted to and 'agreements' concluded with the Company should be cancelled. The third and fourth points called for the extension of the Barotse Reserve to include two further areas: the Caprivi Strip, and 'the land from the headwaters of the Dongwe River down to the place where the Anglo-Portuguese boundary cuts the Zambesi River'. These areas had been expropriated from the

Lozi without even consulting, let alone asking for the consent of, the King and Kuta. Indeed, despite staunch Lozi loyalty to Britain during the war, their only reward had been the handing of the Caprivi Strip not back to Barotseland but over to South Africa as part of the South-West Africa mandate. Moreover, the validity of the land concessions of the 1900s was itself questioned. The petition carefully demonstrated that the extension of the reserve west of the Zambesi, granted in the concession of 1909, had been made an explicit condition by Chamberlain of his confirmation of the concession of 1900, and hence could hardly be used as a bargaining counter for obtaining fresh rights in 1909.

Finally, the petition argued that the original financial arrangement had been that the King was to receive 10 per cent of the hut tax collected, but the Company had 'cleverly planned' that he receive only a fraction of that percentage. Since, in those days, the ruling class had adequate financial resources, they had accepted this unjust settlement. But now, with the cost of living greatly increased, the cattle trade largely ended by the epidemic, free labour almost abolished, and so many of the younger men leaving the country to seek work, 'it is very difficult to keep the same standards of Chieftainship as before'. The Company had, furthermore, reneged on its commitment to endow and maintain schools, improve transport facilities, and the like.

> In the case of schools, although the Company retains 90 per cent of the money collected from the natives, it does not waste or spend anything for the education and civilization of the natives, but it has taken the money which was promised to be their [the King's and indunas'] salary.

The petition asked therefore that the full 10 per cent of the tax be paid to the King, and that 'the Company should help by providing money for the maintenance of the school which has been established by our money'.[43]

Although in its strictures against the Company, its demand for Company funds for schools, and its plea for direct imperial rule, this petition may have obliquely reflected the interests and opinions of all educated Africans in Northern Rhodesia, its basic purpose is accurately described by Gann:

Constitutional change was to be a means of reasserting the chiefly powers of old, relieving the economic position of the Barotse ruling group and enabling them to exact great financial benefits from mining and land settlement.[44]

Moreover, Lozi aggressiveness in pressing their demands was highly displeasing to the Administration. After meeting with Yeta, for example, F. D. Chaplin, the new Administrator, reported that the King's attitude

> did not indicate any great willingness on his part to co-operate with the Administration, and it seems likely that he has been advised to refuse such co-operation in the hope of thereby obtaining a further addition to his salary.[45]

The reference to Yeta's advisers was not merely to his brothers; it included as well a white South African lawyer with whom the Lozi had been in contact and who had not been permitted to accompany them to their meeting with the High Commissioner in Cape Town.[46]

Not even professional legal advice, however, could overcome the determination of the Company, supported by the British government, to block Lozi aspirations. In July, 1921, the High Commissioner sent the King an official reply to the petition of March. The Lozi share of the tax could not be increased. The concessions with the Company could not be cancelled. The reserved area could not be extended. As for the transference from Company to Imperial overrule, the government 'has taken note of your wishes . . . and your request will be borne in mind'.[47]

This major challenge by the united Lozi ruling class, led by its educated new members, to oust the Company's administration and restore its former glories, thus proved an abject failure. Perhaps it was for this reason that they now turned their attention to George Lyons, the local embodiment of all the humiliations and infringements of traditional prerogatives which Company rule had meant. In December, 1921, Yeta openly challenged Lyons on the issue. He called a large general meeting at the capital where, as Lyons admitted, the only complaints made were against the harsh enforcement of the law prohibiting beer-drinking—a law he supported. But this, he explained, was thanks to his own unceasing efforts in the past to have remedied 'the real cause of the recent discontent' —enforced tribute and labour.

Lyons was far from satisfied, however, that the Lozi rulers had genuinely changed their evil ways. As evidence of this, he adduced the recent appointment of Yeta's son, Daniel Akafuna, to the Kuta. Akafuna was, from Lyons's point of view, the worst possible kind of African: educated in South Africa, involved there with black politicians, finally expelled from school for 'open rebellion'. His influence on his father could be expected to be as 'turbulent', his advice as 'pernicious', as Yeta's other young advisers'.[48]

Goode, the Acting Administrator, instructed Lyons to inform Yeta that Akafuna's appointment must be cancelled. Should he refuse, Goode stated,

> It might give the opportunity of telling Yeta that if he chooses his advisers in this way he cannot expect the Government to treat the Council with much consideration, and that his own position will suffer.[49]

Yeta was not intimidated. Daniel Akafuna was not dismissed from his seat on the Kuta. Moreover, the King returned to the attack. The Company's claims to land and mineral rights in Northern Rhodesia were being referred to the Judicial Committee of the Privy Council for judgment. Since those claims were largely based on the concessions granted by Lewanika, the Lozi side of the case should surely be presented, and who could do this better, Yeta asked, than representatives of the Barotse National Government?[50]

When, by July, 1923, these letters remained unanswered, Yeta wrote direct to the Privy Council, setting out 'our points on which we do not accept the claims of the Company to land and mineral rights in North-Western Rhodesia'.[51] In a long, well-documented letter, all the arguments of the preceding seven years were recapitulated. Above all, it stressed that the Company's rights to land and minerals were inextricably tied to its administrative obligations; once it surrendered the latter, it automatically lost the former. Any commercial rights granted to the Company after it ceased to administer Northern Rhodesia should be subject to conditions to be laid down in a new agreement.[52]

This letter received a reply. The Colonial Office informed Yeta that the government and the Company had settled their differences without recourse to the Privy Council. The Crown was to take over the administration of Northern Rhodesia in 1924. This meant that though the Lozi had always been under His Majesty's protection, 'from the 1st of April [1924] onwards they will stand in an even closer and more direct relationship with the Crown'. The Lewanika concessions, however, would not be cancelled and the Company would continue to possess its mineral rights.[53]

This final point effectively undermined whatever satisfaction the rest of the letter might have provided the Lozi ruling class.[54] Perhaps to signal the dissatisfaction, it was at this point that its leaders decided they were no longer prepared to tolerate George Lyons as Resident Magistrate of Barotseland. In December, 1923, the King wrote Goode, the Acting Administrator, requesting Lyons's transfer.[55] The latter was outraged, and with the backing of the High Commissioner demanded an apology to himself and the retraction of the letter.[56] But Yeta would agree to neither until he was shown where his letter was improper; Lyons, for his part, demanded an apology before he was prepared to explain anything.[57] The King insisted that he had not intended to be impolite, unless this simply meant a refusal to accept the High Commissioner's 'advice', or that the Lozi rulers, despite their putative special status, had no right to request the transfer from their country of an undesirable official.[58] In fact, of course, this was precisely the Administration's position, and it was only the sudden death of George Lyons a short time later which prevented a possibly irreparable rupture between the Lozi and the Administration.[59] The accusations against Yeta's régime were not revived by Lyons's successors, R. H. Palmer and P. E. Hall—persuasive evidence that his personal antipathy towards the King's advisers had led him to exaggerate his case—and no other senior official was ever asked by the ruling class to be withdrawn from Barotseland.

In April 1924, direct Crown rule came to Northern Rhodesia. This was the moment for which Lewanika had vainly awaited ever since 1886, and which, after the Company officials began dismantling the old Lozi empire, the entire ruling class agreed was absolutely crucial. Although successive

High Commissioners had consistently supported the Company against the Lozi rulers, even the new elite shared the belief that imperial overrule was the only possible means to the desired end: under a benevolent and economically disinterested government, the former rights and privileges of the ruling class would be restored. If their reactionary goals could not be achieved under His Majesty's paternal government, their entire strategy would have been proved a failure.

Probably, however, they were not over-optimistic that their demands would be acceded to by the new colonial administration. After all, except for a new Governor, Herbert Stanley, most of the Company's local officials were kept on under the new régime. Moreover, although he was naturally pleased at the transfer of Barotseland from the responsibility of the Company to that of the Crown, the King had already expressed 'very much regret' that the Company was to maintain its mineral rights intact.

> Since His Majesty's Government declines to the cancellation of the old Concessions and the making of a new Treaty [Yeta had told the High Commissioner in 1923], the Barotse people feel that the proposed change of Government can only be considered to be theoretical and not practical, because the main objections of the Barotse people were against the terms of the Concessions with the British South Africa Company and its Administration generally. If no effectual change is made, then the protection craved for by the Barotse people has not been attained.[60]

Nevertheless, while it was true that, as Richard Hall has said, in Barotseland the Company had 'left as its monument one of the most neglected territories in Africa,'[61] it was also true that the Lozi alone were explicitly mentioned in the new constitution of Northern Rhodesia, in clauses reaffirming the integrity of the reserved area and guaranteeing the authority of the Lozi King in 'tribal matters'.[62] The Lozi ruling class, then, had little alternative but to put to the test this new régime for which it had struggled for so long.

In August, 1924, Yeta, Ngambela Mataa, and a large number of indunas, at their own request, were granted their first interview with Governor Stanley. The presented him with an

eleven-point petition and a long, six-page document, 'Explanations to Petitions', setting out in detail the grievances and
demands of the previous thirty-five years.[63] In so far as it
included a demand for Lewanika's original programme to
modernize Barotseland, it coincided with articulate African
opinion in Northern Rhodesia. Yet it basically, and naturally,
reflected above all the desire of the Lozi ruling class for the
recovery of its former authority.

Governor Stanley did not reflect the mentality of Company
officials. On the contrary, he was in the vanguard of those
English colonial officers who were beginning to adopt the
policy of 'indirect rule'. For a variety of reasons, it was now
considered that the proper method by which to govern their
colonies was by upholding the status of traditional tribal rulers.[64]
Perhaps 'indirect rule' as applied in Barotseland was not para-
digmatic of its general application by Britain in Africa, though
one suspects that Lugard himself would have approved. For
what is most striking in the Lozi case at least is how marginally
it altered the existing power relationship. Stanley made this
immediately clear. He rejected all the demands contained in
the Lozi petition, though he did so with more patience and
sympathy than the Lozi had become accustomed to from Company representatives. What he offered as compensation for a
restoration of actual authority was an increase in the revenues
of the ruling class to allow its members at least the material
appurtenances commensurate with their theoretical status.

Stanley offered the King £1,000 to surrender his right to a
share of the money received from hunting licences and from
ivory in North-Western Rhodesia outside the reserved area.
He then suggested that in order to preclude further disputes
over the question of exploiting free labour, the King and Kuta
abandon even the limited rights to such labour which had been
granted in the Proclamation of 1906 abolishing 'slavery'. In
return for so doing, Stanley offered the King personally an
annual reimbursement of £500, while the Kuta would receive
£2,000.

Yeta and his advisers accepted this arrangement with
alacrity.[65] They were quick to grasp that the British administration had no more intention than had the Company of
granting them the restoration of authority for which they had

yearned. Failing this, they were prepared to accept Stanley's compromise: affluence would have to compensate for real power. Gradually but perceptibly over the next several years, incessant demands for more money for the ruling class came to replace those for modernizing Barotseland and reviving the authority of its elite therein. In this way, the period during which the interests of the Lozi ruling class happened to coincide with those of the detribalized elite elsewhere north of the Zambesi came to an end. As the latter increasingly pressed to acquire new privileges and greater opportunities within the national administration, the essential parochialism, or tribalism, of the Lozi elite manifested itself in virtual isolationism from the mainstream of African affairs in the remainder of the territory.

To begin with, the grant given as compensation for the abolition of all unpaid labour was deemed wholly inadequate 'to enable those who formerly enjoyed labour rights to live in their accustomed way. . . .'[66] It then emerged that the canal at Lealui was growing dangerously dirty for, although £200 had been set aside from the compensation grant for public works, it had not been cleaned; within six months, all but ten pounds had been spent 'in paying indunas to announce the new law as to unpaid labour' and for paddlers who took Yeta and his party to a meeting with the Prince of Wales.[67] But why was the government not financing such projects, and indeed, why was it not providing roads, court houses, royal barges and houses, adequate clothes and food for schoolboys. The position of the elite was clear: if the government intended to do nothing for the masses of the country, let it at least properly compensate the elite for the powers and privileges it had lost.

> Before the Government came [Yeta stated], we the Paramount Chief and Khotla had a very happy life. Then we lost our tribute, but still we lived well on our cattle and on our unpaid labour. We had great hopes that under the Imperial Government we should recover the rights we had lost, but instead we lost even our twelve days labour. Altogether we have suffered on all sides.[68]

Indeed, it began to seem that the more money the ruling class was able to get, the more it demanded. According to Hall, the Resident Magistrate, it was the members of the new elite, and above all Yeta's private secretary, Mubukwanu Mataa, son of the Ngambela, who were most insatiable in their demands for ever greater governmental subsidies 'to augment their own personal luxury and dignity'.[69] This assessment was reasonable, given their thwarted aspirations, but there is no reason to believe the entire ruling class did not share their sentiments.

In a farewell letter in June, 1927, to Stanley, who was being transferred to Ceylon, Yeta expressed his regret that the Governor was departing before the question of sufficient funds for the Barotse government had been settled. His presentation shrewdly exploited the growing bias among colonial officers towards indirect rule and the preservation of traditional societies.

> We have a form of government according to our native customs [Yeta wrote], and this form of government the British Government allows us to continue . . . . But even if the [British] Government may not wish this power to die out, it will eventually die out if it has no sufficient funds. There is a pressing necessity to fund the Barotse Council . . . [which] has no funds to depend upon in the carrying out of its duties as a governing body.[70]

Stanley was able to promise no more than to ask his successor, Sir James Maxwell, to consider certain salary increases to some of the lowest paid indunas and headmen.[71] The Lozi rulers thereupon decided on a new initiative. As Lewanika had gone to England many years earlier to present his grievances to the King of England, so now, in 1928, it was decided that Yeta should follow this precedent of seeking redress from the man whom the Lozi still believed was the ultimate source of authority in the Empire. Daniel Akafuna, Yeta's son, was despatched to South Africa to encourage Lozi expatriates there—with whom the ruling class had maintained contact[72]—to form an organization to collect funds for the proposed trip to England.

A letter written by the secretary in Kimberley, a bank messenger, of the duly created 'King Lewanika's Memorial Fund', to a policeman who was among the leaders of the Lozi community in Bulawayo, indicates the ambivalent position of the new Lozi elite in terms of the mainstream of African aspirations in south-central Africa. In common with most Africans, it revealed a profound distrust of Europeans: 'whitemen will never do any good for the sake of black men, but . . . they would rather like to see him always down'. On the other hand, while African associations in South Africa, Nyasaland and Northern Rhodesia outside of Barotseland adopted names stressing their nationality or race, the Lozi organization was named after a tribal King. Indeed, the secretary's letter explained that the new 'fund' was named after 'King Lewanika' since one of its objectives was to have the title of 'King' restored to Yeta. Its second objective was to raise money for Yeta's trip to England, since its supporters were certain that the white government of Northern Rhodesia would refuse to sponsor it.

The letter concluded with a stirring appeal to Lozi nationalism: 'Keep the love of our Mother Country at the depth of your respective hearts, that we should all with one consent and unity of mind endeavour to develop or evaluate the Country into a high grade.'[73]

In the event, nothing further was heard from the 'King Lewanika Memorial Fund', and Yeta, for some reason not prepared to spend his own money—although it was undoubtedly adequate—did not go to England. Instead, another of the familiar petitions of protest was sent to Maxwell, the new Governor, but no satisfactory response was received.[74] Lozi resentment was reflected in a song popular at the time of Maxwell's meeting with Yeta in 1928:

> The Governor, Governor, Governor,
> What type of a European
> Is this Governor
> Who has the royal drums
> Beaten for him, the Governor.[75]

The Resident Magistrate reported that relations between himself and the Lozi rulers during 1928 were at a lower ebb than at any time since the death of George Lyons. He claimed that Mubukwanu Mataa, son of the Ngambela, had become not only Yeta's private secretary but his main personal adviser, and that under his influence, 'the Native Government again and again refused to accept the advice or cautions' of the Resident Magistrate. This situation, he said, improved only—

and abruptly—in December, 1928, when Ngambela Mataa and two of his sons, including Mubukwanu Mataa, were arrested and charged with the ritual murder of a woman and her daughter.[76]

A judge sent by the government to try the case found the evidence against the three men to be circumstantial, and all were acquitted.[77] Nevertheless, Yeta dismissed both the Ngambela and his own private secretary, the Ngambela's son, from their posts.[78] His motives for so doing are not clear. Possibly, it was simply because many people in Barotseland believed them guilty.[79] It is also possible, however, that the Ngambela and his sons were the victims of a plot to force them out of office, thus exposing for the first time in a decade internal conflicts within the ruling class which its united front against the government had kept latent. The Resident Magistrate and one of my informants believed that the Ngambela had made himself unpopular, but they could not specify why.[80] Mubukwanu Mataa, the present Induna Imandi, told me that it was true that his father was hated by a number of indunas, and it was they who organized this plot against him. His enemies were 'ambitious and money-loving men', who felt they were getting an inadequate share of the compensation money for surrendering their right to free labour, money which was disbursed by the Ngambela.[81] Although he can hardly be considered an unbiased source, Mr. Mataa's analysis is not implausible. It was true that the subsidies of the King and his immediate entourage were infinitely greater than those of the large majority of the ruling class, and the latter may have considered that the King and Ngambela were not doing their utmost to acquire a fair share for them.

Whatever the truth of the matter—and it is likely that it shall never be known—the dismissals of Ngambela Mataa and his son mark a transitional stage between two eras of Lozi history. During the first half of his reign, Yeta, guided by the new elite and supported by the traditionalist indunas, had first attempted to repudiate Company rule in the belief that, under the direct protection of the Crown, their former powers and authority would be restored. When the Crown finally succeeded the Company in 1924, the Lozi ruling class quickly realized that its aspirations would not be fulfilled, and decided instead that it would have to be satisfied with material manifestations of its status. It therefore produced incessant demands for funds adequate to build the kind of palaces, homes, court houses and barges which would properly demonstrate that its members were at least superior to their subjects. Conspicuous consumption would have to compensate for the absence of real power.

Yet, by the end of the 1920s, even these demands were lessening. From reactionaries, anxious to reconstruct the old order, they turned into conservatives, satisfied to accept the *status quo* which they had achieved. Those progressive interests which the Lozi ruling class had happened briefly to represent were now represented by a handful of young men on the Copperbelt and along the line of rail. In Barotseland itself, the elite shut itself off completely from the currents of African politics in the rest of Northern Rhodesia, concerned primarily with local politics and high living in the midst of what white officials enjoyed calling the 'living museum' which their country had palpably become.

## REFERENCES

1. Messrs. Simalumba and Wina; the latter later became Litia's last Ngambela.

2. Messrs. Zaza, Simalumba, Wina and Mupatu, and *Balovale Commission Report*, 1939, pp. 70–1.

3. Messrs. N. Zaza and Muhali Mutemwa.

4. Mr. Zaza.

5. All the informants named above made this point.

6. Letter from Bouchet, in *News from Barotsiland*, No. 56, Aug., 1916, p. 9.

7. Coillard, Journals, 24 Dec., 1889, ? Aug., 1890, 30 Oct., 1890; Lienard to Boegner, 24 May, 1899, Mackintosh, *Yeta III*, p. 10 and 53; Coillard, *Threshold*, pp. 397, 428, 436; Jalla, *History of the Barotse Nation* p. 73.

8. Lyons to Secretary, Livingstone, 6 March 1919, NAZ KDE 2/21/3.

9. Margaret C. Hubbard, *African Gamble* (New York, 1937), p. 117. Miss Hubbard interviewed Yeta in 1936 when she visited Barotseland to make a film of 'natives in the raw'.

10. Report of Buxton's Visit to Rhodesia, July, 1916, in British Museum, Herbert Gladstone Papers, Vol. xxviii.

11. Annual Report, Barotse District, by Lyons, 1916–17, NAZ KDE 8/1/8.

12. Biographies of Lewanika's sons, submitted by Yeta to Lyons, 18 Oct., 1916, NAZ KDE 2/34/20.

13. *Ibid.* and Induna Imandi.

14. Lyons to Goode, 28 Feb., 1922, NAZ KDE 2/16/1.

15. Induna Imandi, former Ngambela Wina, and Mr. Simalumba.

16. Lyons to Goode, 19 April, 1923, NAZ KDE 2/16/1.

17. Stokes, 'Barotseland', in Stokes and Brown, *op. cit.*, p. 299.

18. Gann, *History of Northern Rhodesia*, p. 183.

19. For the Ndebele, see T. Ranger, 'Traditional Authorities and the Rise of Modern Politics in Southern Rhodesia', in Stokes and Brown, *op. cit.*, ch. 7. For the South African parallel, see M. Benson, *Struggle for a Birthright*, ch. 1–3.

20. For Nyasaland, see J. Van Velsen, 'Some Early Pressure Groups in Malawi', in Stokes and Brown, *op. cit.*, ch. 16. For eastern Northern Rhodesia, see Hall, *Zambia*, p. 113, and Robert Rotberg, *The Rise of Nationalism in Central Africa, the Making of Malawi and Zambia, 1873–1964* (Cambridge, Mass, 1965), pp. 124–7.

21. This point is made forcibly, and indeed is probably overstated, in T. Ranger, 'Tribalism and Nationalism: The Case of Barotseland' (typewritten mss., undated), an essay which Professor Ranger has decided not to publish.

22. Cited in Hall, *op. cit.*, p. 141.

23. Petition by Yeta and the Kuta to Sir L. Wallace, 9 Aug., 1918, NAZ KDE 2/34/14; Wallace's Reply to the Petition, 10 Aug., 1918, *ibid.*

24. Wallace to Buxton, 29 Oct., 1918, NAZ B 1/2/292; also Stokes, *op. cit.*, p. 298.

25. Annual Report for Barotse District for year ending 31 March, 1918, by Lyons, NAR HC 1/3/5.

26. Annual Report . . . for year ending 31 March, 1919, by Lyons, NAR HC 1/3/16.

27. Former Ngambela Wina; also Messrs, N. Zaza and Simalumba.

28. Letters from A. Jalla and Bouchet in *News from Barotsiland*, No. 60, Dec., 1919, pp. 7–10. Confirmed by Messrs. Simalumba and Mupatu.

29. Letters from A. Jalla in *ibid.*, 17 May, 1919, No. 59, p. 10, and May, 1920, No. 61 p. 2.

30. Messrs. Wina, Mupatu and Simalumba.

31. Jalla to Lyons, 4 May, 1920, NAZ KDE 2/13/3; Lyons to Secretary for Native Affairs, 10 May, 1920, *ibid.*

32. Lyons to SNA, 17 Dec., 1919, NAR HC 1/3/16.

33. Annual Report, Barotse District, for year ending 31 March, 1920, NAR HC 1/3/18.

34. Minutes of meeting between Lyons and Kalabo Natives, undated, NAZ B 1/2/292.

35. Minutes of interview between Lyons and Yeta *et al.*, 1 June, 1920, *ibid.*

36. Yeta, the Ngambela *et al.*, to Wallace, 10 Aug., 1920, NAR HC 1/3/18.

37. Report of discussion between Coxhead and Yeta, 25 Oct., 1920, *ibid.*

38. Coxhead to Acting Administrator, 15 Nov., 1920, *ibid.*

39. Stanley to Buxton, 16 Nov., 1917, NAR HC 2/3/1.

40. Wallace to Buxton, 27 Feb., 1920, NAR HC 1/3/17; Financial Statement prepared by Yeta, undated (c. Oct., 1919), NAR RC 3/9/5/4.

41. Gann, *op. cit.*, p. 182.

42. Ranger, 'Tribalism and Nationalism', *op. cit.*, See fn. 23.

43. Petition of Yeta and National Council to High Commissioner, Prince Arthur of Connaught, 31 March, 1921, NAR RC 3/9/5/4.

44. Gann, *op. cit.*, p. 184.

45. Chaplin to High Commissioner, 3 May, 1921, NAR RC 3/9/5/4.

46. Lyons to Goode, 14 July, 1921, NAZ KDE 2/25/9. This is the only reference I found to this man, whose name was not mentioned in Lyons's letter.

47. High Commissioner to Yeta, 26 Sept., 1921, NAZ KDE 2/34/12.

48. Lyons to Goode, 28 Feb., 1922, NAZ KDE 2/16/1.

49. Goode to Lyons, 9 April, 1922, *ibid.*

50. Yeta to High Commissioner, 22 March, 1922, NAR HC 1/3/21; Yeta to Churchill 10 Oct., 1922, *ibid.*

51. Yeta to High Commissioner, 2 July, 1923, NAR HC 1/3/23.

62. Yeta and Council to Judicial Committee of the Privy Council, 2 July, 1923, *ibid.*

53. CO to High Commissioner, 20 Oct., 1923, *ibid.*

54. Yeta to High Commissioner, 18 Dec., 1923, *ibid.*

55. Yeta and Council to Goode, 27 Dec., 1923, NAR HC 1/3/24.

56. High Commissioner to Goode, 1 Feb., 1924, *ibid.;* Goode to Yeta, 2 Feb., 1924, *ibid.*

57. Official Interview held in Resident Magistrate's Court House, Mongu, 22 Feb., 1924, NAR HC 1/3/25.

58. Yeta to Goode, 26 Feb., 1924, *ibid.*

59. Annual Report, Barotse District, 1924–25, NAZ KDE 8/1/6.

60. Yeta to High Commissioner, 18 Dec., 1923, NAR HC 1/3/23.

61. Hall, *Zambia*, p. 96.

62. Northern Rhodesia Order in Council, 1924, No. 324, 20 Feb., 1924, clauses 41 and 43 (3), reproduced in Maxwell Stamp Associates, *History of the Mineral Rights of Northern Rhodesia*, Vol. 2, pp. 337–8.

63. Petition Presented to His Excellency the Governor by Paramount Chief and Kuta, 21 Aug., 1924, and 'Explanations to Petition', NAZ ZA 1/9/47/7.

64. See Stokes, *op. cit.*, pp. 300–1, and Low and Pratt, *Buganda and British Overrule*, pp. 201–8.

65. Transcript of the interview between Yeta and Stanley, 21 Aug.–23 Aug., 1924, NAZ ZA 1/9/47/7.

66. Interview between Hall and Yeta, 6 April, 1925, NAZ KDE 2/34/12.

67. Interview between Hall and Yeta and Ngambela, 6 Oct., 1925, *ibid.*

68. Interview between Hall and Yeta and the Kuta, 13 Dec., 1927, *ibid.*

69. Hall to SNA, 19 Dec., 1927, *ibid*; same to same, 13 Dec., 1928, NAZ KDE 2/16/5.

70. Yeta to Stanley, 29 June, 1927, NAZ ZA 1/9/47/32.

71. Stanley to Yeta, 24 July, 1927, *ibid.*

72. Neither written nor oral sources provided data to illuminate the nature of these contracts.

73. As in the case of Peregrino in 1906, my own notes on this 'Fund' have been mislaid. Again I am indebted to Professor Ranger for my source material, the information on the 'Fund' being from his unpublished essay, 'Tribalism and Nationalism', *op. cit.*

74. Petition of Paramount Chief and Council to Sir James Maxwell, 12 April, 1928, NAZ B 1/3/688.

75. Cited in M. M. Sakubita, *Za Luna Li Siile* (*Our Vanishing Past*) (London, 1958), trans. by D. Nyambe, p. 36.

76. Resident Magistrate to SNA, 13 Dec., 1928, NAZ KDE 2/16/5.

77. Rex vs. the Ngambela and others, 1928–29, *ibid.*

78. Ngambela Mataa to Sylvester, Justice of the Peace, 3 Sept., 1929, NAZ KDE 2/14/2.

79. According to Sakubita, public opinion believed them guilty, *op. cit.*, p. 34. Mr. Berger of the PMS told me that Jalla agreed, but Berger himself is 'absolutely convinced' they were innocent. Of my Lozi informants, Mr. N. Zaza thinks they were guilty, but Messrs. Wina and Mupatu disagree.

80. Mr. Mupatu, and Resident Magistrate to SNA, 10 Jan., 1929, NAZ KDE 2/16/5.

81. Mr. Mataa retired to his village after his dismissal as Yeta's secretary, where he remained until Ngambela Wina asked him to become an induna in 1941. He claims to know the men who framed him and his father, some of whom he says are still alive, but refused to give me their names.

# CHAPTER VI

# THE LIVING MUSEUM

The Lozi ruling class had realized by the middle 1920s that the Crown administration had no intention of restoring the authority which the Company had usurped. It therefore reconciled itself to the fact that its status could be enhanced only by conspicuous consumption, but the government soon enough made it clear that unlimited demands for increased revenues would only be counter-productive: the government might become so impatient that it would withdraw even those grants to which it had previously agreed. Yeta and his Ngambela at least recognized the precariousness of the Lozi position, and as the relations between Lealui and its white overrulers became less acrimonious, internal conflicts within the ruling class began to emerge once again. At the same time, the government became increasingly concerned both about the backward nature of Barotseland and about its imprecise authority over the Lozi. Although it did nothing to alleviate the first problem, it took steps further to consolidate its control over the Lozi rulers.

Yeta, weary with age and the frustrating battles of the first dozen years of his reign,[1] chose for his new Ngambela Mbwangweta Munalula the chief councillor of the Libonda Kuta in Kalabo district. Educated at a local PMS school where he could 'read and write and understand a little English,' Munalula was a pacific man, more interested in accommodating the government than in resisting it.[2]

It is true that in 1930, Yeta presented Gilbert Rennie, the new Provincial Commissioner (as the Resident Magistrate was now styled), with a petition raising most of the issues which had been in dispute since the beginning of his reign,[3] but Rennie refused to take it too seriously. He understood that, since Yeta's authority would never be as great as his father's once was, he would have a 'permanent grievance'. He realized also, however, that Yeta would be 'scared out of his wits if he were told that, because of all his grumblings, His Majesty decided to withdraw all officials from Barotseland and leave him to work out his own salvation'.[4] Rennie accordingly informed the King that, if he reopened the old questions, the Lozi ruling class might find that its powers and revenues would actually be reduced.[5]

At the same time, the new 'West Coast' governor, James Maxwell, who in 1929 introduced indirect rule to all of Northern Rhodesia outside Barotse Province, indicated that he was prepared to treat the Lozi rulers with solicitude and generosity —within the limits of discretion. This nice combination of threat and special attention worked perfectly: together, Yeta and his new Ngambela, with at least the partial consent of the rest of the National Council, resolved that their prime function henceforth was to preserve the *status quo*, to maintain the special position of Barotseland within Northern Rhodesia and of the Lozi ruling class within Barotseland.[6]

So far as one can tell, the new educated elite of the post-war years joined their elders in recognizing the futility of further extravagant demands upon the government, and they too turned their attention inward, concerning themselves largely with the consolidation of their own positions. Indeed, if any Lozi could still be said to represent wider African, as opposed to merely Lozi, interests, it was those with white-collar jobs outside the reserved area. Lozi and Nyasas, who had also, for historical reasons, gained early access to European education, had a virtual monopoly of jobs as messengers, clerks, typists and interpreters in government and commercial service in Lusaka and Livingstone. Similarly, on the Copperbelt, though they constituted only a tiny minority of the African population,[7] the Lozi, with the Nyasas, formed an 'obvious elite'. With the best paid and most prestigious jobs in the mines, the Lozi were in the vanguard of 'progressive' elitist African movements, helping to inspire and giving leadership in the nationally-oriented Native Welfare Associations of the 1930s.[8] Although Yeta succeeded to a certain extent in maintaining the loyalty of these men,[9] it was the Lozi urban elite which was in the forefront of the struggle against the conservative ruling class in Barotseland during the nationalist era of the 1950s and 1960s.

As increasing numbers of Africans were being attracted to urban centres, the colonial office was discovering the stable virtues of traditional African societies. Such societies ought to be preserved, it was argued, but many of them, not least Barotseland, proved to have little worth preserving. Beneath the impressive façade of a state in alliance with the British Crown lay the stark reality of a totally underdeveloped, almost poverty-stricken labour reserve. Under Crown as under Company rule, Barotseland's primary function was to provide cheap labour for the white sectors of southern Africa. The Crown government had not the slightest intention of investing in Barotseland the kind of capital necessary to create the infrastructure of a viable economy.

No one, in fact, was prepared to take the initiative in trying to develop the area. In 1927, Hall, the Resident Magistrate, decided to investigate the economic resources of Barotseland;[10] no Kuta member replied to his request for information.[11] One government official stated with undoubted accuracy that the elite demonstrated 'a total lack of interest in the affairs of the country as a whole except in so far as they manifestly and immediately affect their own pockets and prestige'.[12] But the King and Kuta retorted that the government expected economic development to be financed from the Barotse Trust Fund, whereas they themselves had always considered development to be the legitimate responsibility of the government in accordance with the Concession of 1900.

As for Lozi outside the ruling circle, they too refused to co-operate in Hall's investigation. The older men, Adolph Jalla reported, simply distrusted all white men and their schemes, while 'the younger people', though not irrevocably hostile to the government, were sorely disappointed by its failure to act.

They say [Jalla reported]: Since the Crown Government has succeeded the Chartered Company, we have seen no improvement worth mentioning. We hear no one speak of a railway to Barotseland or of cheaper transport. We have seen no work undertaken for the benefit of the country, or to help the people to earn money without going far away from their homes. What is our good trying to improve or increase the produce of our gardens? . . . Transport is so

expensive that it does not pay to send anything to Livingstone for sale. Why should the government not help to
transport our produce to Livingstone? . . .[13]

The local government officials generally agreed that transport was the critical underlying problem; as one of them
expressed it: 'Experimenting with crops should remain in
abeyance until transport facilities exist.'[14] But the government
would not undertake such a costly project, and by 1930 the
Provincial Commission was forced to report that, 'apart from
the fish industry, which gives employment to a fair number of
natives in their own districts, there is at present no native
industry of much economic importance in the Province.' Even
the cattle industry remained stagnant, not having yet recovered
from the pleuro-pneumonia epidemic or the outbreak of lung
sickness which followed it.[15]

As a result, the overwhelming proportion of Lozi males was
forced to leave home in search of paid employment, whether
as unskilled miners in South Africa or the Copperbelt, farm
workers in Southern Rhodesia or, white-collar workers in
towns along the line of rail. In the Nalolo district in 1927, for
example, it was reported that about half the able-bodied men
were working at various distant centres, while most of the
other half were resting before leaving again.[16] By the end of the
decade, Lozi communities existed in Kimberley and Johannesburg, Salisbury, Bulawayo and Wankie, Livingstone, Broken
Hill, the Copperbelt and lesser Northern Rhodesian towns
outside Barotse Province.[17]

Perhaps this massive migration served to siphon off enough
of the educated and ambitious young men—the natural leaders
of the dispossessed masses—to preclude the growth of a large
class of the discontented. For not even the severity of the
depression threw up a serious group of rebels to challenge the
established ruling classes. Yet its impact was brutal, on a scale
comparable to that of western Canada at the same time, where
economic collapse coincided with unprecedented natural dis-
asters to shake the whole fibre of society. Between 1930 and
about 1936–37, paid employment both in Barotseland and
abroad became increasingly scarce—the recruiting agencies
shut their doors in 1932—while floods, drought and locusts

destroyed four successive crops, and pleuro-pneumonia, anthrax and foot-and-mouth disease terminated the remnants of the cattle trade and the small export trade in skins. Famine, unemployment, and imprisonment or compulsory menial labour for non-payment of the poll tax characterized the life of the average inhabitant of Barotseland during most of the decade.[18]

Only the elite was spared severe hardship during these years. The amount of money in circulation in Barotseland, one official reported, was 'on the whole confined to the ruling classes whose incomes are derived from Government subsidies, and [who] have the sale of milk and other produce to Europeans, and are consequently not seriously affected by the financial stringency'.[19] This privileged position they flaunted blatantly, determined to demonstrate under whatever conditions a style appropriate to their status. In 1935, with the wage level for the few Lozi fortunate enough to find work down to three to five shillings a month, the Barotse government, in a dazzling display of conspicuous consumption, spent £1,300 on 'the maintenance of Lealui', and then showed 'a naïve delight' in divulging the details to the Provincial Commissioner.

To the casual reader [Lane-Poole observed], the expenditures may seem extravagant, even prodigal, but due regard has been paid to the assurance repeatedly given that nothing shall be done to reduce the style and standard of living to which the Paramount Chief has been accustomed. Items such as 'ten fishes a day throughout the year at a penny a piece' read like an excerpt from a manorial account book in the Middle Ages, while the entry 'Two costumes a year for each of 100 maidens working in the Chief's house' reflects an almost oriental glamour upon Yeta's domestic household.[20]

In their frustration and impotence, many—perhaps a majority—of the Lozi turned in these years to the millenarian Watchtower movement. Strict regulation by both white and Lozi officials assured that the movement remained a purely spiritual one, however, and it never achieved influence of any kind in Lozi politics.[21] Insignificant as it was, Watchtower was the only institutional manifestation of mass Lozi discontent

with their lot during the decade of the depression. Still, the
extreme economic dislocation gave birth in at least some minds
to the first tentative stirrings of doubt, a vague and rarely
articulated suspicion that the *status quo* reflected less than the
best of all possible worlds. Partly this was a result of the
flagrant extravagance of their rulers. The depression served to
bring into focus the disparity in standard of living which had
been a function of the introduction of a money economy.
Writing in 1940, Max Gluckman, doing anthropological
research in Barotseland, predicted 'a growing cleavage between rulers and subjects', which he believed had already just
begun to emerge.[22]

Contemporary evidence of this cleavage is not substantial
for whatever the doubts of the mass of Lozi, and whatever the
more acute suspicions of a small number of them, in the end
they resigned themselves to their unhappy fate. The lack of
overt protest was repeatedly remarked upon during these years
by district officers—not without some surprise and relief. 'The
year 1933', the DC, Lealui, wrote, 'will provide the chronicle
of people passive in mood. . . .'[23] Nor was this in fact surprising.
After all, mass uprisings have not resulted from every depression in history; Canadians and Englishmen both elected relatively conservative governments during this decade. Thwarted
aspirations, not a fatalistic resignation to one's lot, breed
revolutions, and the majority of Lozi had no great expectations
from life. 'So', as an informant put it, 'people just quietly
suffered.'[24]

This passivity confirmed the general satisfaction of the
administration with the Barotseland native government. Most
officials on the whole shared Lealui's own belief in the superiority of the Lozi as against most other Northern Rhodesian
Africans, Yeta, the Ngambela and many senior indunas succeeding in impressing government officials with their dignity
and polished manners, their co-operativeness, and their 'sound-
ness'.[25]

Yet the government's attitude was marked at the same time
by negative feelings. 'The Native Government showed very
little drive', Logan, the Chief Secretary, pointed out, 'and the
country as a whole is much more backward than any other
areas [of Northern Rhodesia].' Moreover, 'The District

F

Officer was in an uncertain position, having no power to inter-fere with Native Courts, and little opportunity of initiative'.[26] It was this latter problem—the lingering imprecision in the respective spheres of jurisdiction of the white and black govern-ments—which most disturbed white officials. Uncertain whether the new system of Native Authorities which had been imposed upon the other tribes of Northern Rhodesia in 1929 might conflict with the Lozi's special status, Barotseland alone was excluded from the relevant legislation.[27] The administra-tion had now decided, however, that Barotseland must be brought under the new system, and the subsequent negotiations pointed up once again the ultimately dependent status of its rulers: unlike other tribal chiefs, Yeta would be consulted about and, hopefully, consent to the proposed innovations; yet if he rejected them, they would still be implemented.

The government wished to 'refine' the 'rights and powers' of the ruling class by formally extending its own control over the BNG, especially in regard to its courts and its financial expenditures.[28] Obviously the Lozi rulers were highly reluctant to surrender the independence of their courts or the supple-mental incomes which they derived from court fines.[29] For this reason, the negotiations begun in 1930 by government officials to introduce Native Authorities into Barotseland were not concluded until 1935. Yeta's growing financial difficulties finally forced him to concede. It seems that by 1934, through inept handling of his funds combined with his personal extrava-gance, the King had accrued debts of some £2,500. The govern-ment offered to lend him the money to pay his debts on the condition that he agree not only to the formation of a Native-Treasury to regularize the handling of finances, but also to Native Courts. At the same time, the government agreed to pay the £1,000 which the ongoing law case against the Com-pany had cost the Lozi.[30]

Yeta accepted the *quid pro quo*, but only in the face of strong opposition from most of his indunas.[31] The new ordinances of 1935 formalized and regularized the legal status of the BNG, which now became the senior Native Authority for Barotse Province. They did not, however, qualitatively alter the power relations between the Lozi elite and their white overlords. As Hubert Young, the Governor, assured the unofficial white members of the Northern Rhodesian Legislative Council, the ordinances

> give the Govenor power, in the first place, to direct that an order shall be issued which he thinks the native authority ought to issue but has not issued; and, in the second place, it gives the Governor power to revoke an order by the native authority. . . . This has never been expressly provided for before. . . . The only qualification that is put in is to say that he (the Governor) must have the ordinary manners to consult the Paramount Chief before he does so.[32]

Moreover, the King now had to seek government approval for the appointment and dismissal of indunas, and, as Charles Dundas, the Chief Secretary, emphasized, Yeta's own successor would be chosen with the 'guidance and direction' of the Governor.[33]

By the ordinances, the King and Lealui Kuta became the Supreme Native Authority for the province, while each of the district Kutas was recognized as a Subordinate Authority.[34] But District Commissioners retained wide powers to 'suspend, reduce, annul or otherwise modify any sentence of a Native Court',[35] and they showed little reluctance to exploit these prerogatives. Moreover, for all the new formalization, the nature of the cases heard by the Native Courts hardly changed from the days of Coryndon's 'agreements' with Lewanika. In Mongu–Lealui District in 1946, for example, 90 per cent of all civil cases heard concerned matrimonial disputes, while criminal cases were of the most minor and petty kind.[36]

A similar illusion of power without its substance was built into the new Native Treasury. Into it were funnelled, for the first time, the combined revenues of the King and the Barotse Trust Fund, and from it would come all expenditures. But all expenditures were ultimately controlled by the white administration. The Native Treasury, as the Chief Secretary explained to the Legislative Council, 'will submit its estimates for the year to the Governor, who will approve or not as he thinks fit.[37] This was the reality of 'indirect rule' as applied by the British in Barotseland.

There need be no doubt that many indunas deeply resented the privileges which they lost through the Native Courts and

Native Treasury Ordinances.[38] They lost their traditional right to a direct share of the fines they themselves imposed, receiving instead a salary fixed by the senior Native Authority, the Lealui Kuta. Indunas of the First and Second Class Courts especially suffered a serious decline in income, and none of them was anxious to turn over to the Native Treasury fines collected. The indunas of the Libonda Kuta indeed refused to do so until officials threatened them with prosecution if they failed to meet this obligation.[39]

As the aggrieved indunas understood, their sorry plight was the direct responsibility of the King, his senior indunas, and members of the royal family. For it was in this area that the senior members of the ruling class had a certain real power. One of the chief privileges which the Lozi still retained was the right to accumulate a relatively large amount of wealth, and one of the major privileges of the inner elite of the ruling class was the right to distribute this wealth to lesser indunas and headmen largely as they saw fit.

Compared with any other tribe in Northern Rhodesia, the Lozi rulers were enormously wealthy. In 1938, the Barotse National Treasury collected £13,446, more than ten times the revenue of the next richest treasuries, those of the Bemba and the Plateau Tonga.[40] The major sources of its revenues were its share of the hut tax, its payment for a timber concession to the Zambesi Saw Mills Company, and its compensation for abolishing unpaid labour. For the same year, the King and the Lealui Kuta, with the approval of the Provincial Commissioner, estimated expenditures of £15,200. Of this total, about £2,300 went to the Barotse National School and £2,800 to the missions as educational and medical grants. The remaining £8,666 went towards the salaries and expenses of the ruling class, the only substantial sums going to Yeta, the Mokwae of Nalolo, and the Ngambela. No less significant was the geographical distribution of these salaries. Indunas and royals living in Lealui received £1,800, while only £2,000 went to all the other eight Kutas and £1,629 to the more than sixty-five *silalo* indunas' courts scattered throughout the province. Many minor indunas emerged earning less in their official capacities than many migrant labourers. Thus a very large part of the province's monetary wealth was centralized in the capital, monopolized by the inner elite of the ruling class, the other districts contributing substantially more to the central Treasury than was spent in them.[41]

In general, it was the deliberate policy of the Northern Rhodesian government to support this particular structure of Lozi society. At the same time, as has been seen, there was an ambivalence in the official position: most administration officers wished to preserve the system largely on the basis of the *status quo*, yet arguing for a modification of some of its more flagrant excesses. The members of the Pim-Milligan Commission, for example, after their brief visit to Barotseland in 1937, declared the province to be in 'a condition of stagnation' due largely to the 'multiplicity' of sinecured office-holders. Yet they did not 'wish to see this fine example of native civilization come to an end'. How could the preservation of the system be reconciled with the need to modernize? The necessary alterations, the Commissioners concluded,

> can only be achieved by a slow and careful process within the framework of the Barotse system. Expenses can gradually be cut down as existing officials die and by the combination of indunas' courts. . . .
> At the same time, there is no doubt that Barotseland does stand in need of financial assistance from outside. There is much educational as well as health and veterinary work to be done and no resources at present in Barotseland to pay for it. . . . It is not possible to acquiesce in the continuance of the present stagnation. Efforts should be made and money provided by the Government to deal with the more urgent requirements of the province.[42]

The wheel, then, had come full circle. Lewanika's enthusiasm for the modernization and development of his country had been thwarted by the Company's determination to impose its control with the minimum expense. By the late 1930s, the British government's new concern for the material welfare and economic development of its colonial subjects collided with the Lozi rulers' sole interest in asserting their 'special status' by conspicuous consumption, since it was evident they would not be allowed to do so in terms of real political power.

Nevertheless, government officials convinced themselves that Yeta and the Ngambela at least—if not many other indunas—appreciated the need for reforming the Barotse government and for improving the economic lot of the masses.[43] Their conversion may well have been genuine; in any event, adequate incentives were offered to tempt both men to acquiesce in most government suggestions. Above all, once the ordinances were implemented, permission was granted by the government for Yeta and the Ngambela to visit England to attend the coronation of George VI, towards the cost of which the government contributed £300.[44] It seems reasonable to assume that the trip was to fulfil two very practical functions: it would be in the nature of a reward for accepting the Native Authorities and an inducement for carrying out the necessary administrative reforms once they returned.

The trip further exacerbated the hostility of the many indunas who had—unlike the King himself—been adversely affected by the new ordinances. But for Yeta it was the fulfilment of a dream he had cherished since his father's journey in 1902. He had, as we have seen, been refused permission to travel to England shortly after his accession, but had never thereafter, as a missionary put it, ceased 'wearing down the Mongu Magistrate with continued requests on the subject. . . .'[45] Now, for reasons already suggested, the old man was formally invited to the Coronation as a 'Distinguished Visitor'.

In May, 1938, Yeta, accompanied by the Ngambela, his official secretary Godwin Mbikusita, and an interpreter, reached England. Their schedule included, besides the Coronation itself, a private audience with the new King, a special service at the French Church in London, and, at the end, three days in Paris visiting the headquarters of the PMS.[46] But unlike his father, Yeta did not have a political meeting with the Colonial Secretary.

The trip seems to have been considered a great success on almost all sides—the King and Ngambela, the administration, the PMS, and the mass of Lozi who perhaps felt that the honour bestowed upon their ruler reflected upon the entire nation. The general satisfaction, however, was not quite universal and, as the PMS journal put it, was 'somewhat dampened' by the knowledge that a 'cabal' had apparently tried to overthrow Yeta in his absence.[47] Considerable mystery and internal contradictions characterize the abortive coup, though it certainly exposed the deep personal internal conflicts which had long riven the Lozi elite.

A *prima facie* case was not difficult to make against most of the alleged plotters. The chief among them was said to be Yeta's second son, the ambitious, well-educated Edward Kalue. Many white officials considered him an 'extremist' and blamed him as well for Yeta's many debts; under their strong pressure, he was replaced as the King's private secretary by Godwin Mbikusita.[48] In 1937, Kalue was apparently bitterly resentful that Mbikusita, and not he, was chosen to accompany Yeta to England.[49] It seems too there was a rivalry between father and son involving the affections of a local woman.[50]

Induna Nambayo of Lealui was related to Atangumbuyu, whom Yeta deposed in 1935 as Mokwae of Nalolo and replaced with his own daughter, Mareta Mulima; Nambayo was said to be seeking revenge on her behalf.[51] Godwin Mbikusita's grievance was even more obvious: Yeta refused to recognize his claim to be a son of Lewanika. Moreover, Mbikusita's driving ambition and his curious involvement in the urban politics of Northern Rhodesian Africans[52] lent credence to the belief that he was capable of colluding with Kalue in the hope of becoming the latter's Ngambela had their plot succeeded.[53] It is more difficult, however, to speculate as to the motives of the two remaining accused plotters—Chief Liatitima of Lukulu and Yeta's half-brother Mboo Lewanika.

After months of vacillation on the part of both the Boma and Yeta,[54] 'certain documents', unfortunately never specified, were discovered proving Kalue to have been the instigator of the plot. The Governor, who had to hand down the final judgment, accepted the Kuta's decision that Kalue be banished from Barotse Province. Presumably the documents also implicated the other accused, with the exception of Chief Liatitima, for the Governor upheld the Kuta's sentence against them. Mbikusita was not again to hold a post in the Barotse government, while Nambayo was dismissed from his indunaship and he and Mboo Lewanika were banished to their respective villages. Only the sentence against Liatitima was modified. He alone of the four accused (not including Kalue) had appealed to the Kuta against its original judgment against him, but to no avail.[55] The Governor, however, revoked the

Kuta's order deporting Liatitima, though he confirmed the sentence that he lose his chieftainship of the Lukulu Kuta and his salaries as chief and as member of the royal family.[56] Yet, so far as is known, no policy difference divided the alleged plotters from their putative victims. Kalue may have exploited the resentment against the apparent subservience of Yeta and the Ngambela to the government, but there is no evidence that anyone at any time demanded firmer resistance to the administration. Indeed, the Provincial Commissioner was intially asked to use his powers to depose the King,[57] Liatitima had appealed to the former against the decision of the Kuta,[58] and Mbikusita was hardly the man to lead an anti-white crusade. Nor is there evidence to suggest that Kalue and his 'cabal' were less conservative and more socially-conscious than the King and Ngambela. The entire incident, in fact, may be viewed as a case study vindicating the widespread Actonian cynicism among Lozi of the corrupting nature of power.[59]

For it is arguable that it was a measure of Yeta's greatness as King that he survived in power for over two decades before open opposition to his rule manifested itself. This was, to be sure, a measure as well of the security of his position under the protection of a white government. But it also suggests a real shrewdness in balancing the forces within the ruling class, in— if not satisfying—at least not wholly alienating either the old conservatives or the ambitious educated elite. He had persuaded them of the prudence of accepting a status for their country which, if hardly like the old days, was at least demonstrably better than that of most other tribes in Northern Rhodesia. By the late 1930s, however, the concensus seemed to be shattering. New interests and old resentments were leading to renewed doubts about the wisdom of Yeta's policy of prudence.

The troubles in Balovale District served once again to underline the hollowness of the sovereignty of the Lozi ruling class. Throughout the decades, Lozi officials in the area had been in conflict with the patriotic sensibilities of both the Lunda and Luvale peoples.[60] Finally, in 1938, the government believing that a physical conflict between the two groups was not impossible,[61] announced the appointment of a commission to investigate the entire question.[62]

This was a severe blow to the Lozi. Here was their ally, the British government, considering whether to excise from the Lozi two of their alleged vassal tribes over whom British control had originally been asserted by virtue of the Company's concessions with Lewanika. Whether this humiliation was sufficient to rupture the institutionalized relations between the Barotse government and the Crown government remained to be seen. Gluckman, after all, considered that 'the absence of conflict in White-Lozi relations was remarkable',[63] though it is true that he had previously worked in Zululand.

Moreover, the options to Crown government were distinctly unattractive. Like all other Northern Rhodesian Africans, the Lozi informed the Royal Commission of 1938–39 in unequivocal terms of their antipathy towards Southern Rhodesia's 'native policy' and their consequent opposition to any proposal of amalgamating the two Rhodesias. The Lozi case to the Commission was put by a series of individuals who reflected an accurate cross-section of the Province's political and social elite, including Yeta himself, a Kuta judge, a teacher, a chauffeur and a policeman. The overwhelming conservatism of these elitists was striking. They all stressed the impotence of chiefs south of the Zambesi, and all expressed their hopes that Barotseland would continue in its special status within Northern Rhodesia under the direct protection of the Crown.[64] The Commission showed considerable sympathy for the Lozi position. Its report recalled and reaffirmed the Crown's treaty obligations to the King, and recommended that 'due regard' should be had for his privileged position should amalgamation be agreed to.[65]

But though there were thus grounds for ruling class complacency, there were yet already perceptible by 1939 signs of serious potential conflict. Labour migration, for example, temporarily slowed down by the depression, had revived to an unhealthy extent,[66] and it was not long before many young men returned from the tough mining compounds of Johannesburgh flaunting their contempt for traditional authority, white and black alike. At the same time, class cleavages were perceptible within the Province. Although not yet dangerous. Gluckman noted tensions between, on the one hand, the unprivileged—the peasants, the powerless yet increasing group of

skilled men, clerks, and artisans, and the poor minor councillors
—and, on the other, a rich, insensitive and autocratic inner
group of the ruling elite. Moreover, the impotent petty
bourgeois began questioning the hitherto accepted economic
social and economic superiority of local whites.[67]

Finally, a clash between the Barotse government and the
Northern Rhodesian government was growing less unlikely.
It was not merely that the Crown was considering excising
Balovale District from Barotseland. For the Bledisloe Commissioners, like those of the Pim–Milligan Commission, while
generally sympathetic to the maintenance of the political
status quo in the Province, had been shocked by its economic
backwardness. 'We could not fail to note,' they reported, 'that
in many respects, notably in the provision for medical services
and education, the Barotse Province falls short even of the
comparatively low standard obtained in other parts of Northern Rhodesia.'[68] They therefore recommended that the colonial
government, while respecting the terms of the Concession of
1900, 'actively pursue' an agreement with Yeta to modify some
of its provisions 'so as to permit of more effective administration
and development in the interests of the Barotse people'.[69]

Before any such approach could be made, however, World
War II broke out, and the war effort took priority over reforms
in Barotseland. Moreover, early in 1939, Yeta was struck down
with paralysis which deprived him of his speech.[70] Although
he was not expected to survive long, in fact Yeta, like Charles II,
was 'an unconscionable time dying'. Gordon Read, the Provincial Commissioner, saw in the situation an opportunity to
extend the Boma's influence even more widely over the
Barotse government. Read had Ngambela Munalula appointed
as Acting Paramount Chief, and although he was to be advised
by an ad hoc body of three senior Lozi, Read was able to keep
their influence, as well as that of the Moyoo, Yeta's first wife,
to a minimum. Read worked hand in glove with the Ngambela,
and, as a result, the Barotse government was, according to Mr.
Berger of the PMS, more in the hands of the Boma at this time
than at any other period since Company rule was initiated.[71]

Unfortunately for Read, Munalula died in January, 1941.
From the names selected by the Kuta, the mute king indicated
his preference for Kalonga Wina.[72] Wina had been born in

1878, the son of a Lealui induna. He spent five years at the PMS school in Kazangula, where he became a Christian. In 1903 he joined the Kuta in Sesheke as its clerk and as interpreter to Yeta. Two years later he married one of Lewanika's daughters and was promoted to a higher rank in the Sesheke Kuta, where he remained until he was called to succeed his father as Induna Wina Lioma at the Lealui Kuta. In 1936, Wina was chosen to be Daniel Akafuna's chief councillor at the new Balovale Kuta, a position he held until the British government ordered the disbanding of the Kuta in 1941. Married into the royal family, a close personal friend of Yeta, generally considered to be a clever and natural leader, it was his involvement in the Balovale crisis which finally made him the obvious choice for the job. He was seen as a man who, unlike Munalula, would not be servile to the Boma, who would 'be able to restore the glory that Lewanika once gave Barotseland'.[73]

Gordon Read predictably resented Wina's appointment.[74] Through Induna Solami, Yeta signified his wish that Wina also succeeded Munalula as Acting Paramount,[75] a wish the Provincial Commissioner grudgingly approved.[76] Wina had no intention of respecting Gordon Read's suggestion that, like Munalula, he disdain the co-operation of the Moyoo. Though he maintained several senior indunas as his official advisers,[77] he in fact formed a kind of diumvirate with Yeta's wife and for the next four years successfully contrived to keep the King's own intervention in affairs of state to a minimum.[78]

Nevertheless, Wina shrewdly minimized his unpalatability to the Boma, first, by passively accepting the Crown's decision to excise the Balovale District from Barotseland,[79] and secondly, and most importantly, by co-operating in the only sphere that really mattered to the administration in these years, the war effort. What was expected from the Lozi was political stability and a certain assistance in facilitating the war effort through enlistment for service, providing farm labour, producing rubber and selling cattle. Led by Wina and members of the royal family, the Lozi fulfilled these expectations to the satisfaction of the territorial government.[80]

Yet there were distinct gradations in the enthusiasm shown for the British side. The most active loyalists were from the ruling elite. The mass of Lozi probably had only a dim grasp of a war being waged many thousands of miles away.[81] But among three other sections of the Lozi community, the war was giving rise, as with most other African peoples, to a new self-consciousness, with results not yet easy to foresee.

The new spirit was articulated most clearly by the Lozi lower-middle class, the small elite of educated men who, though materially privileged because of their white-collar jobs, yet were politically dispossessed. Because many members of the Lozi ruling elite, unlike their counterparts in the rest of Northern Rhodesia, were educated and literate, the Kutas were to a considerably extent able to cope with their tasks and meet the demands of white officials without the assistance of educated clerks. Although there were exceptions to the rule, the Barotse government remained largely in the hands of the traditional aristocracy.[82]

Unlike the educated elite of the 1920s, the majority of this second group of 'new men' were not the sons of royals and indunas. Unlike the former as well, the new group was concerned with the wider questions of race and nationality as opposed to narrower issues concerning Barotseland alone. In their isolation, the handful of educated Africans working in Mongu had already banded together in 1939 to form the Mongu–Lealui African Welfare Association, modelled on the many similar associations which proliferated throughout Northern Rhodesia and Nyasaland during the decade. The 'Aims and Objects' of this eminently moderate body were

(1) To promote co-operation and brotherly feeling between Africans in Northern Rhodesia;
(2) To encourage the spread of civilization by education, industrial and agricultural development;
(3) To protect and further African interests generally.[84]

The aspirations of its members were clearly reflected in one of its first meetings, held a year after the Boma agreed to recognize the Association in 1943.[84] Significantly, it took place in the office of the DC, Mongu. Consistent with its isolationist policy, the Barotse government had refused to set up in Barotseland one of the Provincial Councils which the central government was instituting in the other provinces for the purpose (*inter alia*) of nominating African representatives to the legislative Council. The Association's members strongly urged the formation of such a council in Barotseland for, they explained,

> The masses of the educated class in this province is not playing its part within the scope of African advancement. We quite realize the powerful authority of the Barotse Native Government, but this Association feels it most essential that free people with sound education in this Province should also be encouraged to hobnob with their fellow africans [sic] in other provinces in the enhancement of the african [sic] interests.[85]

There is no evidence that the Lozi rulers heeded the suggestions of the Association, but neither is there doubt that the latter's members spoke for many of the Province's emerging middle class. A schoolteacher in rural Senanga, for example, recalls that he and a small number of his friends heard about and were highly influenced by such wartime phenomena as the Atlantic Charter, the Four Freedoms, and the struggle to liberate small nations.[86]

Missionaries too discovered during these years for the first time the depth of Lozi mistrust and even hatred for Europeans. Mlle. Marie Borle, teaching teenage girls, remembers her pupils pointing out that whites claimed to be bringing peace and civilization to Africa, yet were at that moment destroying each other and much of the world as well. Were the whites, they asked, then to destroy the black people as well? When a Lozi soldier appeared claiming that he had been killing Europeans, the girls were openly 'ecstatic'. It was, Mlle. Borle noted, wholly remarkable that Lozi girls had the temerity to express such sentiments in front of a white teacher.[87]

Returning soldiers, then, were a second element in the growth of African self-confidence, in Barotseland as in the rest of the continent. During the war, as the mission journal put it, they had received 'an education of a different kind! and their eyes have been opened to many things hitherto unknown to them'.[88] 'They have seen new ways of life and have acquired new ideas, and with them, new desires. . . .'[89]

Returning labourers were similarly affected. For the first time since Lozi labour migration had commenced on a serious scale, migrants were returning home flaunting their contempt for authority by refusing to demonstrate their respect for and servility to local Europeans through bowing and clapping.[90] Many government officials considered these men to be 'hooligans . . . filled with ideas of their own importance'.[91] This short-sighted and superior attitude was shared by the Lozi rulers, whose response to it was simply to increase the number of indunas' visits to schools, reminding the pupils that continued respect for whites must be shown since the Lozi were universally known for their good manners which were a sign of being civilized.[92]

In any event, such problems seemed peripheral to the central political issue of the time. For Yeta had neither recovered nor died; he remained paralysed and speechless. From Wina's accession to early 1945, it was he, as Acting Paramount Chief, who held ultimate responsibility in Lealui. In theory, all decisions came from him after consultation with the King; in fact, during these years, it was the Moyoo who interpreted, and insisted that she alone was capable of interpreting, her husband's wishes as signalled by his hand motions. According to both Boma and PMS sources, the Moyoo had acquired 'an absolutely decisive influence over affairs of state which has led to suspicion and resentment alike in the Kuta and outside it'.[93]

The alternatives to this obviously unsatisfactory situation were clear: a revamped structure for carrying on with Yeta incapacitated, or the latter's resignation and the appointment of a new King. Either solution implied considerably jockeying for positions of influence, and for months the capital was wracked, in the words of J. P. Burger of the PMS, with 'intrigues . . . animosities and jealousies. . . .'[94] Finally, in June, 1945, Glennie, the Provincial Commissioner, decided that decisive action was imperative to end the crisis. Yeta was to resign immediately and a successor was to be appointed.[95] The sick old man sadly agreed to abdicate, indicating his wish that his half-brother Imwiko succeed him.[96]

Perhaps the King received a certain consolation from the many expressions of tribute which he received from those senior government officials whom he had always respected: the Secretary of State, the Governor, the Secretary for Native Affairs.[97] Nor can it be doubted that the sorrow of his people was genuine and widespread. They respected him as their King, but they also loved him as a man.[98] Perhaps indeed he abdicated just in time. The end of the war was a watershed in all the colonies in Africa; a new era was beginning. Yeta, child of an earlier generation, was hardly the man to lead his people happily into it. Essentially his mentality was closer to his father's and to that of the missionaries and even colonial officers whom he had known and with whom he had worked. For all his struggles against European rule during the first half of his reign, he had continued to respect white men as such, to think in terms of 'natives' and the Empire. He had become, in short, an anachronism. Social reform and political equality —the keynotes of the post-war colonial world—were beyond his comprehension. The question remained, however, whether his successor could make the transition more smoothly.

## REFERENCES

1. Mr. E. Berger of the PMS.

2. J. Gordon Read, 'Mbangweta Munalula: Ngambela of Barotseland', 18 Jan., 1941, typescript, in RLI Collection, Barotseland Historical Manuscripts; letter from Coisson in *News from B. and B.*, No. 11, Dec., 1930, p. 16.

3. Yeta to Rennie, 17 Nov., 1930, NAZ ZA 1/15/H/1/5.

4. Rennie to Chief Secretary, 21 March, 1931, *ibid.*

5. Chief Secretary to Rennie, 21 April, 1931, *ibid.*

6. Messrs. Berger, Wina and Zaza. The Lozi were, however, throughout the decade, involved in a protracted dispute with the Company, which wanted Yeta's agreement of 1927 with Minerals Separation Limited abrogated. A compromise settlement, unsatisfactory to all parties, was reached only in 1938. See Maxwell Stamp Associates. *History of the Mineral Rights of Northern Rhodesia*, Vol. 1, pp. 78–91, Vol. 2, pp. 343–430.

7. Of some 17,000 African employees on the Copperbelt, only 870 were from Barotseland in 1937. A. Pim and S. Milligan, *Report of the Commission Appointed to Enquire into the Financial and Economic Position of Northern Rhodesia* (hereafter *Pim–Milligan Report*), Colonial No. 145, App. VI, p. 362.

8. A. L. Epstein, *Politics in an Urban African Community* (Manchester, 1958), p. 236; Hall, *Zambia*, p. 115.

9. Epstein, *op. cit.*, p. 40 *et seq.*

10. Hall to all officials, etc., 5 Aug., 1927, NAZ KDE 2/5/1.

11. Hall to Board of Management, Barotse Trust Fund, 28 Jan., 1928, *ibid.*

12. Tour Report of Director of Native Education, 2 Sept.–16 Oct., 1926, *ibid.*

13. Jalla to Hall, 28 Dec., 1927, NAZ ZA 1/9/47/33/2.

14. Hall to Board of Management, 28 Jan., 1928, NAZ KDE 2/5/1.

15. Annual Report, Barotse Province, 1930, NAZ ZA 7/1/13/3.

16. Report on Nalolo Sub-District by Hudson, 1927, NAZ KDE 2/5/1.

17. Report by Commissioner of Police on Lozi Migrants, ? Nov., 1928, NAZ KDE 2/30/4; Hall to SNA, 6 Nov., 1928, *ibid.*

18. J. P. Burger to Director, 19 June, 1935, PMSS; Lane-Poole, 'Report on Barotse Province', in *Northern Rhodesia Native Affairs Annual Report, 1935* (Luska, 1936), p. 83 (hereafter NRNAAR); *News from B. and B.*, March, 1934, p. 7, and Jan., 1935, p. 5; Trapnell and Clothier, *Soils . . . of North-Western Rhodesia*, para. 208; Gluckman, *Economy*, pp. 112–19.

19. Annual Report, Lealui District, 1933, NAZ ZA 7/1/16/3.

20. Lane-Poole, 'Report on Barotse Province', NRNAAR, 1936. p. 85.

21. Annual Report, Barotse Provinces, 1933, NAZ ZA 7/1/15/2; DC Lealui, to Lane-Poole, 4 Oct., 1934, NAZ ZA 1/9/62/1/6; Reports on Watchtower Meetings, 1932–7, *ibid*; Lane Poole, 'Report, 1936', *op. cit.*, pp. 83–4.

22. Gluckman, *Economy*, p. 111.

23. Report for Lealui District, 1933, NAZ ZA 7/1/16/3.

24. Mr. Simalumba.

25. P. J. Law to his father, 20 Aug., 1932, Rhodes House. P. J. Law, Personal Letters from Northern Rhodesia, 1932–36, Mss Afr. s. 393, folio 2; also Reports from Provincial Commissioner and District Commissioners, 1931–4, NAZ ZA 7/1/14/2–5.

26. W. M. Logan, 'Native Administration in Northern Rhodesia', *Race Relations* (Johannesburg), Vol. VI, No. 2, 1932, p. 52.

27. J. M. Thomson, NRNAAR, 1930, p. 8.

28. Minute by Governor Storrs, 29 Sept. 1934, NAZ ZA 1/15/H/1/1; Thomson, NRNAAR, 1931, p. 9.

29. For a comprehensive analysis of the Lozi legal and judicial system, see Gluckman, *The Judicial Process among the Barotse of Northern Rhodesia* (Manchester, 1955), and *The Ideas in Barotse Jurisprudence* (New Haven, Conn., 1965).

30. *Balovale Commission Report*, 1939, pp. 182–7; see fn. 6, above.

31. Former Ngambela Wina.

32. Northern Rhodesian Legislative Council Debates, No. 27, 27 Oct., 1936, pp. 94–5.

33. *Ibid.*, p. 122.

34. *Barotse Native Government Orders and Rules* (English version, Lusaka, 1957 edition).

35. J. Gordon-Read, 'Report on Barotse Province', NRNAAR, 1937, pp. 92–3.

36. A. F. B. Glennie, 'Report on Barotse Province', *Colonial Annual Reports*, 1946, copy in Mongu Boma Files.

37. Debates, 27 Oct., 1936, p. 96.

38. Former Ngambela Wina and Mr. Mupatu.

39. J. Gordon Read, 'Barotse Province', NRNAAR, 1937, p. 93.

40. Audrey Richards, 'The Political System of the Bemba Tribe, North-Eastern Rhodesia', in Fortes and Evans-Pritchard, *African Political Systems*, p. 116; *Pim–Milligan Report*, 1938, p. 195.

41. *Pim–Milligan Report*, 1938, pp. 193–5; Gluckman, *Economy*, p. 100.

42. *Pim–Milligan Report*, pp. 195–7.

43. *Ibid.*, p. 196; foreword by Logan, Chief Secretary to NRNAAR, 1938, pp. 1–2.

44. *Balovale Commission Report*, p. 187.

45. Burger to Director, 1 July, 1936, PMSS.

46. *News from B. and B.*, Jan., 1938, pp. 8–12 and 17–18.

47. *Ibid.*, Jan., 1949, p. 14.

48. Burger to Director, 3 Nov., 1937, PMSS.

49. *Ibid.*, and Mr. E. Berger, who was then at the PMS's Lealui station.

50. Chief Liatitima and Mr. Berger.

51. Messrs. Simalumba and Mupatu, and Burger to Director, 13 Oct., 1937, PMSS. I interviewed the former Induna Mambayo, now Muimui Anakandi, but he refused to discuss this incident in any way.

52. See Hall, *Zambia*, p. 118, and Rotberg, *Nationalism*, p. 132.

53. According to Mr. Berger.

54. Burger to Director, 3 Nov., 1937, 24 Nov., 1937, 17 March, 1938, PMSS.

55. Chief Liatitima, who later became a strong supporter of UNIP.

56. Burger to Director, 17 March, 1938, PMSS.

57. *Ibid.*

58. Chief Liatitima.

59. Virtually all my informants explained that men in power were always threatened by others jealous of that power. Gluckman records the same sentiments in almost all his works on the Lozi.

60. *Balovale Commission Report*, 1939, pp. 107 and 129–33, and Mr. Wina, who was appointed chief councillor to Akafuna at Nawinda.

61. *Report*, pp. 179 and 185.

62. *Report of the Commission Appointed to Examine and Report Upon the Whole Question of the Past and Present Relations of the Paramount Chief of the Barotse Nation and the Chiefs Resident in the Balovale District both East and West of the Zambesi River with Special Reference to the Ownership of Land and the Method by which the Tribes Have Been Governed and to make Recommendations for the Future*, Sir Philip J. MacDonnell, Commissioner (Luska, 1939). This report remained 'strictly confidential', and the Lozi did not learn until 1941 that Balovale District was to be excised from Barotse Province.

63. Gluckman, *Economy*, 1941, p. 119.

64. *Report of the Rhodesia and Nyasaland Royal Commission* (Bledisloe Commission), Cmd. 5949, 1939, pp. 168–9, 175–6, 218, 235–6.

65. *Ibid.*, pp. 235–6.

66. Ibid., pp. 184–7; R. Philpott, 'Mongu-Mulobezi Labour Route', *Rhodes–Livingstone Journal*, No. 3, June 1945, pp. 50–4; Gluckman, 'Barotse-land: Where Western Civilization Has Brought Poverty', *Libertas*, July, 1945 (typescript copy at RLI).

67. Gluckman, *Economy*, pp. 120–1.

68. *Bledisloe Commission Report*, p. 235.

69. *Ibid.*, p. 167.

70. *News from B. and B.*, No. 7, March, 1940, p. 4.

71. Mr. Berger; also Messrs. Wina, Mupatu and Simalumba, and Gordon Read, 'Mbangweta Munalula', *op. cit.*

72. According to Wina himself.

73. Messrs. Zaza, Simalumba and Berger. The quotation is Mr. Berger's.

74. Read to Yeta, 16 April, 1941, Wina Dossier, Boma Files.

75. Solami to Read, 16 April, 1941, *ibid.*

76. Read to Yeta, 19 April, *1941, ibid.*

77. Mr. Wina.

78. Mr. Berger.

79. See Northern Rhodesia Government Gazette, Vol. xxxi, No. 38, 9 July, 1941, General Notice No. 398.

80. A. F. B. Glennie, 'Report on Barotse Province', *Colonial Annual Reports,* 1946, copy in Boma Files.

81. Glennie, 'Report', 1946, *op. cit.*

82. Gluckman, *Seven Tribes,* pp. 57–8.

83. Mongu–Lealui African Welfare Association Draft Rules, Boma Files, Provincial Administration, 1939–53.

84. DC, Mongu to PC, 23 Dec., 1943.

85. Minutes of a Committee Meeting of the Association, 21 Dec., 1944, *ibid.*

86. Mr. Simalumba.

87. Mlle. Borle.

88. *News from B. and B.,* No. 14, May 1947, p. 3.

89. *Ibid.,* No. 13, March, 1946, p. 2.

90. Messrs. Simalumba and Berger and Mlle. Borle.

91. See, for e.g., Philpott, 'Mulobezi–Mongu Labour Route', *op. cit.,* p. 53.

92. Mr. Berger witnessed such occasions in his schools.

93. Glennie to Chief Secretary, 20 June, 1945, Boma Files, Retirement of Paramount Chief Yeta Dossier; also Mr. Berger.

94. Burger to Director, 18 July, 1945, PMSS.

95. Glennie to Chief Secretary, 20 June, 1945, *ibid.*

96. Seguin to Glennie, 19 June, 1945, *ibid.*

97. Secretary of State to Yeta, undated, Boma Files, *op. cit;* Governor's Message to Yeta, undated, *ibid; Mutende,* July, 1945.

98. Mr. Berger.

# CHAPTER VII

# THE CONSOLIDATION OF TRIBALISM

The Acting Provincial Commissioner, Glennie, moved rapidly to have the National Council confirm Imwiko as Yeta's successor.[1] Imwiko Lewanika was then sixty years old. He was the son who Lewanika had sent to school in England early in the century, where he completed Standard VII. In 1916, he had been the choice of certain indunas to succeed his father, one of the reasons perhaps that Yeta appointed him to be chief of Sesheke, where he remained until 1945. There he is said to have developed an impressive reputation for his cordial relations not only with his indunas but with the educated men and common people as well. If opposition to his becoming King was minimal, however, probably part at least of the reason was the expectation that, given his age, his reign would be relatively brief.[2]

Whatever Imwiko's aspiration as King may have been, the framework within which he was to operate during his reign was firmly imposed upon him by the central government. This was made unmistakeably clear by Glennie, now the Provincial Commissioner. Plans mooted prior to the outbreak of the war and postponed both because of it and Yeta's illness, he announced, were now to be implemented. Above all, the Barotse government was to be reformed so that all its members 'will have a definite job of valuable work to do', and a programme of economic development, financed by the British government's 'big gift of money to the Empire', was to be commenced.[3]

In retrospect, it is clear that the new administrative reforms proved too little too late, and were largely irrelevant in terms of the real political demands of the post-war era, while the development scheme created expectations which it never had the resources—financial or human—to fulfil. Glennie, however, forced the Kuta to accept changes in both areas, thus incurring widespread hostility towards himself and to the new King.[4] Although he began his term believing that the Lozi, unlike other tribes in the colony, 'must be convinced' before reforms were imposed upon them,[5] he soon decided that changes must be wrought 'in the face of a jealous conservative opposition which seeks to cling to every crag and cranny of advantage and to yield no iota of privilege without a struggle'.[6]

Perhaps because their own interests were not directly affected, perhaps realizing that opposition was futile, Imwiko and his coterie of advisers agreed to Glennie's proposed reforms, though with little enthusiasm.[7] But among many of the political elite, the reaction was predictably hostile. For a large number of indunaships were abolished, and with them the titles, salaries, and privileges possessed by their holders.[8] Moreover, the Kuta was seriously offended by Glennie's insistence that representatives of two outside groups be appointed to the National Council: those of the younger educated men not belonging to the ruling class, and those of the many small, non-Lozi tribes in the province.[9]

In 1947, Glennie 'pushed upon' Imwiko the revival of the Katengo council[10] which had been dormant for more than half a century. It was to be resurrected as an advisory body which would forward recommendations to the National Council. Initially its members were to be appointed by the five district Kutas in consultation with the DCs and with the approval of the Provincial Commissioner, but one of the five appointees from each district was to retire annually and be replaced by a member elected by universal adult male suffrage.

The new council, duly implemented, was a failure from the first. Most indunas resented its very existence, their hostility increasing as the promised elections resulted in a number of ambitious teachers and clerks joining the Katengo.[11] The Kuta largely ignored the Katengo's recommendations,[12] while the Provincial Commissioner forbade it to discuss important political matters or express anti-white sentiments.[13] In short, the government's administrative and political reforms left the politically dispossessed white-collar group wholly unsatisfied, heightened the conflict between the latter and the traditional elite, and increased the resentment of both groups against the white administration.

In its attempts to raise the level of Lozi technology and the living standards of the mass of the population, it was only barely more successful. The economic position of the Province was no less depressed after the war than before it. Peasant farmers were producing barely enough crops for their own subsistence. Employment opportunities for both the skilled and unskilled remained minimal. The extent of labour migration was such that many villages were left literally with only women, children and old men.[14] 'There is no remedy to this evil', Glennie acknowledged, 'except an extensive programme of economic and social development which will provide within the Province higher wages, better conditions, and a wider variety of occupations.'[15]

To that end, using Colonial Development and Welfare Funds, the central government decided in 1947 to establish a Development Centre in Barotseland south of Sefula at Namushakende. Lewanika's modernizing schemes seemed at last about to be realized, but Imwiko and Wina met strong resistance to the entire venture from many indunas.[16] While they were prepared to lease to the government a large tract of land for the purpose, the Kutas of Lealui and Nalolo both believed the scheme was merely 'another white man's trick' to 'steal Lozi land' and distribute it to white settlers, and to do so with the connivance of their own leaders.[17] Fearing, therefore, a 'sell-out' by the white government, perhaps in collaboration with the King and Ngambela, the Kutas refused to lease the required land, and Imwiko and Wina signed the formal document on their own initiative.[18]

As a result deep rifts appeared at the capital between the Kuta and the King, two informants estimating that 'at least three-quarters' of his indunas were hostile to Imwiko.[19] When, therefore, he took ill and suddenly died in June, 1948, an atmosphere already existed in which rumours of foul play found ready acceptance. Perhaps the true story will never be known. For, though the official medical reports stated that Imwiko had died of a stroke,[20] many—probably a majority—of Lozi believed at the time and continue to believe that his brother Mwanawina, desperate to become King, was responsible for having Imwiko poisoned.[21]

The King's death created a serious power vacuum in the

Barotse government. That events in Africa were picking up momentum was reflected not only in the distant Gold Coast but in Northern Rhodesia itself, where the first African National Congress was formed in the year of Imwiko's death.[22] To the Northern Rhodesian government, therefore, his loss was a serious blow. For he had been considered a 'gentle, dignified African ruler of the type that is in danger of disappearing in the colonies today,'[23] which meant that he embodied traditional values while acquiescing in the strictly limited reforms which the government asked of him.

It was not clear that his likely successor would prove as 'reasonable'. Fox-Pitt, the Acting PC, considered Mwanawina to be not only obstinate and inflexible but—very mistakenly—unintelligent as well. Fox-Pitt first suggested that Yeta's daughter, the Mokwae of Nalolo, be appointed to the kingship, but was warned that a female ruler would never be tolerated.[24] He then settled upon Masheki Akashambatwa, son of Akashambatwa Lewanika, whom he considered less conservative than Mwanawina.[25] (Fox-Pitt stood out among government officials for his liberalism; he later joined the ANC). As the election conclusively proved, however, on certain matters of significance the Lozi ruling class possessed real power. Mwanawina defeated Masheki by 76 votes to 4, and was installed as Paramount Chief of Barotseland.[26]

Mwanawina was Lewanika's fourth son, born around 1888. He received his early education at PMS schools in Barotseland before his father sent him in 1908 to Lovedale College in South Africa for five years. He returned to become secretary and interpreter to Lewanika, soon gaining a reputation as a loyal supporter of the Empire; as we have seen, he was the only one of the King's sons to volunteer in 1916 to lead Lozi porters across Northern Rhodesia to the East African frontier. He remained one of Yeta's senior advisers until 1937, when he was appointed to be the first chief of the newly-created Mankoya Kuta, where he successfully resisted Nkoya demands for greater freedom from Lozi overrule. Again during World War II he won the gratitude of the government by encouraging rubber production and collecting cash contributions in his District for the war effort. In 1946, these services were formally recognized by the award of the King's Silver Medal for Chiefs.[27]

It was precisely because he had shown himself to be a firm Lozi patriot, as in the Mankoya controversy, and yet was warmly regarded by the British government, that the vast majority of the ruling class chose Mwanawina. For they now expected him to appeal to the metropolitan government against the importunities and demands of local officials to continue the reforms initiated under Imwiko. 'It is said,' noted J. P. Burger, 'that despite his gentleness, he knows what he wants. . . .'[28]

What he wanted was to make substantial changes both in policies and in personnel. He began with the latter, setting in motion the machinery to enable him to dismiss Wina as Ngambela and Francis Suu as Administrative Secretary of the Native Authority. Mwanawina and Wina had first clashed when the latter had supported Mwene Mutondo of the Nkoya in his dispute with the former.[29] Moreover, the King was convinced that Wina and Suu had voted for Masheki against himself.[30] Finally, he was anxious, as we shall see, to appoint as Ngambela his son-in-law, Akabeswa Imasiku.

It was easy enough, in the charged atmosphere of the time, for Mwanawina to show less self-interested reasons for dismissing the two men. Wina was said to have exploited Yeta's illness to increase his own powers, and was denounced for not following him into retirement. He was charged both with poisoning Imwiko and for failing to take proper care of him as he lay dying, as well as with accepting the white man's claim that Imwiko had died of a stroke.[31] He was condemned for accepting Glennie's reforms of the Barotse government, since these were considered to be attacks on the 'house of kingship' itself.[32] Wina and Suu were similarly accused of trying to undermine the prerogatives of the National Council in their own interests by seeking the Boma's support for the election of Akashambatwa.[33]

Mwanawina spent a month co-ordinating and consolidating the opposition to the Ngambela,[34] then informed Glennie that, since 'a multitude of many people of this country' and the Barotse National Council 'agree . . . in having no confidence in . . . the two men, that they should no longer continue in service of Barotse Native Government'.[35]

Having achieved his first objective, Mwanawina now attempted to appoint as Ngambela Akabeswa Imasiku, his son-in-law and chief councillor at the Mankoya Kuta. Glennie, however, favoured Muheli Walubita, and 'advised' Mwanawina that if he chose Imasiku over 'the older and more experienced Walubita, strong public opposition would be aroused, and he would be accused of favouritism'.[36] Walubita, the fifty-one year old chief councillor of the Sesheke Kuta, really belonged, like Mwanawina himself, to an earlier era. He was therefore a man to whom the Paramount Chief could reconcile himself, and by accepting Walubita as Ngambela, he could avoid a showdown with Glennie.[37]

This problem concluded, J. P. Burger of the PMS wrote hopefully, 'the long period of instability' was over.[38] Such optimism, however, was highly misplaced. In general, as we can now see, Barotseland could not achieve genuine stability until its several factions came to terms with the post-war world, a process which proved arduous indeed. Moreover, in the years following Mwanawina's accession, the currents disrupting Lozi life were many and complex. As Glennie recognized, the extraordinary events of 1948 had stimulated political consciousness to an extent 'hitherto unknown outside an exclusive circle'.[39] Factions within the royal family challenged the King; the educated elite challenged the political elite; the latter challenged the Boma, and all Lozi challenged the central government on the question of amalgamating the two Rhodesias. Since most of these conflicts occurred simultaneously, the Lozi participants often found themselves united and divided at one and the same time, all factions, for example, coming together against amalgamation, then splitting off again on more parochial political issues.

The question of amalgamating Northern and Southern Rhodesia produced most cohesion among Lozi of all classes and factions. In 1938, the Bledisloe Commission had discovered in no uncertain terms the unanimity of Lozi hostility to any connection with a Southern Rhodesia dominated by white settlers.[40] That attitude had now not only hardened, but had been channelled into a demand for a positive alternative: if amalgamation took place, the Lozi would demand to secede from Northern Rhodesia and be made a full protectorate along the lines of the High Commission Territories south of the Limpopo.

As the demands for amalgamation by white unofficial members of the Legislative Council increased after the war, so did Lozi opposition to the proposal intensify. In June, 1948, the National Council met in Limulunga for the specific purpose, as Ngambela Wina told the assembly, of submitting their views on 'one important matter', the demand for a Barotseland Protectorate. One after another, chiefs and indunas rose to warn against the consequences of amalgamation and to demand a genuinely self-governing protectorate 'such as Lewanika always wanted'.[41] This position, moreover, was supported by the Mongu African Welfare Association, whose members denounced the evils of white rule in Southern Rhodesia, vowed to resist the imposition of amalgamation at all costs, and demanded full protectorate status for Barotseland.[42]

The accession of Mwanawina in no way altered Lozi opinion on the subject. The new King quickly made it clear that being loyal to the Crown and Empire was a very different matter indeed from accepting the whims of the white community in Northern Rhodesia. As a result, Gilbert Rennie, the Governor, flew to Lealui to reassure the King and Kuta that no change in the territorial constitution would be made 'without prior consultation and agreement with the Paramount Chief and his Council'.[43] Rennie's visit was followed in 1949 by that of Arthur Creech-Jones, Labour's Secretary of State for the Colonies, who repeated all of the Governor's assurances.[44]

It was presumably in the light of these firm reassurances that the demands of the Lozi rulers were modified. Rather than a separate protectorate, detached from Northern Rhodesia, they now began talking in terms of being recognized as the 'Barotseland Protectorate' within the protectorate of Northern Rhodesia, with all their rights under the various agreements of the past reaffirmed in writing by the British government.[45]

This may be seen as a shrewd tactical move by the Lozi ruling class. For what it meant was that it was prepared to compromise on its most extreme demand, secession, in return for a restoration of its lost glories of the past. Within months of his accession, Mwanawina caused to be drawn up a petition setting out all the grievances of which his father and Yeta had so frequently complained, save only that it excluded their 'progressive' demands for modernizing and developing the country. The petition was concerned solely with the restoration of the powers and privileges of the traditional elite.

Although emphasizing that the Paramount Chief and his people 'remained unswervingly loyal, as always, to the Crown', the petition declared that many rights of the King and Kuta had been forcibly wrested from them. Why should the jurisdiction of the Kutas be limited to minor offences instead of to 'all cases between natives'? Why need the Governor approve all appointments to and dismissals from the several Native Authorities? Why should expenditures of the Native Treasury be subject to 'the directions and approval' of the Governor? Finally, the petition drew attention to the profound dissatisfaction of the Lozi that, under the supposed protection of the Crown, their country had shrunk to a mere rump, with losses on their western frontier in 1905, of the Caprivi Strip in 1909, and of Balovale in 1941.[46] When Labour's new Colonial Secretary, James Griffiths, visited Lealui in 1951 to discuss the Federation issue, the Lozi rulers cleverly indicated that they could not give the matter their full attention until questions of their status and rights had been definitively settled.[47]

Mwanawina's initiative in reopening the grievances of an earlier generation succeeded in uniting the Lozi ruling class against the white government. Unlike Lewanika at several stages in his reign, Yeta during the 1930s, and Imwiko in his short time, Mwanawina seemed to be fighting for the rights of the entire ruling class, rather than for those of its inner elite at the expense of its less influential members. Neverthelesss, once the common enemy, the white government, was no longer the paramount problem, the community divided into a number of mutually hostile factions. Above all, two groups were dissatisfied with their status within Barotseland: the members of the Mongu Welfare Association, and various members of the royal family who were vying for the succession.

The election of Mwanawina had unfortunate implications for two groups within the royal family. In the first place, being the third successive son of Lewanika to become King, princes by other lines had effectively begun to lose the chance of gaining the throne.[48] Secondly, the hopes of the children of Yeta and Imwiko, once so high, were frustrated by their uncle's accession, since his own sons were receiving the positions and favours they once foresaw for themselves. This frustration was equally felt by the many children of Lewanika's many other sons. Yet among neither group was all hope abandoned, since the succession could theoretically revert to any of them upon the death of Mwanawina, who was after all over sixty years old. In consequence, intriguing and scheming became the order of the day, a number of indunas attached to the various princes apparently playing a leading role.[49]

This is the general explanation of the serious internecine political conflict which convulsed Lealui during most of 1949 and 1950. It is, however, difficult to suggest exactly which factions or individuals were involved. The major incidents were three cases of arson during 1949 directed against the property of Ngambela Walubita and one of Mwanawina's daughters. With the full co-operation of the Boma, the Barotse government imposed a curfew on Lealui and the Paramount dismissed several indunas. However, Glennie reported, 'no sooner has one purge been accomplished than signs of disaffection appear in a different quarter'. He agreed that those responsible were 'cliques of indunas and others connected with the ruling families', adding obscurely that 'Such forces are altogether reactionary and have, in effect, adopted a "back to Lewanika" slogan. . . .'[50]

I know of no other evidence which alludes to, let alone clarifies, this matter.[51] One may perhaps speculate that as part of their strategy to win support for their claims to the throne, certain princes, assisted by a number of indunas, adopted the classical political ploy of accusing their enemies of being inadequately patriotic. Conceivably, their pressure may have pushed Mwanawina into demanding more forcefully the restoration of the traditional rights and powers of the ruling class, in competition with the 'cliques' mentioned by Glennie.

By 1950, however, with only one case of suspected arson in Lealui, large purges of indunas ceased. Nevertheless, the Paramount Chief and his coterie remained extremely insecure, and general unrest continued to characterize the atmosphere at the capital.[52]

A more organized opposition to the Barotse native government, though of a distinctly muted kind, came from the self-styled 'African intelligentsia' of the Mongu African Welfare

Association. Its hundred-odd members were English speaking clerks in the Boma, white stores, recruiting agencies, and even BNG, school teachers and medical orderlies, as well as a number of prince consorts who worked for their livelihood. Many had been to schools in Basutoland and South Africa, others had worked on the line of rail, and some had been as far afield as Uganda. The large majority of them were Lozi, but an important minority had migrated from Nyasaland.[53] Indeed, the Association was marked by internal rivalries between these Nyasa and the Lozi,[54] not surprising in view of the fact that it had been transformed from the moderate proto-nationalist elitist organization which it had been in the early 1940s into a conservative and tribalist pressure group, sharing the political elite's resentment of the diminution of Lozi sovereignty under white 'protection'.[55]

In fact, the only real criticism by the Association of the BNG was that it ignored the members of the Association. Most of the latter shared the conviction that their higher education gave them the same natural right—indeed the duty—to be involved in the decision-making process as tradition gave to chiefs and indunas. Their basic complaint, as the Association's Lozi president, Daniel Mukoboto, a Boma clerk, put it, was that 'the young educated Malozi were neglected by the Barotse Native Authority in not obtaining their views on matters affecting the Barotse Nation as a whole'.[56]

The sole *raison d'être* of the Association, then, had become to promote the immediate and specific class interests of its members within Barotseland. Its basic assumptions were almost entirely identical with those of the ruling elite; it wanted little more than to share its power. This explains the Association's support for Mwanawina's petition. It was, in consequence, a relatively easy faction to undermine. In the next few years, in what appears to have been a deliberate policy decision, Mwanawina began inviting senior members of the Association to fill clerical posts in the BNG,[57] and it is striking how many members of the Welfare Association in the 1940s were employees of the BNG by the 1950s.[58]

Like the Boma, however, Lealui could obviously absorb only a limited number of the alientated 'intelligentsia'. A large number of the latter continued, therefore, to leave Barotseland in search of better employment or higher education in the urban areas along the line of rail. Indeed, through most of the 1950s, Lozi remained the largest single tribal group at Munali in Lusaka,[59] the most important secondary school in Northern Rhodesia and, like Achimota College in the Gold Coast and Fort Hare in South Africa, a breeding ground for future African political leaders.

Among those educated young men who were not absorbed into the ruling class and who chose not to migrate, alienation and resentment increased. One District Officer told a touring official in 1953 that many people, white and black alike, doubted whether any development was possible in the province 'without changing fundamentally the Barotse Native Government. You would be surprised if you knew what a great undercurrent of discontent with the BNG there is among the so-called intelligentsia. . . . But they are afraid to speak.'[60]

Indeed, aside from absorbing a number of outspoken clerks, Mwanawina seemed determined to antagonize all but a tiny minority of his subjects. By 1951, he seems to have succeeded in purging the Kuta of those elements remaining loyal to other branches of the royal family, and in their place installed his own close relatives. Always nepotistic and highly centralized, the BNG became even more so under his rule. All important decision-making, and even many minor ones, became concentrated in the hands of Mwanawina and his principal advisers.[61]

The new Katengo Council, the great symbol of the government's determination moderately to democratize the BNG, was almost completely ignored by the ruling elite.[62] Nor did the latter co-operate with the white officials in charge of the Namushakende Development Scheme.[63] The general consequences of these authoritarian and obstructionist practices was to leave the Province, both politically and economically, a back-water.

On the whole, the ruling elite was quite satisfied with this condition. The Kuta, carefully reorganized by Mwanawina personally, shared his desire to isolate Barotseland as much as possible from the main currents of Northern Rhodesian life. Thus, for example, Mwanawina's appointees to the African Representative Council, an advisory body which had been created by the central government in 1946,[64] were given explicit instructions that their role was to be a purely passive one. 'This policy', as Glennie understood 'is not designed to integrate Barotse interests too closely with those of the country as a whole. . . . The Barotse leaders evidently wish to drive as lonely a furrow as possible.'[65]

Indeed, it can hardly be doubted that Mwanawina, like Yeta in the 1930s, wished nothing more than that the ruling class should live in splendid isolation. The difference was that Mwanawina's splendour was on a vastly greater scale than that of his half-brother. Thanks to fees paid by the Zambesi Sawmills Company for working the teak forests in Sesheke District and by WNLA for its labour recruits to the Rand mines, the Barotse Native Treasury showed a balance at the end of 1951 of £102,000, most of which went to pay salaries and for the proper upkeep of Lealui.[66]

Glennie and the central government were highly dismayed by the callous conservatism of Mwanawina and his court. In contrast to Imwiko's reign, however, they were no longer schemes upon a reluctant tribal elite. Because they decided they needed its support in other more critical areas, government officials were forced to tolerate a great deal from the Barotse government to which they were opposed. Above all, they considered it important, in terms both of wider public opinion and of influencing other chiefs in the territory, to win Mwanawina's approval for the Federation of Rhodesia and Nyasaland. Secondly, they wanted him to help keep Lozi on the Copperbelt out of the considerable agitation then being conducted against Federation. In neither area did he fail them.

In 1952, as Henry Hopkinson, the new Colonial Secretary, reminded Mwanawina, 'when there was much stupid talk of political strikes and disturbances [against Federation by the ANC and the African Mineworkers' Union] . . . you told your peoples to have nothing to do with such foolishness. . . .'[67] Although his intervention further exacerbated tensions on the Copperbelt between the mass of Bemba miners and the minority of elitist Lozi clerks,[68] Mwanawina's 'wisdom', Hopkinson assured him,'has not passed unnoticed.'

Now, partly as a reward for his 'wisdom' in this matter and partly as an inducement to have him approve of Federation, the government began to move closer towards meeting some of

Mwanawina's demands. Governor Rennie came to Lealui to announce that the jurisdiction of the courts of the Paramount and the Mokwae of Nalolo would be extended and that he was 'considering' granting to the Paramount the sole right to appoint and dismiss indunas.[69] Shortly thereafter, the Colonial Secretary, Harry Hopkinson, also flew to Lealui to announce to a full meeting of the National Council that he agreed to the recent proposal that the Lozi's protected status be formalized by its becoming, instead of 'Barotse Province', the 'Barotseland Protectorate', and the Provincial Commissioner becoming the 'Resident Commissioner.'[70]

Mwanawina could hardly have demanded greater safeguards than these. Yet so great was Lozi hostility to white rule that, after Hopkinson's speech, Ngambela Walubita felt it necessary to repeat that Federation was 'entirely opposed by all [Lozi] people . . . not wanting to associate with S[outhern] R[hodesia]'. Another induna reported to Hopkinson that 'illtreatment of Africans in SR made Barotses on Railway Line and here be against Federation', while Mwanawina himself remained unconvinced that the laws of the settler-dominated Federal Parliament would not prevail over those of the Northern Rhodesian Legislative Council.[71] This continued to be the official position of Lealui as late as February, 1953.[72]

In April, 1953, Governor Rennie again flew to Limulunga. He addressed a public meeting of about 500 people, of whom precisely eight raised their voices in favour of Federation.[73] He then conferred privately at length with Mwanawina and his senior advisers. Rennie used, Ngambela Walubita later stated, 'words to cheat us'.[74] He emphasized repeatedly the proposition than since the Queen approved the Federation, opposition to it was tantamount to being disloyal to the Queen. Mwanawina later said he was unable to resist this argument.[75]

At the conclusion of the meeting, the Paramount Chief and Kuta issued a statement declaring that if Federation was decided upon, they would raise no objections provided that

(1) Rights under the Lewanika Concessions are preserved by an appropriate provision in the Federal Constitution, and
(2) That that part of Northern Rhodesia known as Barotseland be styled or declared by Order in Council as the Barotseland Protectorate.[76]

In fact, the Governor had already acknowledged that these demands would be met.[77] At about the same time, Glennie announced that the government would no longer have the right to approve the appointments of indunas to and their dismissals from the BNG.[78]

While officers of the central government promptly spread the news of Mwanawina's decision in order to 'give a lead to other more hesitant tribes', and other Lozi denounced the decision as reactionary and arbitrary,[79] the Paramount Chief himself, accompanied by Ngambela Walubita, flew off to London to attend the coronation of Elizabeth II and to receive a Coronation Medal.[80]

The trip to London was presumably in the nature of a reward for Mwanawina's decision. Whether, in the event he had refused to accept Federation, Governor Rennie was prepared to deport him to London as, in not wholly unsimilar circumstances, Sir Andrew Cohen deported the Kabaka of Buganda, is not known. As a result of his stand, the Kabaka suffered temporary deposition and deportation. He thus greatly increased his public popularity and, as a direct consequence, his political influence in the Ugandan struggle for independence.[81] Because Mwanawina's decision seemed to be contrary to the interests of his people, he effectively isolated not merely his 'Protectorate' from the rest of Northern Rhodesia but himself from all his subjects save the tiny minority of the ruling class. During the nationalist struggle of the 1960s, he was shown to be highly unpopular among the great majority of his people, thus making it virtually impossible for the British government to uphold his interests against the African nationalists'. The responsibility for this rested solely with him and his advisers. For he too remained suspicious of the intentions of the white leaders of the new Federation, suspicions which were increased by the speeches of Godfrey Huggins and Roy Welensky demanding full independent status.[82] Yet at no time was he prepared, either in 1953 or later, to attempt to reach any accommodation with the forces opposing Federation. This was a strategical error of the greatest consequence. For even though he had not shown the courage of the Kabaka in 1953, he might still have salvaged something of his personal popularity. Had he made concessions to his moderate internal opponents during the 1950s, they may not have aligned themselves with the nationalists. Had he later agreed to co-operate with the latter, he might have won for himself a position comparable to that temporarily achieved by the Kabaka in independent Uganda. But his unyielding intransigence assured the ultimate destruction of the remaining rump of a formerly powerful empire.

These shattering events were put in motion moderately enough after Federation had begun. In Barotseland, the 'main agitator', as a white official described him,[83] was Newo Zaza, an elected member of the Katengo Council, a position he effectively exploited to voice his criticism of the BNG.[84] In 1954, his brother Clement returned from Bechuanaland where he had achieved considerable distinction as a supervisor of schools.[85] Together they won over several other educated Lozi in the area, and, apparently eschewing the local Welfare Association, began a systematic attack on the BNG.[86]

At about the same time, a small group of Lozi on the line of rail had banded together as the 'Barotse National Association'. Initiated by the ubiquitous Godwin Mbikusita presumably to prove that urban Lozi supported the BNG, it was soon taken over by a faction hostile to the Paramount Chief. Under Sekeli Konosi, a Lusaka businessman, the BNA began a 'truculent and abusive' campaign against the BNG.[87]

Although there was apparently no initial collusion between the Zazas' small group in Barotseland and the BNA, their virtually indentical criticisms of the Lozi ruling class inevitably brought them together. Their essential aim was to reform, rather than restructure, the existing administrative and political apparatus. They considered the BNG a family compact. A large percentage of indunas were, since the purges of 1949 and 1950, relatives of the Paramount Chief. The opinions of unrelated indunas went unheeded. The Katengo Council was contemptuously ignored. The welfare of the inner ruling elite alone was their sole concern. A large part of the best agricultural land in the flood-plain was kept in their own hands. Public money from the Native Treasury was being squandered for private uses, such as the redecoration of the palaces of the chiefs. The masses received few benefits from the BNG. The most capable people, if they were of humble origin, were excluded from the inner circle of power. In short, the Barotse government, according to its enemies, was callous, corrupt, and it excluded them.[88]

The Zaza brothers' programme called upon Mwanawina to abdicate and demanded a new constitution and the election of a new Paramount who would be obliged to abide by it. Their proposed constitution, hardly a radical manifesto, did not call for democratic government. Elected Katengo members were to share decision-making with traditional indunas, and the new Paramount, as a constitutional monarch, would be bound by their decisions.[89]

However conservative these reforms—which essentially demanded an alliance between the educated and the traditional elites—they predictably infuriated the Lozi rulers. Mwanawina is said to have threatened to dismiss Newo Zaza from the Katengo and to banish his whole village from Barotseland,[90] but public opinion apparently deterred him from such drastic retaliation.[91] The two brothers forged ahead with their campaign. They solicited, with apparent success, pledges of support from most of the Mongu 'intelligentsia'. They also approached Glennie, the Resident Commissioner, realizing his powers to enforce reforms was far greater than their own. Glennie, it is said, expressed sympathy with their arguments, but counselled patience since, he pointed out, the old man was not expected to live much longer. He would not be pushed too far, however. When the Zazas persisted in demanding from him immediate action, Glennie firmly warned them that their activities could be interpreted as a conspiracy against the Paramount Chief, for which serious punishment could be meted out.[92]

Yet even Ngambela Walubita, conservative as he was, strongly opposed Mwanawina's transformation of the Kuta into a family compact. Moreover, the Paramount Chief was increasingly determined to have as Ngambela his niece's husband, Akabeswa Imasiku, whom he had nominated as one of the Lozi members to the African Representative Council. Under this pressure, Walubita finally resigned early in 1956,[93] but the appointment of Imasiku proved awkward. 'There is among the people,' wrote Coisson of the PMS, 'a strong feeling' against him,[94] presumably including those indunas who felt isolated from the inner elite of the ruling group. They nominated Muleta, chief councillor of the Libonda Kuta, and Godwin Mbikusita, a supporter of Federation who had recently returned from a course on Moral Re-Armament in Switzerland. On the advice of the Boma, a secret ballot was conducted not only among the members of the National Council, but among Lozi on the line of rail. The ballots of both groups were then counted by Mwanawina and the Natamoyo, his brother, who announced a large majority for Imasiku, with Mbikusita second and Muleta last.[95]

This method of selection made the Paramount patently susceptible to accusations of fraud, and the then Treasurer of the BNG told me that in fact Imasiku was not chosen correctly and that he was not 'the people's choice'.[96] Certainly Sekeli Konoso of the Barotse National Association was infuriated by Imasiku's appointment. He wrote to Mwanawina, demanding that the Paramount resign,[97] and to the Zaza brothers informing them that he intended personally to come to Lealui to protest.[98]

Thus forewarned, the Zazas began mobilizing their supporters. It was a fascinating group, for virtually all its key members—Newo Zaza, Yuyi Mupatu, Francis Suu, J. K. Kapota, Muimui Anakandi—had long-standing personal grievances against Mwanawina.[99] However much they may also have agreed with Konoso, they all clearly had other interests in supporting him.

Konoso arrived in Barotseland early in 1956, but after being refused permission to address the Kuta, returned to Lusaka where he continued a sustained attack against the BNG.[100] In October, Mwanawina, with the approval of the Resident Commissioner, decided to charge Konoso for distributing pamphlets in Barotseland defaming and insulting the Paramount Chief.[101] In January, 1957, Konoso appeared before the Lealui Kuta accompanied by some thousands of his supporters.[102] While the large crowd loudly demanded the dismissal of Ngambela Imasiku, the Kuta sentenced Konoso to three years in solitary confinement, a sentence later reduced by the Federal High Court to six months' imprisonment with hard labour.[103] Following this drastic sentence, Konoso's supporters demonstrated in protest at the Mongu Boma, as a result of which about ten of them—including the Zaza brothers, Yuyi Mupatu, and Francis Suu—were convicted in the Mongu

Magistrate's Court for disorderly conduct and received light fines.[104]

The immediate result of this debacle was a decision by the central government to appoint a commission to consider reforms in the BNG. Such a commission, it was hoped, might mollify Konoso's supporters while prodding Mwanawina to make certain concessions to his opponents. But reforms were not to be imposed on the Paramount; he was too invaluable an ally against African nationalism to alienate gratuitously. His special status was accurately reflected in the conservative nature of both the Lozi and European appointees to the new commission, and by the absence of any representative of the Konoso–Zaza faction. The reaction to its formation by many Lozi was reported by J. P. Burger of the PMS: 'This is a family council, composed of the relatives and friends of the king, and will lead to nothing.'[105]

This forecast proved precisely accurate. After interviewing hundreds of witnesses, the commissioners concluded that

> the present framework of the Barotse Native Government, being suitable for the conditions existing in Barotseland at present and being adaptable to changing conditions in the future, should remain the basis on which any future developments are built.[106]

The many proposals to elect members to the BNG were dismissed as impractical;[107] those demanding that the BNG be more representative of public opinion were marginally more fruitful: the Commission recommended that five members of the Katengo Council 'should become full members of the National Council in meetings of that Council dealing with motions from the Katengo Council'.[108] The Kuta accepted the recommendation, as well, not surprisingly, as the general conclusion of the Report that 'the pattern of the Barotse Native Government should remain unchanged.'[109]

Glyn Jones, the Resident Commissioner, reacted to the Report with the same complacency as did the Kuta, although pointing out what the Report had signally failed to stress, that many witnesses expressed great dissatisfaction at Mwanawina's policy of appointing to the BNG men who were 'elderly, reactionary and incapable of appreciating' the need for changes.

'The younger educated Malozi,' he acknowledged, 'were not being encouraged to assume posts of responsibility because the existing councils showed resistance to the transfusion of new blood into themselves.'[110]

The Rawlins Commission satisfied none of Mwanawina's critics. A long, lugubrious letter written in March, 1958, by J. P. Burger, one of the more politically-aware of the PMS missionaries, provides a shrewd and accurate assessment of the prevailing political climate, and is therefore worth citing at some length.

It has been calm here for several months [Burger wrote]. Since the [Konoso] troubles in January, 1957, a European detective has been placed in Mongu, with African assistants, to follow the developments in the situation. . . . He is watching the upper schools, and the teachers, for propaganda they could pass to their students . . . .

The Government is behind Mwanawina. He himself has learned nothing, it seems . . . [and is] badly seconded by his Ngambela . . . .

Faithful to Government policy . . . it [the Rawlins Commission Report] makes the most superficial recommendations in order not to weaken the authority of the Paramount Chief. Whereas . . . the idea of the reign of one person has become contemptible . . . . They [his opponents] complain that the Paramount Chief pays no attention to their [Katengo councillors'] reports and that he takes no account of the opinion of his people.

Moreover, groups of Lozi from Bulawayo to the Copperbelt want to have their voice heard, but this has so far been refused. They now threaten not to pay their levies [to the BNG] if their right to be heard is not recognized.

Everywhere, in Barotseland as on the line of rail, the word democracy is solemnly being pronounced. One can only applaud.

But Mwanawina is insensible to the signs of the times. Recently, when he arived at Limulunga [the winter capital], we were struck to see that he received virtually no royal salute. When we asked our people [i.e. Lozi Christians] about it, they said 'This is good, this is progress!'[111]

Lozi informants confirmed this analysis.[112] If Mwanawina was respected in his capacity as King, he was unloved as a man.

This distinction between the man and his office was apparent in the demands of Konoso and the Zaza brothers, who were in a real sense defending the integrity of the kingship against an unjust King. Mwanawina could hardly have been unaware of his unpopularity. Nor could he have failed to realize that the failure of Barotseland materially to benefit from Federation vindicated the suspicions of those who had always opposed it. A new hospital in Mongu was not considered adequate compensation for closer association with and potential control by white settlers in Southern Rhodesia.[113] Mwanawina, however, continued to remain indifferent to the widespread current of antagonism against him, refusing even to accept the advice of the PMS that he establish some kind of information or propaganda agency through which to explain his position to his subjects both at home and abroad.[114]

Yet, as both he and the National Council made clear in 1957 and again in 1958, he shared their general suspicion of the Federal government, of Welensky's continuing demands for dominion status for the Federation,[115] and of the demands of white Northern Rhodesians for a new constitution giving themselves greater powers at the expense of the Lozi ruling class.[116] By this stage, however, the Federal government had perceived that in Mwanawina it had a devoted ally and apparently firm bulwark against the forces of African nationalism. For in May, 1958, Welensky paid a formal visit to Mongu, where he guaranteed the Paramount Chief and Kuta against any interference in Barotseland's affairs by his government.[117] Many Lozi resented any dealings with Welensky,[118] but Mwanawina's disdain for their opinions was presumably grounded on his faith in government support for his position. Nor, so long as white power was predominant in Northern Rhodesia, was such faith misplaced. One white liberal described Barotseland as 'probably the most backward part of Central Africa, or the most unspoilt, depending on your point of view'.[119]

The point of view of most white officials was obvious enough. It may not unfairly be represented by the words of M. C. Billing of the Lusaka Secretariat, who observed with maudlin sentimentality that 'the whole set up of life in the Barotse plain . . . is something which has a flavour of its own', while acknowledging, on a less romanticized level, that 'There is no doubt at all that the chiefs are . . . a stabilizing influence when many responsible Africans are not a little bewildered by the ebb and flow of political propaganda'.[120] Because the government felt that Mwanawina's good will was necessary to retain his 'stabilizing influence', it was not prepared to impose measures upon him against his will, a form of solicitude it showed to no other chiefs in Northern Rhodesia. His special status—and the means by which the central government tried to win his consent to important moves—was demonstrated once again in connection with the territorial elections of 1959. Throughout the previous year, Mwanawina had refused to allow a Lozi to stand in the Barotseland Protectorate, one of the minority of special constituencies reserved for Africans. Lealui was not prepared to take any steps which might reduce its own powers. As a result, the Paramount had informed Welensky, 'It is not our custom to get mixed up in other parliaments. Our custom is to deal with all matters through the Paramount Chief and the Kuta.'[121]

At the beginning of 1959, the Queen's New Year's Honour List included the name of the Paramount Chief, who now became Sir Mwanawina Lewanika III, KBE—the first and last African in Central Africa to be so honoured.[122] Rather than crude bribery, J. P. Burger interpreted the award as an implicit assurance to Mwanawina from the British government that recognizing the Legislative Council would not be a step towards infringing the powers of the Kuta.[123] This point could not have been lost on Mwanawina. Presumably, too, he was made aware that, since all his indunas and recognized headmen were eligible to vote, he had effective control of the seat. Moreover, he discovered an impressively 'modern' yet loyal candidate in the person of Kwalombota Mulonda, a graduate in education from Makerere in Uganda, now a teacher at the Barotse Secondary School who had earlier acted briefly as Administrative Secretary to the BNG.[124] For all these reasons, Mwanawina agreed that Barotseland would participate in the elections, and in March, 1959, Mulonda duly 'romped home', receiving 382 of the 571 votes cast for the three candidates in the constituency.[125]

Mwanawina appeared then to be at the peak of his career. Indeed, he enjoyed more prestige and privileges than any King of Barotseland had done since Coryndon's arrival in 1897. His conservative and isolationist policies made him indisputably the most important chief in Central Africa. Honoured by the Queen, respected and flattered by government officials, wooed by the Prime Minister of the Federation personally, his position seemed as impregnable as that of the Federation itself. Only the large majority of his subjects and the African nationalists were against him, and those winds of change were blowing—as he, his court, and his white supporters very soon discovered to their dismay—in their direction.

## REFERENCES

1. Glennie to Chief Secretary, 25 June, 1945, Boma Files, Retirement of Yeta Dossier.

2. Mr. M. Kawana, a senior induna of the Sesheke Kuta under Imwiko; Mr. G. M. Mukande, formerly Central Treasurer of the BNG, appointed by Imwiko; Mr. Simalumba.

3. Copy of Glennie's speech, undated, Boma Files, op. cit.

4. Glennie remained PC of Barotseland for eleven years. Mr. Mukande described him as 'tough and humourless'. He epitomized the white officials' ambivalent attitude towards Barotesland, on the one hand cherishing its isolation and conservatism, on the other considering the BNG too inefficient. See His 'The Barotse System of Government', *Journal of African Administration*, Vol. IV, No. 1, Jan., 1952, pp, 9–13, and 'The Administrative Officer Today: Barotseland', *Corona*, Vol. 2, No. 3, March, 1959, pp. 86–88.

5. Glennie, 'Report on Barotse Province', in *Colonial Annual Reports*, 1946, copy in Boma Files.

6. Glennie, 'Barotse System of Government', *op. cit.*, p. 9.

7. Messrs. Mukande and Kapota.

8. Glennie, 'Report', 1946, *op. cit.*

9. Glennie, 'Report', 1946, *op. cit;* Glennie, 'Reports on Barotse Province', *NRNAAR*, 1947, p. 72, and 1948, p. 68; Acting PC to Welfare Association, 10 July, 1948, Boma Files, Provincial Administration, 1939–53.

10. Harry Franklin, *Unholy Wedlock: The Failure of the Central African Federation* (London, 1963), p. 221.

11. R. S. Burles, 'The Katengo Council Elections', *Journal of African Administration*, Vol. 4, No. 1 Jan., 1952, p. 15; Glennie, 'Report', NRNAAR, 1948, p. 69.

12. Messrs. Mukande and Berger.

13. Franklin, *op. cit.*, p. 221, and Mr. Mupatu, who was one of the appointees to the new council.

14. This situation still obtained when I was in Barotesland in 1965.

15. Glennie's Report, 1946, *op. cit.*

16. Glennie, 'A Note on the Barotse Province and Some Current Questions', 25 Aug., 1952, marked 'Confidential', Boma Files.

17. Messrs. Wina, Mupatu, Mukande, Simalumba and Berger all agreed on this point.

18. Fox-Pitt, 'Barotse Province', NRNAAR, 1947, p. 75.

19. Messrs. Arthur and Newo Zaza.

20. Glennie, 'Report', NRNAAR, 1948, p. 70.

21. Messrs. Njekwa, Kapota, Mupatu, Mukande, Arthur and Newo Zaza.

22. Hall, Zambia, pp. 124–6; Rotberg, Rise of Nationalism, p. 212.

23. Cited in News from B. and B., March, 1949, p. 3.

24. Mr. Berger.

25. Burger to Director, 27 July, 1948, PMSS.

26. Same to same, 29 Aug., 1948, ibid.

27. 'Biographical Note on Paramount Chief Mwanawina III' in Notes on the Barotseland Protectorate and its Districts (anonymous, 3 July, 1956), Boma Files.

28. Burger to Director, 28 Sept., 1948, PMSS.

29. Messrs. Wina and Walubita. The latter succeeded Wina as Ngambela.

30. Burger to Director, 27 July, 1948, PMSS, and Messrs. Mupatu, Makonde, Kapota and Berger. The latter was told this by Mwanawina himself.

31. Burger to Director, 29 Aug., 1948, and 11 Oct., 1948, PMSS.

32. Gluckman, Seven Tribes, p. 39.

33. Statement by Induna Katema, 23 Sept., 1948, Boma Files, Daniel Mukoboto Dossier.

34. See Boma Files, Mukoboto Dossier and Ngambela Wina Dossier; Glennie, 'Report', NRNAAR, 1948, p. 70; also Mr. Mupatu, then a relatively senior induna of the Lealui Kuta.

35. Mwanawina to Glennie, 12 Oct., 1948, Boma Files, Ngambela Imasiku Dossier.

36. Glennie to SNA, 29 Nov., 1948, Boma Files, Wina Dossier

37. Mwanawina to Glennie, 27 Nov., 1948, and Glennie to Mwanawina, 27 Nov., 1948, Boma Files, Wina Dossier; also Mr. Walubita.

38. Burger to Director 26 Dec., 1948, PMSS.

39. Glennie, 'Report', NRNAAR, 1948, p. 71.

40. See Chapter 6.

41. Minutes of the National Council Meeting, 4 and 5 June, 1948, Boma Files, Barotse Native Authorities Conference.

42. Minutes of Association Meeting, 9 Sept., 1948, Boma Files, Welfare Association Dossier.

43. Glennie, 'Report', NRNAAR, 1948, pp. 70–1.

44. ibid. for 1949, p. 82.

45. Glennie, 'Report', NRNAAR, 1949, p. 82; Glyn Jones (Acting PC), 'Report', ibid., 1950, p. 91.

46. Cited in 'A Note on the Barotse Province and Some Current Questions', 25 August, 1952, Boma Files.

47. *ibid.*, and Glennie, 'Report', NRNAAR, 1951, p. 80.

48. Gluckman, *Seven Tribes*, p. 41.

49. These perceptive insights are suggsted in Glyn Jones (Acting PC), 'Report', NRNAAR, 1950, p. 92.

50. Glennie, 'Report', *ibid.*, 1949, 82.

51. There are no references to it in either the Boma of PMSS files, nor were any Lozi informants forthcoming on the subject.

52. Jones, 'Report', 1950, NRNAAR, p. 91.

53. Data from Mr. Daniel Soko, himself a Nyasa, once a prominent member of the Association who now runs a small shop in Mongu, and Mr. Arthur Zaza.

55. Association's 'Memorandum of Rights and Privileges of Barotseland Not Respected by N. Rhodesian Government,' 9 Sept., 1948, Boma Files, Welfare Association Dossier.

56. Minutes of Association Meeting of 3 June, 1948 and 9 Sept., 1948, *ibid.* The Boma Files contain no documents relating to the Association after 1948. Mr. Soko told me that it continued its activities into the early 1950s, but was unable to recall the issues with which it was concerned.

57. Glennie, 'Report', NRNAAR, 1952, p. 86.

58. This is confirmed by Messrs. Soko and A. Wina. Daniel Mukoboto, for example, became Mwanawina's private secretary in the late 1950s, until he was murdered in mysterious circumstances in 1961.

59. Glennie, 'Report', NRNAAR, 1955, p. 92.

60. Peter Fraenkel, *Wayaleshi* (London, 1959), pp. 102-4 ,108.

61. Glennie, 'Report', NRNAAR, 1951, p. 80. Also Mr. Newo Zaza, see below.

62. *ibid.*, p. 81, and 'Note on Barotse Province . . . ', 25 Aug., 1952, *op. cit.*

63. 'Note on Barotse Province', *op. cit;* Jones, 'Report', NRNAAR, 1950, p. 91; Glennie, 'Report', *ibid.*, 1951, p. 93.

64. Gann, *History of Northern Rhodesia*, p. 385.

65. Glennie, 'Report', NRNAAR, 1949, p. 85; also Mr. Mataa (Induna Imandi), who was one of the appointees to the ARC.

66. Glennie, 'Barotse System of Government', *op. cit.*, p. 13; 'Note on Barotse Province', *op. cit.*

67. Hopkinson's Speech, 5 Aug., 1952, reported in NR Information Department Press Communique No. 626.

68. Epstein, *Politics in an Urban African Community*, pp. 133-4, 144, 236.

69. Glennie, 'Report', NRNAAR, 1952, p. 86.

70. Hopkinson's speech, *op. cit.*

71. Record of Meeting between Secretary of State and Chief and Council, 2 Aug., 1952, Boma Files, Proposals for Closer Association between Central African Territories Dossier.

72. Meetings between Glennie and Chief and Council, 7 Feb., and 14 Feb., 1953, *ibid.*

73. Burger to Director, 29 April, 1953, PMSS.

74. Mr. Walubita.

75. The interpretation given by Mwanawina to Harry Franklin,

*Unholy Wedlock*, p. 220, is identical almost to the word with that given me by Mr. Walubita.

76. Cited in Glennie to all Barotse Province DCS, 20 April, 1953, Boma Files, Closer Association Dossier.

77. Copy of Rennie's address to the Legislative Council, 16 April, 1953, in *ibid.*

78. Glennie, 'Report', NRNAAR, 1953, p. 96.

79. *Ibid.*, pp. 93–4.

80. *Ibid.*, p. 93, and *News from B. and B.*, 1953, pp. 10–11.

81. Low and Pratt, *Buganda and British Overrule*, App. 1, and A. I. Richards, 'Epilogue', in L. A. Fallers *The King's Men* (London, 1964), pp. 359–64.

82. Rotberg, *Rise of Nationalism*, p. 254.

83. Confidential, unsigned, undated memorandum, probably by Glennie, in Boma Files.

84. Mr. N. Zaza.

85. Mr. C. Zaza.

86. Mr. N. Zaza.

87. Confidential memorandum, *op. cit.*

88. Messrs. N. and C. Zaza, Mupatu, Simalumba and Mukande. The writer of the confidential memorandum, *op. cit.*, concurred. The 'key positions' in the BNG, he wrote, 'are filled by the powerful landowners. Thus you have a baronage poised between the Chief and the Lozi polloi who do not matter a damn. All very medieval . . . . The BNG is reasonably benevolent provided the requirements of the royal family and the interests of the cabal which forms the cabinet are first met.'

89. Mr. C. Zaza.

90. Mr. N. Zaza.

91. M. Mainga, 'The Origin of the Lozi', in Stokes and Brown, *Zambesian Past*, p. 241, fn. 3.

92. Messrs. Newo and Clement Zaza independently gave identical testimonies on the matter.

93. Messrs. Walubita, Kapota, Arthur and Newo Zaza, Mukande.

94. Coisson to Director, 3 May, 1956, PMSS.

95. Mr. Lifunana Imasiku, son of Ngambela Imasiku, and assistant personal secretary to Mwanawina, 1951–61, personal secretary 1961–66.

96. Mr. Mukande.

97. Coisson to Director, 5 Sept., 1956, PMSS. Mwanawina showed the letter to Coisson.

98. Mr. C. Zaza.

99. Messrs. L. Imasiku, Mupatu and Kapota, and Wina and Suu to Glennie, 12 July, 1953, Boma Files, Wina Dossier.

100. J. F. Hayley, 'Report on Barotseland Protectorate', NRNAAR, 1956, p. 80. Glennie retired in October, 1956, after eleven years in Barotseland.

101. Mwanawina to RC, 26 Oct., 1956, Boma Files, Correspondence between RC and Paramount Chief.

102. Glyn Jones, RC, 'Report', NRNAAR, p. 88.

103. Burger to Director, 6 May, 1957, PMSS.

104. Messrs. Mupatu and C. Zaza, who were fined £5 and £9 respectively, and Jones, 'Report', *op. cit.*, p. 88.

105. Burger to Director, 12 June, 1957, PMSS.

106. *Report of the Committee to inquire into the Constitution of the Barotse Native Government together with the comments thereon of the National Council* (Lusaka, 1958), p. 3.

107. *ibid.*, p.2.

108. *ibid.*, p. 5.

109. *ibid.*, p. 15.

110. Jones, 'Report', *op. cit.*, p. 88.

111. Burger to Director, 31 March, 1958, PMSS.

112. Messrs. Mukande, Mupatu and Simalumba.

113. Messrs. Walubita, Mukande, A. and C. Zaza, Mupatu and Simalumba.

114. Messrs. Berger and Graebert.

115. *Northern News*, 18 Nov., 1957.

116. G. Clay, RC, 'Report', NRNAAR, 1958, p. 80.

117. *Northern News*, 20 May, 1958.

118. Mr. L. Imasiku.

119. Peter Fraenkal, *Wayaleshi*, p. 92.

120. Billing, 'Government Policy in the Utilization of Indigenous Political Systems', in R. Apthorpe (ed.), *From Tribal Rule to Modern Government* (Lusaka, 1959), pp. 1–3, 11.

121. *Northern News*, 20 May, 1958.

122. Hall, *op. cit.*, p. 238.

123. Burger to Director, 4 Jan., 1959, PMSS.

124. Clay, *Annual Report*, 1962, copy from Boma Files.

125. Editorial note by Apthorpe in his *From Tribal Rule to Modern Government*, pp. 67–8. The other two candidates stood as independents, apparently receiving the support of those white-collar Lozi who were eligible to vote but who numbered fewer than indunas and headmen.

# CHAPTER VIII

# TRIBALISM VERSUS NATIONALISM

The positions of both the Lozi ruling class and the Federation of Rhodesia and Nyasaland seemed invulnerable in 1959. In fact, the imminent destruction of both was signalled—for those who cared to see—the previous year when Dr H. K. Banda returned to Nyasaland and a militant group of Northern Rhodesia's African nationalists broke away from Harry Nkumbula's African National Congress. The Northern Rhodesian militants formed the Zambian African National Congress (ZANC), which in October, 1959, became the United National Independence Party (UNIP).

Early in 1959, the Northern Rhodesian government banned ZANC. Several of its non-Lozi leaders were restricted to Barotseland, an action which has been described as a 'cardinal mistake' on the part of the government,[1] and which reflected the delusion of white officials that rural Africans would not be susceptible to the nationalists' message, and that the Lozi would not succumb to the lure of 'alien' Africans.

It is true that after Konoso's conviction early in 1957, organized opposition to the Barotse native government had dissolved. Yet its conservative critics remained dissatisfied, though leaderless,[2] and an underground group of ZANC supporters already existed by 1959.[3] Although the former faction was concerned primarily with local as opposed to national politics, as Lealui and the Federal government became increasingly identified in the public mind, it found itself moving inexorably towards the tiny minority which supported the larger nationalist movement. The consolidation and expansion of the two groups was a direct result of the politicizing efforts of the ZANC restrictees during 1959. Through unceasing propaganda, they created an ever-widening network of contacts with the result that, by the end of their period of restriction, they could count upon the dedicated support of the African middle class—teachers, clerks, storekeepers—in Mongu, Senanga and Seseke.[4]

Moreover, the rusticated nationalists won considerable public gratitude for their involvement in the case of the mysterious murder of Akashambatwa Imwiko, son of the late King Imwiko. Many UNIP supporters and personal opponents of Mwanawina maintained at the time, and continue to believe, that the Paramount was responsible for Akashambatwa's murder. Probably the truth of the matter can never conclusively be proved. But the important political fact is that many Lozi were convinced of Mwanawina's responsibility, believed that Boma officials were bribed to help conceal his complicity, and saw that it was UNIP leaders who kept the affair in the headlines, forcing the government at least to pretend to be carrying out a thorough investigation.[5]

Although the sordid affair was eventually closed with the murder unsolved, its consequences were long felt. For it was among the major early causes of political polarization in Barotseland. To the many Lozi who believed in Mwanawina's guilt, the case appeared to be sufficient vindication of the UNIP charge of deliberate collusion between the Boma and the BNG to perpetuate injustice and the rule of the traditional clique in Lealui. Moreover, UNIP's involvement in the case made it seem the sole viable organization within which conservative and radical Lozi alike could unite, for very different reasons, against the ruling elite and its Boma protectors.

On the other hand, UNIP's role assured for it the underlying hostility of the large part of the Lozi ruling class. This was not wholly inevitable. Aside from the Paramount and the Ngambela, most of the Lozi elite were treated as racially inferior by many district officials, and consequently shared with UNIP and its supporters a bitter resentment of white racialism.[6] As Chief Liatitima said, 'All our traditions were spoiled by the whites since we were forced to give them the same forms of respect we should give only to Chiefs'.[7] Since at the time the possibility of a nationalist victory in Northern Rhodesia seemed infinitely remote, the ruling class had either to gamble and support UNIP, or take their stand against what some of its members called black 'extremists',[8] which meant remaining on the top rung of the Barotseland elite though at the lowest level of the white hierarchy. Like a majority of their counterparts in Africa when faced with the same choice, the traditional Lozi rulers opted for the latter alternative. As Lewanika had long before appealed to the British Crown against Lobengula's Ndebele, so now did his son continue to repose his security with Her Majesty's government against Kenneth Kaunda's 'alien' nationalists.

In practice, this meant that no political parties were allowed to operate in Barotseland, and UNIP was refused permission by the BNG to hold meetings in the 'Protectorate'.[9] Apparently with government encouragement,[10] indunas were sent through the countryside to vilify UNIP, break up its meetings, and arrest its partisans who were then fined by the local Kutas.[11]

Mwanawina was not yet, however, prepared to join with Welensky against the territory's nationalists. Although the Monckton Commission's *Report* of 1960 reaffirmed Barotseland's 'special position',[12] Lealui was no longer so easily satisfied. In August of 1960, the National Council asked Britain to allow Barotseland to secede from Northern Rhodesia and the Federation and be proclaimed a protectorate directly under the British government on the lines of the High Commission Territories.[13] This decision caused a tremendous uproar among the nationalists,[14] who believed it revealed the Lozi rulers to be as hostile to African nationalism as to white domination.[15]

Ngambela Imasiku hotly denied that secession was a reaction to the fear of a nationalist victory. Such a contingency was, he asserted, quite irrelevant, since 'We do not consider ourselves a part of Northern Rhodesia or as a protectorate within a protectorate. We are a different country and a different people. We have our own government.'[16] As a statement of fact, this declaration was entirely accurate. So far as Lealui was concerned, the attachment of Barotseland to Northern Rhodesia was fortuitous, an administrative convenience initiated originally by the Company when North-Western and North-Eastern Rhodesia were amalgamated and continued by the successor colonial government. Barotseland had existed as an independent national entity long before the creation of Northern

Rhodesia, and was legally and historically entitled to maintain or to dissolve the attachment as its rulers wished.

In terms of political reality, however, historical rights were beside the point. Even the *Northern News*, hostile but reconciled to black rule in the future, recognized this truth. It cogently pointed out the fundamental weakness of the Lozi position: their demand for independence, it foresaw,

> if there is the expected nationalist majority in the Northern Rhodesian legislature . . . could develop into a full scale secession conflict on the lines of Buganda or Katanga. Poor, primitive and isolated, the 'protectorate within a protectorate' scarcely occupies the same key position as these two secessionist provinces do in Uganda and the Congo.[17]

Moreover, as the *Northern News* acknowledged, Barotseland represented 'a remnant of old-style tribal rule which offends modern pan-African thinking'.[18] In particular, Lealui's stand was intolerable to those UNIP leaders who were Lozi, not least, perhaps, because a number of them were Lozi aristocrats who —like so many of Konoso's supporters some years earlier— happened to have personal grievances against Mwanawina. The resistance to secession, for example, of Arthur and Sikota Wina, sons of the former Ngambela; Liatitima, former chief of Lukula; and Princess Nakatindi, Yeta's daughter, was surely compounded of elements of personal antipathy and the aristocrat's belief in his natural right to rule as well as of nationalist principles.

Moreover, most Lozi on the line of rail seemed antagonistic to the BNG. Although Sekeli Konoso was now allied with Lealui,[19] in November, 1960, the Barotse National Society formed a new organization, the Barotse Anti-Secession Movement:[20] BASMO was little more than a specifically Lozi front organization for UNIP,[21] and its leaders warned the government that, if Barotseland were allowed to secede, the 'chaos and discord' which would result would be 'much worse' than that which the secession of Katanga had produced in the Congo.[22]

Nevertheless, both Gervase Clay and his successor as Resident Commissioner, Heath, while acknowledging that 'a minority of the educated Africans [in Barotseland] have been attracted by the shouts of the nationalists', continued to believe that 'the

1. Lewanika in England, 1902. Front row: interpreter, King Lewanika; Back row: Alfred Bertrand, Adolph Jalla, Ngambela Mokamba, Lewanika's son-in-law.

NOEL 1904 — 1ᵉʳ JANVIER 1905

Cette bonne nouvelle du royaume sera prêchée dans le monde entier.
*Matth. XXIV 14*

...e que vous faites, faites-le de bon coeur, comme pour le Seigneur
et non pour les hommes.
*Col. III. 23*

Mr. Coillard
dans sa pirogue

2. A Christmas card in honour of Coillard.

3. Birds'-eye view of Lealui village and the flooded plain at the 1965 Kuomboka ceremony. The royal barge Nalikwanda is in the foreground right.

4. The Cabinet of the reformed Barotse National Council after the Katengo elections of 1963. Front row (left to right): the Ngambela (H. N. Noyoo); the Litunga (Sir Mwanawina Lewanika III); the Household Steward (Amba). Back row (left to right): K. Mulemwa (Finance); Councillor S. Liyoka (Transport and Works); Clr. K. Mutondo (Natural Resources); Clr. N. Situtu (Education); and Mr. K. Mulonda (Administrative Secretary).

5. President and Mrs. Kaunda and Litunga Mwanawina on the royal barge during the 1965 Kuomboka ceremony.

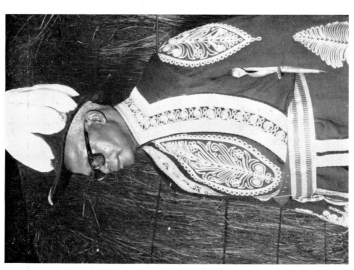

6. Litunga Mwanawina arrives at the winter capital, Limulunga, during 1965 Kuomboka ceremony. He is wearing the admiral's uniform which Chamberlain presented to his father in 1902. The royal paddlers are immediately behind him.

7. The Litunga Mbikusita Lewanika II.

vast majority of the inhabitants of the Protectorate' supported the BNG.[23] With this backing, Mwanawina and the Ngambela flew to London in April, 1961, to demand secession from Iain MacLeod, the new Colonial Secretary. MacLeod refused; clearly the British government was not prepared thus to provoke the nationalists in order to preserve Barotseland's status. MacLeod did, however, reaffirm Britain's previous commitments, and proposed as well to entrench 'the special rights and benefits of the Barotse people' in Orders in Council. Moreover, it was announced that the Lozi Paramount would henceforth be styled the *Litunga*—'earth', owner of the land—of the Barotseland Protectorate. A half century earlier, the Company had withdrawn Lewanika's right to be called 'King' in order to reduce him to the same status as that of the other chiefs of Northern Rhodesia; now, in order to elevate Mwanawina above his peers, the Company's successors were distinguishing him with the supreme title of the Lozi themselves.

MacLeod's compromise satisfied no one. The Litunga still demanded secession, while UNIP saw the new concessions as part of an imperialist plot to divide and rule.[24] The Boma continued to stand solidly behind Mwanawina, while he contrived to provoke UNIP on every possible occasion. The party remained illegal in Barotseland, its local supporters being able to maintain only clandestine links with their leaders in Lusaka. BASMO organizers from Lusaka were immediately deported. Nalumino Mundia, a senior UNIP official and a Lozi, was imprisoned in Mongu for a month for defying a deportation order.[25] Finally, Godwin Mbikusita's influence with the Litunga seemed to be increasing, for he acted as the spokesman for the BNG on several occasions during the year.[26] Already anathema to all nationalists as a UFP member of the Federal Parliament, Mbikusita's interventions on behalf of Mwanawina served further to intensify UNIP's determination to smash Barotseland's *ancien régime*.

In November, 1961, the party decided to send Mundia and two Lozi royals, Liatitima and Ngombala Lubita, back to Barotseland. In Mongu, Mundia was served with a deportation order, but refused to obey it. He did accept the consequent summons to appear before the Kuta, arriving in Lealui with a large group of vociferous supporters. Alarmed by the hostile crowd, Ngambela Imasiku telephoned Mongu to demand that the police come and arrest Mundia.[27] A white inspector duly arrived with a small contingent of police and, at the Kuta's behest, ordered Mundia to withdraw and the crowd to disperse. A riot ensured—the first in Barotseland under white rule—ending only after the police used tear gas against the crowd. While Mundia and Liatitima successfully appealed the sentences handed them by the Mongu Magistrate, some of their less prestigious supporters were less fortunate. The Kuta sentenced a large number of people to three months' imprisonment while the Mongu Magistrate jailed eleven men for eighteen months on charges of rioting.[28]

The riots, the trials, and the apparent alliance between the Kuta and the Boma aroused great interest in Barotseland generally and spurred the local UNIP supporters to begin a serious, if illegal, campaign of organizing and propaganda for the Northern Rhodesian elections due in 1962.[29] Yet the more hostile UNIP's attitude towards the Litunga became, the more valuable an asset did he appear to Roy Welensky. Early in 1962, Mwanawina's personal secretary, Lifunana Imasiku, who was also the son of the Ngambela, claims to have met Welensky in Salisbury. The Prime Minister suggested to him a plan for a new Federation incorporating Southern Rhodesia, the Copperbelt, Katanga and Barotseland. Welensky offered to arrange a personal meeting if necessary between the Litunga and Tshombe, but Mwanawina rejected the scheme, fearing it would alienate his white friends in Lusaka and London.[30] Welensky was undeterred, however, and in February, 1962, put roughly the same proposition to Duncan Sandys, the Colonial Secretary: he would agree to the secession of Nyasaland and North-eastern Rhodesia in return for a new Federation, in which Southern Rhodesia would provide the talent, the Copperbelt the wealth, and Barotseland the labour as well as a co-operative African ruler.[31] Sandys apparently adopted this 'manifestly absurd'[32] scheme of a new Federation with Barotseland as its Bantustan. Accompanied by Godwin Mbikusita, he flew to Barotseland and, after conferring with the Litunga, left with a signed document formally requesting Barotseland's secession from Northern Rhodesia 'while remaining within the Federation'.[33]

To UNIP, these negotiations were merely a transparent manoeuvre to 'play off' the Lozi rulers against the nationalists.[34] Sikota Wina, UNIP's publicity chief, declared that 'If Mwanawina breaks away he will be doing so illegally and we will be justified in overthrowing him'.[35] Sandys, however, soon reneged on the alleged agreement, and announced that it 'would not be in the interests of the Barotse people to pursue the question of separation at this stage'.[36] Nevertheless, even after Sandy's repudiation of the scheme, secession, within or without a Federation, remained Lealui's demand, as Godwin Mbikusita busily intrigued behind the scenes encouraging the Litunga not to capitulate.[37]

Immediately thereafter, in his capacity as one of Welensky's two African parliamentary secretaries, Mbikusita accompanied his Prime Minister to London for talks with R. A. Butler. They were informed that Northern Rhodesia and Nyasaland would be allowed to secede from the Federation, but Barotseland would not be permitted to secede from Northern Rhodesia. Mbikusita legitimately pointed out to Butler that this meant the British government was breaking its treaties with Lewanika, while Welensky, a recent convert to the African cause, added that 'the Barotse have been sold down the river'.[38]

Thus, for the first time since Lewanika had looked to the 'Great Queen' for protection, the Lozi ruling class was faced with no alternative but to rely for support on local white settlers against both the British government and threatening alien Africans. The Litunga publicly announced that 'If extremists [UNIP] come to power in Northern Rhodesia, we will not be interested in associating with the Government'.[39]

In April, 1962, with Mbikusita back in Barotseland, Mwanawina summoned the National Council for a meeting from which emanated a new tactic: although secession was still the final goal, the Lozi rulers nevertheless agreed to accept the new constitution for Northern Rhodesia and allow political parties to organize for the territorial elections in 1962.[40] The last decision unquestionably reflected the consensus that, in the words of the *Northern News*, though 'a class of collar-and-tie African civil servant or clerk might want more say in the Barotse Government, neither UNIP nor Congress have [sic] any appreciable following in Barotseland'.[41]

Given this premise, the Boma had put strong pressure on the BNG to recognize UNIP,[42] while the united Lozi ruling class concluded that if its candidates in the forthcoming elections defeated the nationalists, Britain would be forced to concede to the demand for secession. The initiative for creating a traditionalist political party to this end came not, as has sometimes been thought, from Welensky and Mbikusita,[43] but from the National Council itself. Its meeting had reaffirmed the policy of secession on the grounds that UNIP threatened to destroy the kingship, depose the indunas, and integrate Barotseland into Zambia. To meet this threat it had been decided to found 'a Party pledged to free Barotseland from UNIP rule and make it not a part of Northern Rhodesia'.[44] Only the intervention of the Resident Commissioner prevented an official declaration of Kuta support for the Sicaba (National) Party.[45] Mwanawina and his indunas remained officially neutral, though they were in fact obviously relying on the party to demonstrate to Britain mass support for secession.[46]

Three Land Rovers plus £200 in cash were given to the Sicaba Party by 'friends' of Godwin Mbikusita who had 'pledged themselves to secede Barotseland from Northern Rhodesia'.[47] It was palpably obvious to all who Mbikusita's 'friends' were;[48] the appearance in Barotseland during the last month of the campaign of Mr. George Addicott, a public relations man from Salisbury, to work for the Sicaba Party, merely confirmed what was already known.[49] Nevertheless, Lealui pretended that it was not being supported by Welensky's United Federal Party, the Sicaba supporters clearly preferring to await the results of the election before repudiating the campaign assistance.[50]

Yet no real campaign was launched for the Sicaba's two candidates, old Francis Suu, who had recently been reinstated in the Litunga's good graces, and Griffiths Mukande, the much younger and energetic treasurer of the BNG. For both Lealui and the UPF shared the illusory hope expressed by the *Northern News* that 'the lower roll Barotseland voter will make it his business to find out how his Paramount Chief would like him to vote—and do so'.[51]

Indeed, UNIP itself shared the view that Barotseland— which the *Northern News* described as 'the tribal museum-piece of Africa'[52]—was one of its weakest areas. In consequence, its propagandists, both Lozi and non-Lozi, and including Kenneth Kaunda himself, took great care to reassure the old ruling class that a UNIP government would interfere neither with the Litunga's personal position nor with Barotseland's 'protectorate' status.[53]

This was a shrewd tactic, for it revealed UNIP's awareness that it had two very different sources of support within Barotseland: the dispossessed white-collar group and the traditionalist opponents of the Litunga. Its campaign to woo both elements was virtually flawless. Its candidates were Arthur Wina, Mubiana Nalilungwe, and Dr. Masekwa Nalumango. All were university graduates, Wina was the son of the former Ngambela, and Nalumango the son of an induna. Their appeal thus lay not only to the aspiring middle classes; they offered at the same time a traditional form of leadership to the Lozi voters who respected the kingship but resented the present incumbent.

Moreover, building on its formerly illegal branches in the Protectorate, UNIP Lozi leaders from Lusaka, created an efficient election organization[54] through which they proclaimed its 'double-edged' struggle against both white domination and 'crumbling, anachronistic feudalism'.[55] The status of the Litunga and the Protectorate would remain unaltered, but Barotseland, to its own great economic advantage, would remain within Zambia. UNIP's development plans promised more schools and agricultural development centres, more and better roads, and—very rashly—a railway from Mongu to Lusaka.[56] In short, it was the essential modernizing programme which Lewanika had devised many decades earlier. Once again, through UNIP, the dynamic and educated elements of the Lozi aristocracy were offering to lead the nation out of its backwardness and isolation, with the qualification, as Ranger has pointed out, that 'the failure of the Lozi establishment to modernize and develop the country on its own meant a realization that the desired progress could only be achieved within the wider Northern Rhodesian frame-work,'[57] even if this necessitated undermining one's own Litunga.

The franchise was still qualified. It effectively included African civil servants and teachers on the one hand, indunas and headmen on the other. While UNIP ensured that a majority of the white-collar elite registered, the number of the latter group who put their names on the voters' roll fell far below the government's expectations. Not surprisingly, therefore, Arthur Wina overwhelmed Francis Suu by 1,057 votes to 65, while Nalilungwe received 688 to 69 for his ANC opponent and 42 for Mukande of the Sicaba Party.[58]

This was a stunning defeat for Mwanawina and the ruling class, and resulted in a serious breach within the traditionalist camp. Three of Sicaba's leading members, including Suu, publicly announced their resignations from the party. Already during the campaign, they acknowledged, they had discovered that

> Some of the big people and masses of the people [had] joined UNIP one by one. Eventually we found that wherever we went in Barotseland, people had become all UNIP members. Even in the Chiefs' villages, there were none on the side of freeing Barotseland from Northern Rhodesia.

Moreover, they pointed out, they had helped create the party to free Barotseland from the control not only of UNIP but of the Federal government. Yet they had discovered during the campaign that 'some of us were trying to make our party a part of the Federal Party. It was not until the last moment when we realized this, for Mr. Rabb of the Federal Party came and said all the material we used belonged to the Federal Party.' Consequently, they had decided 'in sorrow to dissolve the Sicaba Party'.[59]

Some of its members, however, refused to be dissolved.[60] The party executive was reorganized, and Ngombala Lubita, a son of one of Lewanika's daughters, became its president. Lubita had been an active UNIP supporter until December, 1962, when Munukayumbwa Sipalo, a leading Lozi UNIP official, was attacked with a petrol bomb. Virtually all Lozi in UNIP alleged that the Bemba members of the party were responsible for the incident. While the majority of Lozi in UNIP decided that they would not let themselves be pushed out of the party, and thereby allow the Bemba to dominate it,[61] Lubita and a number of others resigned in protest. He returned to Barotseland to become the president of, as he claimed, a wholly unaligned Sicaba Party opposing the incorporation of Barotseland into Zambia.[62]

The Litunga continued to give unofficial support to the party and official endorsement of its secessionist policy.[63] At the same time, however, the new UNIP–ANC coalition government of Northern Rhodesia determined to reform the BNG. To begin with, the Katengo was to become a wholly elected body, with or without the co-operation of Lealui.[64] The Kuta was outraged,[65] and four times in the following four months announced, then cancelled, dates for an election the outcome of which was no longer faced with equanimity. Indeed, UNIP's victory in 1962 had made secession seem more vital than ever, and Mwanawina succeeded in receiving another invitation from R. A. Butler for a further round of talks in London.[66] To UNIP's chagrin, Mwanawina flew to London accompanied not only by his new, strongly traditionalist Ngambela, Silumelume Siyubo, but by Mbikusita and L. K. Wilson, a Salisbury lawyer whom Mbikusita had hired to prepare the Lozi case for secession.[67]

Not even Wilson's legal expertise, however, could sway the British government. As the *Northern News* understood, after the election results in Barotseland in 1962 'Britain can only conclude that the Litunga's monarchy is an anachronism and that, like others in Africa, it must eventually yield. . . .' If this meant reneging on earlier agreements with Lewanika, political realities allowed no other solution.[68] Butler told the Litunga that Britain could not afford to finance Barotseland if it were divorced from Northern Rhodesia,[69] and the meeting therefore seemed to be a victory for UNIP.

This development clearly increased the significance of the Katengo elections, which had finally been set for 15 August, 1963. Since universal suffrage now obtained, the election would establish whether the Litunga could legitimately claim to represent his subjects in a democratic sense. 'The real issue', as the *Northern News* said, 'is the constitutional future of Barotseland.'[70] Yet the Lozi ruling class hardly bothered to run an election campaign. After an abortive alliance with ANC, Prince Ngombala Lubita had dissolved the Sicaba Party,[71] but the ruling class made no effort to establish a substitute for it. The Kuta merely approved nominees for eighteen of the twenty-five Katengo seats, thus giving UNIP eight seats at the outset by default.[72]

In contrast, UNIP's campaign was once again relatively well organized at every level. Kaunda and other cabinet ministers addressed public meetings, while voters in many villages were personally canvassed.[73] Political interest had grown remarkably in a few short years. The UNIP candidates stressed that secession would create great economic hardship; a vote for UNIP was a vote for remaining part of a free, prosperous Zambia: a nice balance of pragmatism and orthodox nationalist principle which succeeded beyond UNIP's most optimistic predictions. The party won every one of the eighteen contested seats, gaining 84 per cent of the 25,000 votes cast.[74] Not even the Boma doubted that the results were a profound blow to the secessionists.[75] Arthur Wina declared that 'If ever there was a danger of a Tshombe emerging on the Northern Rhodesian political scene, [the] elections have nipped his growth in the bud'. The Lozi people, Wina concluded, had 'shown clearly . . . their desire to have things that everybody else [in Zambia] has', including 'freedom from feudalistic or colonial rule [and] the chance of bettering their living conditions'. To this end, he called for radical reforms of the BNG and immediate discussions of 'the future of the treaties between Lewanika and the British Crown . . . [in] an independent and free Zambia'.[76]

The Litunga clearly feared these new developments. His own people having deserted him, he again turned to Europeans in his struggle against African nationalism. He began a correspondence with Patrick Wall and Roland Bell, Conservative Members of Parliament, and S. B. Cook, a Conservative lawyer in London, all known supporters of Tshombe, asking them to put pressure on their government to allow Barotseland to secede.[77] At the same time, through Mbikusita, L. K. Wilson, the Salisbury Lawyer, was invited to delve in the Lealui archives for evidence to support the ruling class's demands.[78]

As a result of his research, Wilson produced three documents. The first was a detailed record of the guarantees of Barotseland's status as set down in the several concessions signed by Lewanika, and thereafter repeatedly reaffirmed by successive Governors and Secretaries of State and enshrined in the Constitutions of 1924, 1953 and 1961.[79] The second document presented the Lozi case for a protectorate along the lines of the High Commission Territories, based on Barotseland's legal rights, its existence as a nation prior to the creation of Northern Rhodesia, the failure of the colonial government to develop Barotseland, the unsuitability of western democracy for African conditions, and the ostensible material advantages of becoming an independent protectorate.[80] Finally, Wilson produced a detailed written constitution for the new 'Protectorate of Barotseland'.[81]

Wilson's activities were conducted without undue publicity, not only to avoid provoking UNIP, but also because, after the Katengo elections, a number of the old guard had resigned themselves to the inevitability of their fate, some of them actually giving up their indunaships.[82] Indeed, Mwanawina himself apparently wished to find a *modus vivendi* with UNIP by this stage, but was deterred by the intransigence of an influential minority of extremists who still believed secession was possible; the extremists are said to have included Mbikusita, Ngambela Siyubo, the Natamoyo (Mwanawina's half-brother), and several senior indunas. In public, however, they agreed that the best tactic was to concede that secession would not be granted and called instead for a kind of semi-independent status for Barotseland which would continue to share 'common services' with Zambia.[83]

Against the traditional elite were pitted the apparently united UNIP nationalists of Barotseland and the central government. Conflict between the two sides was demonstrated immediately, when a Lozi delegation had to be chosen to meet government representatives to discuss the future of Barotseland. After an acrimonious dispute in which Hastings Noyoo of Senanga led the elected Katengo councillors out of their first session of the National Council,[84] the Council agreed that five of the thirteen Lozi delegates to the Livingstone talks would be elected members, the other eight being what the latter called 'traditionalist stooges'.[85]

The UNIP government representatives at the talks, Arthur Wina and Simon Kapepwe, were anxious that a quick agreement be reached, since they believed Britain would not allow the elections preceding full independence without Barotseland's consent.[86] They naturally looked to the UNIP Katengo councillors to co-operate with them to this end, but discovered, for the first time, that Barotseland UNIP was comprised of men who intended to be both Lozi patriots—tribalists—and nationalists. The traditionalist indunas argued, predictably, that if they were to remain part of Zambia at all, it must be on the condition of virtually complete local autonomy. Kapepwe and Wina were more chagrined to find that Hastings Noyoo's group differed only in degree, not in kind. The elected councillors wanted to be 'part and parcel of Zambia', but with Barotseland's special status remaining intact and indeed being enshrined in the Zambian constitution.

This totally unexpected development forced Wina and Kapepwe to make important concessions to the Lozi in order to preclude complete failure and the possible postponement of the national elections as a result. It was agreed that Barotseland would remain part of the wider territory and participate in the 1964 elections, but the 'final' discussion of Barotseland's relationship with independent Zambia was postponed to a later date.[87]

Returning to Barotseland, the elected councillors now determined to carry through the deposition of Ngambela Siyubo in order to replace him with an elected man. A series of furious debates in the National Council between the UNIP councillors and its traditionalist members was followed by a near-violent demonstration in Lealui against Siyubo,[88] and on 18 October he announced his resignation. The elected councillors demanded that their leader, Hastings Noyoo, become Ngambela, but the traditionalists, speaking for the Litunga, refused to consider such an appointment. The two factions eventually agreed to compromise by selecting Muleta, the chief judge of the Libonda Kuta, as acting Ngambela. Muleta, however, soon discarded his reputation for judicial impartiality and privately agreed that secession remained the only genuine hope of saving Barotseland from the nationalists.[89]

Nevertheless, the tactic in public remained one of apparent willingness to compromise. The Litunga accepted the Lusaka directive that a Working Party be established, consisting of representatives of both factions in the National Council, to make recommendations for the radical reform of the BNG. Although the two groups did reach 'a remarkable degree of agreement on most of the proposals for reform', on the critical point of the future composition of the National Council their interests widely diverged: the elected councillors demanded a majority for themselves while the traditionalists called for parity of representation between the two factions. With no obvious means to reconcile these conflicting views on the spot, both groups agreed in January, 1964, to submit the issue to Lusaka for arbitration.[90]

This was the second occasion since the Livingstone talks on which Lealui had recognized the legitimacy of the central government. For in December it had presented a memorandum setting out its ideas for the future relationship of Barotseland and Zambia for consideration by the Lusaka government. The memorandum, a revised version of L. K. Wilson's draft, expressed the wish of the Lozi rulers to 'achieve the closest possible integration with Northern Rhodesia which will permit the individuality and traditional institutions of Barotseland to remain'. This objective could be assured only if Barotseland's special status were written into the new constitution. The memorandum then proceeded to outline the precise responsibilities and prerogatives which would remain in the hands of the National Council, concluding finally with the request that the Northern Rhodesian government formally accept 'responsibility for the financial support and economic development of Barotseland'.[91] Here was the weakest point in Lealui's case for secession and UNIP's strongest bargaining counter, for the central government was then contributing some £250,000 annually to the Barotse government.[92]

Clearly if Barotseland must be associated with Zambia— and Lealui was not yet persuaded that it must—the acceptance by UNIP of these proposals would have gone far to assuage the sensibilities of the ruling class. Apparently the Litunga and his advisers did believe that a UNIP government would accede to their demands, and it was for this reason that they did not participate in the national elections of January, 1964.[93] Of UNIP's seven candidates in Barotseland—who included such sons and daughters of the traditional ruling class as Arthur Wina, Dr. K. Konoso and Princess Nakatindi—all but three won by acclamation, the others scoring resounding victories.[94]

Presumably fearing that these results would stiffen UNIP's resistance to his demands, the Litunga's thoughts returned again to total secession. During the Katengo election, UNIP leaders had accused Lealui of seeking the help of South Africa and Portugal against the nationalists. In January, 1964, Prince Ngombala Lubita—former member successively of ANC, BASMO, UNIP, the Sicaba Party and again ANC—undertook a journey apparently to determine if assistance from these sources would be forthcoming.[95] Lubita claims the initiative for the trip came from the Litunga, but the latter's private secretary claims that Lubita was the instigator.[96] In any event, it is clear that Mwanawina arranged that WNLA, the local labour recruiting agency for the Rand mines, should provide the Prince with a free air journey to Johannesburg. At that time, WNLA was recruiting some five to six thousand men annually from Barotseland for South Africa, who received there about five pounds per month.[97] Lubita carried with him a letter from the Litunga to Gemmill, WNLA's general manager in South Africa, asking that WLNA's attestation fee to the BNG be raised from 11s. 6d. to 24s. per head, an increase of about £5,000 a year, and concluding that 'it is my wish and my people's wish that we continue with our friendship as it was before'.[98]

Lubita claims to have met Gemmill in Johannesburg. Already WNLA must have been concerned that a UNIP government would repudiate its contract to recruit cheap labour in Barotseland,[99] and Lubita underlined for Gemmill the threat implied in Mwanawina's letter. As a result, WLNA agreed to raise its attestation fee as the letter requested.[100]

Lubita also claims that the Litunga wished him to visit sympathetic government officials in South Africa, Rhodesia, Portugal and France to seek financial and military aid for the Lozi ruling class. He indeed insists that from South Africa he was flown in a private plane to Paris and 'other places', but refused to divulge further details; no other source either confirmed or denied this story. But the Litunga's private secretary, Mr. Imasiku, corroborates Lubita's claim that, through WNLA, the latter met on his return journey in March, 1964, with a representative of the Verwoerd government in Katima Molilo, in the Caprivi Strip on the border of Barotseland, for the purpose of obtaining South African military and financial assistance for Barotseland. Here Lubita ended his story, but Mr. Imasiku went on to say that the South African representative agreed to station troops in Katima Molilo, preparatory to a military invasion of Barotseland for the purpose of 'freeing' it from Zambia. Mr. Imasiku in fact claims that a South African Police Depot was established at Katima Molilo immediately thereafter, but the Litunga in the end refused to endorse this bizarre scheme for making Barotseland into a Bantustan of South Africa, while Lubita decided to return once again to the UNIP fold.[101]

Now, in part because he had decided to appear reasonable and conciliatory in public, and partly because he had come to realize that the elected Katengo councillors were less dangerous than he had originally feared, the Litunga agreed to implement certain reforms in the BNG which Lusaka had decided upon after assessing the dispute between the traditionalists and the elected councillors of the Working Party. Hastings Noyoo was elected deputy Ngambela, while the twelve appointed departmental indunas were replaced by five elected councillors each in charge of a department—finance, education, social services, natural resources, and transport and communications. These five men in effect formed the Cabinet, and with the Litunga and Acting Ngambela Muleta constituted the formal ruling body in local government.[102]

After the January elections UNIP had taken sole possession of the central government, and it now seemed to have won effective control of the Barotse government as well. The next round of talks, however, made it clear once again that the elected councillors were tribalists as well as nationalists. The Lozi delegation to Lusaka, led by the Litunga, included three elected and three traditional councillors, and the central government's representatives were obviously shocked to discover that they presented a united front. The elected councillors refused to follow the party line, insisting as forcibly as the traditionalists that Barotseland would join Zambia only if its special status were recognized. In the end, it was the central government which was forced largely to capitulate. The memorandum presented at the end of 1963[103] was essentially agreed to, and Kaunda and the Litunga issued a joint communique declaring that 'Northern Rhodesia and Barotseland will go forward to independence as one country'.[104]

It was not to be so easy, however. The Litunga had insisted

that the agreement formally be incorporated into the Zambian constitution, but here UNIP drew the line. No other tribe in the territory had received so much special attention in the nationalists' advance towards full independence, and to single out the Lozi in the constitution was a flouting of UNIP's 'One Zambia, One Nation' motto to an extent the party—and particularly its Bemba members—was not prepared to accept. As a compromise, the Litunga and Kaunda agreed upon a formal treaty to be signed by the British, Barotse and Northern Rhodesian governments.[105]

It seemed, then, that UNIP was willing to conciliate the traditionalists, but that it was not prepared to tolerate the breach of party discipline by the three elected councillors at the Lusaka talks. Hastings Noyoo and his two colleagues were consequently suspended from the party for six months,[106] a punishment which offered the Litunga an obvious opportunity to consolidate the two factions in the National Council against the central government. Instead, he did precisely the opposite. Five days after the suspensions were announced, Mwanawina presented his slate of the twenty councillors which Lusaka had decided he could appoint to the 45-member National Council. Each of his nominees was a known political opponent of UNIP; eight had unsuccessfully stood against UNIP candidates in the Katengo elections of 1963, and at the top of the list stood UNIP's major *bête noire*, Godwin Mbikusita.[107]

Two of the elected councillors who had remained loyal to the national party, Saxon Liselo and Likolonga Masosa,[108] grasped this chance to reunite the UNIP councillors. On 4 May, the National Council convened, and the elected members combined to demand that seventeen of the Litunga's twenty nominees, including Mbikusita, be replaced.[109] On 5 May, the Litunga received an invitation from Duncan Sandys, who had replaced Butler as Minister responsible for Central Africa, to send a delegation to London, where Sandys and Kaunda were already conferring.[110] All the National Council members wished to accept this invitation, but they were unable to agree on the composition of the Lozi delegation. The elected councillors unitedly demanded that the delegation consist entirely of their representatives, a demand the appointed members naturally rejected. By 7 May, the Council was completely deadlocked,[111] and the Litunga announced that for internal reasons, it was impossible for him at this stage to go to London at all.[112]

This decision provoked the sending of two urgent telegrams to the Litunga, one from Roland Bell, MP, and S. B. Cook, who had been appointed as his advisers by the Conservative government, the other from the Under-Secretary of State in the Commonwealth Relations Office. Both messages strongly urged the Litunga to get his delegation to London immediately, lest at the conclusion of the independence conference with Sandys, Kaunda would demand to settle the position of Barotseland with or without the participation of Lozi representatives.[113]

On the following day, 12 May, the National Council reconvened. Given the urgency of the situation, the meeting finally agreed to a three-man delegation consisting of the Litunga, Acting Ngambela Muleta, and Deputy Ngambela Noyoo; John Wilson, the Boma officer who had been seconded to the BNG as Administrative Secretary the previous November, would accompany the delegation. The two factions also agreed that the delegation would press for an agreement along the lines reached at the Lusaka talks, and that such an agreement must be written into the new Zambian constitution.[114]

On 15 May, the Litunga and his party flew to London where they met with Sandys and Kaunda. They found that the latter was prepared to accept the Lusaka agreement, but would on no condition agree that it be entrenched in the constitution. On the advice of Roland Bell, the Conservative MP, the Lozi representatives agreed to a separate treaty. Sandys, Kaunda and Bell all explained that Britain was prepared to sign such an agreement not as a participant but only as a witness. It was clear at the time, however, and became increasingly evident in the following months, that the Lozi failed to grasp the crucial distinction. For this reason, though they were disappointed that the agreement would not be incorporated into the constitution, they considered that they had won a substantial victory.[115]

On 18 May, Kaunda and the Litunga signed 'The Barotseland Agreement, 1964', Duncan Sandys adding his signature 'signifying the approval of Her Majesty's Government'. Its purpose was to establish Barotseland's position within Zambia in place of the earlier agreement between Britain and Barotse-

land which would be terminated when Northern Rhodesia
became fully independent in October. To this end, Barotseland
was to become an integral part of Zambia with its traditional
rights preserved, and the Litunga was to retain powers over
local government matters greater than those granted to any
other chief in Zambia.[116] The reason Kaunda was prepared to
grant such privileges to the Lozi, and why he insisted on a
separate treaty rather than a clause in the constitution, is quite
clear. As Mr. Clement Zaza, UNIP's political assistant in
Barotseland, openly acknowledged a year later,

> The Barotseland London Agreement was agreed upon
> merely as a passport to enable Zambia [to] integrate.
> Barotseland and proceed to Independence as one country.
> After all, the Zambian Government has no moral obliga-
> tion whatsoever to respect or honour the said Agreement.[117]

The three Northern Rhodesian groups involved in the London agreement, then, shared contradictory hopes as to its
future implications. To the UNIP government, it was a simple
expedient which it could, if necessary, repudiate in imposing
its authority over Barotseland. To the Litunga, it was the
means to preserve the traditional prerogatives of the Lozi
ruling class. To the elected councillors, it was a further step
towards usurping the positions and privileges of the traditional
elite. There was never any doubt that, in the end, Zambia was
going to rule Barotseland. UNIP was initially prepared to allow
this process to transpire gradually and gently, but the intransigence and unco-operative attitude of both factions of the
National Council assured that it came swiftly, brutally, and
definitively.[118]

During the following five months, the internecine warfare
which raged between the elected and traditional councillors
consumed virtually all time and attention at the capital. As a
result, by the time of Zambia's formal independence on 24
October, 1964,[119] none of the reforms of the BNG demanded by
the UNIP government had been implemented. A month later,
Hastings Noyoo was elected Ngambela by the National
Council, and installed by a reluctant Litunga only after he was
seriously threatened by Sikota Wina, UNIP's Minister of Local
Government and a Lozi.[120]

The Litunga's capitulation averted an immediate confrontation between Lealui and Lusaka, but perhaps gave UNIP the false impression that its will would henceforth prevail. When, a short time later, the government announced that a Provincial Development Commission would be set up to co-ordinate development projects in Barotseland, all but five loyal UNIP members of the National Council united to protest against the decision as an infringement of the rights of the BNG under the Barotseland Agreement. It was this decision by the Council which caused Lusaka finally to lose patience with the Lozi councillors, while it made the two factions within the Council realize that their common interests outweighed their disagreements. In January, 1965, with only a handful of UNIP loyalists dissenting, the Council announced that the time was not propitious for reforming the Barotse government; indeed, the Council declared, its real objective was to make Barotseland a 'sister state' of Zambia, part of a loose federation in which the Zambian government was to pay the bills for but have no control over the Lozi.[121]

Lusaka refused to take this challenge seriously, however, and went ahead with some of the reforms which it had been openly discussing for the past months. In February, 1965, the judges (indunas) of the several Kutas were informed that as of 1 July they would fall under the jurisdiction of the Ministry of Justice, and in March the government announced that capital development projects would henceforth be carried out not through the Kutas but through the Bomas. When the chief officer of the Senanga District Local Authority was instructed to move his organization from the Nalolo Kuta to the Senanga Boma, the Mokwae of Nalolo demanded an urgent meeting of the National Council. On 28 May, with only a handful of dissenters, the Council resolved never to move the Local Authorities from their existing sites to the Bomas nor to hand over jurisdiction of Lozi judges to the Ministry of Justice. It decided to present a memorandum to the central government rejecting all further reforms and accusing it of breaking the 1964 Agreement.

UNIP could hardly tolerate such provocation much longer. Already the councillors' total absorption in political machinations had resulted in the failure of virtually all of Lusaka's development plans. In December, 1964, funds had been

H

allocated for water schemes, access roads to courts, artesian wells and agricultural drainage canals; by the middle of 1965 the Lozi authorities had not begun a single one of these projects.[122] In May, the government announced that a total of £1,500,000 was to be spent in Barotseland under its Transitional Development Plan,[123] and there was a real fear that the implementation of the various projects would be forestalled by the Council. This fear may well have had a political component too, for one could sense in the province a growing resentment against UNIP, rather than the traditional elite, for the failure of independence to bring any immediate tangible benefits.

At the Council meeting on 28 May, it had been decided to refuse all further co-operation with Lusaka—Francis Suu declared that the Lozi would 'resist to the death' any encroachment on their rights—and the Ngambela was given authority to seek widespread publicity for the grievances of the newly united elites in Lealui. In June, Zambian newspapers were rife with sensational stories of the rift between Barotseland and the UNIP government. A number of senior ministers, led by Arthur Wina, flew to Mongu, where Wina informed the Ngambela that the National Council must either co-operate or go to jail. Noyoo agreed,[124] and Wina publicly announced that the National Council had made a full apology for 'misinterpreting the Government's policy'.[125]

A fortnight later, the Ngambela openly repudiated the apology.[126] This was Lusaka's breaking point. As a direct consequence of Noyoo's statement, the government decided to introduce its Local Government Bill, abolishing the National Council and replacing it by five district councils, initially appointed by the Minister of Local Government, later to be elected.[127] 'Just Another Chief Now', headlined the newspapers,[128] and though the Litunga was promised that he would remain 'the final authority in Barotseland in all matters concerning the allocation of land', [129] this assessment was accurate.

The Litunga lost the right to appoint councillors and judges (now separate functions), his control of the Barotse Treasury, and his right to reject legislation of which he disapproved. The central government paid the salaries of the royal family and the Litunga's household staff, and the President's office itself was the source of his own annual income of £10,000.[130] In short, Mwanawina's power base was cut from under him, he was totally dependent on the men he was trying to resist, and these facts he understood completely.[131]

The reaction in Lealui was predictably furious. Chiefs and indunas gathered in the capital to discuss ways of resisting the new measures. They considered starting a new party to promote their interests,[132] and, still failing to grasp either constitutional or political realities, wrote letters to friends in London demanding the intervention of the British government.[133] Godwin Mbikusita, then working in Southern Rhodesia, was asked to return to lead the opposition; he did not do so, and if he had, the Resident Minister, Mr. Jose Monga of Southern Province, was prepared to deport him from Barotseland. Although some councillors understood that they were provoking potentially dire consequences for themselves, a vocal minority, led by the Natamoyo and Induna Luyanga, was attempting to persuade the Litunga that all was not lost.[134] Luyanga openly told me that the Lozi had many white friends in London, Washington, Katanga and Johannesburg to whom they could still appeal, and if Barotseland was to be destroyed, their friends would help them destroy Zambia in the process. Luyanga and the Natamoyo were indeed trying to convince the Litunga to write the necessary letters of appeal to these 'friends'.[135]

The government, however, was not to be deterred. It was then quite prepared, had the need arisen, simply to arrest and imprison all the dissidents. In October, 1965, President Kaunda signed the order bringing into force the Local Government Bill, and on 1 November, Sikota Wina published the statutory instruments abolishing the National Council, setting up the five District Councils, and announcing the names of their nominated members.[136] Shortly before, Parliament had approved the Chiefs Act, effectively giving the President unilateral authority to recognize or withdraw recognition from any chief in Zambia; the Litunga of Barotseland was explicitly mentioned as falling under the provisions of this Act,[137] and there then seemed no reason to doubt, first, that it would be applied if Lealui continued as a centre of opposition to Lusaka, and secondly, that Mwanawina's successor would in effect be chosen by the central government.

Yet Barotseland retained its power to influence and disturb

the Zambian body politic to a degree incommensurate with its small numbers and economic stagnation. Several factors account for its continuing dissidence and its disproportionate influence. The new alliance of the traditional and educated elites remained irreconcilably hostile to central government control. Moreover, given Lozi pride and self-consciousness together with popular disappointment with the developmental fruits of independence, it was not difficult to mobilize mass opinion against Lusaka. It was widely felt that the Lozi people had been deceived into sacrificing their traditional rulers and repudiating their heritage in return for unfulfilled electioneering promises. Moreover, resentment was perceptibly increasing against the new UNIP appointees in Barotseland, both Lozi and non-Lozi; it was impossible not to contrast their sudden, conspicuous affluence with the negligible impact which independence had made on the lives of ordinary Lozi farmers and fishermen. If indeed they were touched at all by the new order, many Lozi soon became its victims. In 1966, Sipalo, the Lozi Minister of Labour, prohibited all further recruitment by WNLA in Barotseland, thus in a single blow depriving the area of its single greatest source of cash income.

Finally, growing friction within UNIP between its Lozi and Bemba members functioned so as to exacerbate anti-nationalist sentiment in Barotseland. Undue Bemba influence in the national government was widely held to be responsible for Barotseland's continuing neglect. It was true that having four Lozi members of the Cabinet was far more than the province's population strictly warranted, but this was the President's mechanism for demonstrating that his government was ethnically balanced. When, for example, conflict of interest charges were raised against Mundia and Nalilungwe, Kaunda immediately promoted two other Lozi to replace them in the cabinet. But Mundia was not to be disposed of so easily. In March, 1966, he helped found and became leader of the United Party, a more attractive haven than the ANC for Lozi who opposed UNIP, including those miners who, having lost the opportunity to work in South Africa, were billeted by the government in a special compound on the Copperbelt.

In August, 1967, at UNIP's national conference at Mulungushi, the precariously maintained façade of party unity was publicly exposed. In elections to the party's Central Committee, Bemba and Tonga delegates joined to defeat candidates from Eastern and Barotse Province, including Arthur Wina and Muna Sipalo. The two were involved in a consequent cabinet shuffle but Sipalo initially refused to be demoted. Protesting against growing Bemba power in the party, he submitted his resignation which, he said, ought to start a 'chain reaction'.[138] However, the subsequent rumours that the Wina brothers intended to join Mundia, Sipalo, and, perhaps, the Litunga against UNIP, proved unfounded. But talk of secession continued to be widespread. Not even a five-day visit by the President to attend the 1968 Kuomboka ceremonies was adequate to assuage Lozi sensibilities. If anything, their alienation from the centre was increasing with the feeling that the Lozi cabinet ministers, by not quitting the party after their defeat at Mulungushi, had sold out Lozi interests and capitulated to Bemba domination of the government.

If UNIP's Lozi were losing their power base in Barotseland, its Bemba leaders were pleased to take advantage of the situation. Such was the hostility by this time between these two factions within the national elite that the Bemba now contrived, according to a senior member of the government,[139] to put Godwin Mbikusita in the House of Chiefs as a stepping stone to his becoming the next Litunga of Barotseland. Putative son of Lewanika, ardent secessionist, ally of Welensky, Sandys and Tshombe, the 'chameleon' to the Lozi and the *bête noire* of all Zambian nationalists—such was the man the old Bemba nationalists wished to use against their erstwhile Lozi colleagues. Presumably Mbikusita's appointment to the House of Chiefs would be taken as an indication of the rejection by the Lozi people of their own ministers. Both the latter and other cabinet members protested bitterly to Kaunda that Mbikusita must be regarded as a grave security risk in the light of his extensive white contacts in southern Africa and Barotseland's strategic geographical position. But in the face of Bemba pressure plus his own reluctance to provoke Barotseland, the President sanctioned Mbikusita's appointment to the House of Chiefs. At about the same time, Mbikusita's status as a Lozi royal was further legitimized, for the Litunga, his presumed step-brother, named him the new Natamoyo, or Minister of

Justice, in the Barotse government. The significance of the move was twofold: the Natamoyo is one of the senior titles in the traditional political system and its bearer is the only councillor of the Chief who must be of the royal family.

For both the Lozi remaining in UNIP and for the health of the nation, affairs continued to degenerate. On the Copperbelt, UNIP organizers were being thwarted in the compound set up for Lozi miners; most of the latter were sympathetic to Mundia's United Party, and tension between the two sides grew to dangerous proportions. Finally, in August, 1968, a clash between UNIP and UP supporters led to the deaths of two UNIP officials. The new party was thereupon banned and its leaders, including Mundia, were restricted. Many Lozi were convinced that it was the Bemba who were responsible for depriving them of the party they favoured.

In November, 1968, Sir Mwanawina Lewanika died; he was around eighty years old and had been head of his people for two decades. He had never yielded in the overriding purpose of his reign, the preservation of those few privileges which remained to the traditional Lozi ruling class. Of course he failed to secure this goal. Nevertheless, his impact was undeniable. His greatest monument was the extraordinary amount of vexation which his insignificant labour reserve had caused the nationalist movement. Indeed, even in death he remained a dangerous enemy. The ANC tried to make political capital by charging that UNIP had not provided the old man with adequate hospital treatment and was therefore responsible for his death.

Even more palpable, on 15 December, to the shock of most and the dismay of many, Godwin Mbikusita was installed as Mwanawina's successor, and in the presence of President Kaunda. The President had received contradictory advice from his Lozi ministers and advisers. Some believed the election was irregularly conducted and that Mbikusita ought not to be recognized. A number argued that to attend the installation ceremony was to legitimate the selection, others that it would on the contrary symbolize UNIP's control of the proceedings. Kaunda rejected the first group and compromised between the latter two: he attended the ceremony but declined to make the speech for which he was scheduled, 'apparently because of the rains'.[140]

These deliberations were not held in isolation. Four days after Mbikusita's installation, Zambia had its first election since independence. Mbikusita's appointment and Kaunda's compromise must be seen then in the perspective of campaign strategies. The real opposition to UNIP in Barotseland came from the banned United Party, functioning under the legal banner of the ANC. Its spokesmen charged that the Bemba controlled the national government, that the Lozi ministers had sold their people out, and that in consequence the development of Barotseland had been stultified. Mundia himself, though in restriction, was one of the ANC candidates, and there was clearly close collusion between ANC/UP and the local traditionalist and educated elites; the former UNIP Ngambela, Hastings Noyoo, was another ANC candidate.

As for the ruling party, it was so isolated from public opinion in the province that it blithely believed its former support still obtained. It did not. While the government was easily re-elected, ANC candidates won eight of the eleven Barotseland constituencies with 61 per cent of the votes cast. Mundia and Noyoo were both elected, and at least one of the other ANC winners was a known secessionist. Among the defeated UNIP candidates were three of the four Lozi cabinet ministers, Arthur Wina, Sipalo and Konoso—Sikota Wina was easily re-elected from his Copperbelt constituency—as well as Nali-lungwe, Sakubita, and Princess Nakatindi.[141] Moreover, the results could only be seen as an implicit endorsement of the selection of Mbikusita as the new Litunga.

The overriding factor which was responsible for a defeat of such magnitude for the ruling party is surely clear; the belief that Barotseland had failed substantially to benefit from Zambia's independence because of Bemba domination of the central government. As Lozi on the line-of-rail told me shortly after the election, only the 'de-Bembaization' of UNIP and a serious development effort can bring Barotseland back into the national fold. The importance of regaining Lozi loyalty to the concept of a united Zambia can hardly be exaggerated. In the election Southern Province returned all but one ANC candidate; much of the western and south-western borders of Zambia are thus in anti-government hands. Since ANC leaders want to stabilize relations with South Africa, since they are alleged to have received campaign funds from south of the river, and since Mbikusita's record is well-known, the threat of a black fifth-column within Zambia is far from chimerical; a white one, of course, has always existed. Here is the obvious leverage possessed by the white governments of the Southern African Complex for convincing Kaunda if not of the necessity for an actual rapprochment, at least to cease facilitating the activities of the liberation movements.[142]

To reintegrate these provinces, then, must be one of Lusaka's overriding priorities. And since the Southern Province situation is more enigmatic than that of Barotseland, it is the latter which must be the initial target area. Yet early in 1969 it seemed that the Zambian government intended to follow precisely the opposite course. According to a senior member of the government, the cabinet had already decided that the Lozi were to be punished, not placated, for their imprudence in electing 'former Johannesburg waiters' to replace 'some of the best brains in President Kaunda's former cabinet'.[143] The intention was virtually to cut Barotseland off from all public funds and all development projects, to show it in no uncertain terms that, in the President's words, 'it pays to belong to UNIP'.

Opponents of such a course of action feared, however, that it could only heighten Barotseland's sense of alienation from Zambia and concomitantly make it more susceptible to overtures from subversives within and racialists without. Indeed, Mbikusita's installation and UNIP's election defeat almost immediately revived talk in Barotseland of secession and of renewing southern African links. However, UNIP claims that the security risk is being stringently controlled. To be sure, there seems little likelihood that the defeated ministers are interested in co-operating with their dissident compatriots against the central government. Moreover, after the elections, the government stationed fifteen plainclothes intelligence officers in Lealui to maintain a close surveillance of activities there. I was told that if they uncover evidence to connect Mbikusita with those Lozi who were seeking southern African assistance, the President would use his powers to depose the Litunga.[144] Aside from this effort, it was said, 'we're going to let Barotseland stew in its own juice.' In fact, the events of 1969 proved to be even more complex than many had expected.

Barotse Province in the event received its fair share of development projects,[145] but the nation as a whole suffered from a pervasive malaise. Britain's failure to end Rhodesia's UDI embittered race relations along the line of rail and twisted the national economic priorities. Probably a majority of Zambians had failed to benefit materially since independence, while the urban areas were being flooded by unemployable school dropouts. The resulting discontent was diverted at the popular level into mindless attacks on the official opposition party, members of the Watchtower sect, the white Chief Justice, Asian traders and shopkeepers, and mini-skirts. Within the governing party, although few knew it at the time, these tensions were reflected in a growing hostility by all sections against the Bemba who, especially since the election, were deemed to have become even more ambitious and self-aggrandizing than before.[146]

The crisis dramatically came to a head in August. On the 11th, the National Council of UNIP began its annual meeting. It was an open secret that representatives from seven of the eight provinces, including a faction of the Bemba themselves, were to introduce motions of non-confidence in the nation's leading Bemba, Vice-President Kapepwe. Instead, the President took over the meeting. In a major speech, he declared that Zambia was 'virtually at economic war' with powerful vested interests in Britain, South Africa and the United States; that he had sent units of the Zambian Air Force, Army and Police to guard unspecified installations in the country; and that he was nationalizing the copper industry. Among other reforms of the party and government that he proceeded to announce was the forefeiture by the Litunga of Barotse Province of his remaining concession rights. He then abruptly terminated the meeting.[147]

On 14 August, President Kaunda told an interviewer that the South African Broadcasting Corporation had been broadcasting messages in Afrikaans to whites in Zambia promising that South African troops would intervene in the event of anti-white incidents on the Copperbelt. To preclude such a pretext for South African aggression, he announced, he was sending UNIP leaders to the Copperbelt to ensure there were no demonstrations.[148]

On 25 August, Kapepwe, who had been under strong pressure from all of his non-Bemba colleagues and from junior ministers representing all Zambian ethnic groups, announced his resignation. A few hours later Kaunda announced that, exercising his legitimate prerogative, he had abolished UNIP's Central Committee and was taking personal control of the party. He warned that divisive forces were seeking to destroy the 'very fabric of the party and the nation', and accused certain unnamed party leaders of fostering sectional interests.[149]

On the following day, the President's personal airplane crashed as it attempted to leave Lusaka. Kaunda was not aboard but the four men who were, all British, were killed; the investigating team was examining the possibility of sabotage. Later the same day he announced that he was reshuffling his cabinet and taking on several new portfolios for himself; while Kapepwe complied with the President's request to withdraw his resignation, his personal loss of power and influence was undeniable. At the same time, Kaunda unexpectedly announced that Barotse Province would thereafter be known as Western Province and that its traditional rulers would lose their authority over the area's wild life and fishing rights.[150] For the first time since independence, all eight provinces were to stand on an equal footing.

Old Bemba nationalists and old Lozi traditionalists were thus hit simultaneously. For the latter the formal blow fell in October when the government introduced a bill to cancel the Barotseland Agreement of 1964 and abolish all the rights, liabilities and obligations which attached to the Agreement. The bill was violently attacked by ANC members from Western Province[151] while eight Lozi traditionalists petitioned the President personally to drop the bill. They included such old friends of Mbikusita as Ngambela Imwaka, Suu, Lipalile and Muyangwa, and their central argument was quite sound; without the 1964 Agreement, they pointed out, the traditional Lozi leaders would never have agreed to remain part of Zambia, and the Agreement could not, therefore, now be rescinded unilaterally without breaking faith.

It was generally agreed that these indunas were speaking on behalf of the new Litunga, but from him directly there was no comment. His position was seen to be a difficult one. He had been elected to his post because he was seen as the one man who could successfully stand up to UNIP. Clearly he was failing to do so; yet he was apparently reluctant now to assume the leadership of the resistance to the central government. On 15 October the second reading of the bill was overwhelmingly passed by Parliament.[152] At the same time it passed new land tenure legislation which transferred control over the use of land from the Litunga to the state. The resulting fury in Lealui was hardly surprising. If the Litunga lost control of the land he lost everything. And this was now the case.[153]

Given the realities of African nationalism, it was predictable that the work of the British South Africa Company was completed by a black government. The formal destruction of the old kingdom of Barotseland was now total; it became merely one among eight provinces of independent Zambia. In retrospect, one can see that this was the logically necessary result of the initiative taken by Lewanika eight decades earlier. Had his vision of creating a modern state along western lines been fulfilled, the outcome might have been somewhat altered. But because the Company had decimated his empire, and because it was the policy of neither the Company nor the British government to develop modern nations in black Africa, Barotseland had long before been transformed into a backward, isolated and essentially insignificant labour reserve, comprising only one-sixth of the land mass and containing less than one-tenth of the population of Zambia.[154]

Yet it is unlikely that in the event anything could have reversed its fate. Not even larger and economically more viable kingdoms such as those of the Ganda and the Ashanti could escape the inexorable fate implicit in the nationalist creed.[155] 'One Zambia, One Nation' was irreconcilable with the continued existence of a privileged traditional elite, and the failure of that elite to attempt to accommodate itself to the new order —as Lewanika had recognized that it was necessary to do when faced with white power—assured that its formal destruction came sooner rather than later.

It was exactly eighty years since Lewanika had signed the Ware Agreement. His successors were left with nothing but their status, an unshakeable belief in the superiority and special destiny of the Lozi, the loyalty of many of their people, and their good white friends in southern Africa. A very special effort will be needed by the central government to woo the majority of Lozi back into the national fold. But it is far from clear that even if the will existed the means could be found.

At the end of 1969, President Kaunda accused South Africa of intending to use its western-supplied military equipment 'against Zambia and all other independent African countries determined to make African Independence a reality'.[156] Early in 1970 Mr. Ian Smith threatened to cut off Zambia's power supply if Kaunda's government continued to assist the 'terrorist incursions into Rhodesia'.[157] Zambia is now arming itself at great expense against the threat from the south, though one hopes its government will not have to choose between aiding the liberation movements and being attacked by South Africa. At the same time, there is to be a concerted effort in the area of rural development. The President has described 'the yawning gap between the urban and rural people' as 'Zambia's most vexing and explosive problem'.[158] But until now, most third world nations, including Zambia, have found it incomparably easier to modernize their armed forces than their peasantry. If Zambia of all African countries does not succeed in both areas, the consequences may well be felt by the entire world.

## REFERENCES

1. Harry Franklin, *Unholy Wedlock*, p. 220.

2. Mr. C. Zaza.

3. Messrs. Mbanga Mutemwa and Hastings Noyoo, who became Ngambela in 1964 representing UNIP.

4. Messrs. C. Zaza, M. Mutemwa, Noyoo and Simalumba.

5. Prince Ngombala Lubita, Messrs. N. and A. Zaza, Kapota, Mupatu and Lifunana Imasiku; *Northern News*, 19 Jan., 1960, 23 May, 1960; Clay, *Report*, 1960.

6. Mr. M. Kawana, formerly a senior induna, Sesheke Kuta; L. A. Ambanwa, Chief Judge, Sesheke Kuta; M. Timwendela, induna, Sesheke Kuta; Y. Mupatu, formerly induna, Lealui Kuta.

7. Chief Liatitima.

8. E.g., Mwendaweli Lewanika, Chief of Mankoya District, in *Monckton Commission Report*, App. VIII, Evidence Vol. 2, p. 246.

9. Under Order No. 8, Public Meetings, in BGN *Orders and Rules*, English version (Lusaka, 1957), p. 11.

10. According to Franklin, *op. cit.*, 220.

11. Induna Kawana at Sesheke told me Chief Lubinda selected him 'to go out to the poeople of his district and talk against UNIP'.

12. *Report of the Advisory Commission on the Review of the Constitution of Rhodesia and Nyasaland*, Cmd. 1148 (London, 1960).

13. Clay, *Report*, 1960

14. *African Mail*, 22 Nov., 1960.

15. *Northern News*, 3 Dec., 1960.

16. *Ibid.*, 2 Dec., 1960.

17. *Ibid.*, 6 Dec., 1960. Pratt had made the same distinction between Buganda and Barotseland earlier; see Low and Pratt, *Buganda and British Overrule*, pp. 299–300.

18. *Northern News*, 6 Dec., 1960.

19. *Ibid.*, 22 Jan., 1959, and Memorandum by Konoso in *Monckton Commission Report*, p. 70.

20. *African Mail*, 22 Nov., 1960.

21. Prince Ngombala Lubita, one of its officials.

22. *African Mail*, 27 Dec., 1960.

23. Clay, *Report*, 1960; Heath, *Report*, 1961.

24. *African Mail*, 18 July, 1961; *Northern News*, 5 April, 14 April and 22 April, 1061; Heath, *Report*, 1961.

25. *African Mail*, 13 June, 1961.

26. *Northern News*, 16 May, 1961; *African Mail*, 25 July, 1961.

27. Mr. L. Imasiku.

28. *African Mail*, 16 Jan., 1962; Chief Liatitima, Prince Lubita and Mr. L. Imasiku.

29. Mr. H. Noyoo.

30. Mr. L. Imasiku.

31. Sir Roy Welensky, *Welensky's Four Thousand Days*, (London, 1964), pp. 318, 322–3.

32. Franklin, *Unholy Wedlock*, p. 219.

33. *Ibid.*, pp. 216–22; *African Mail*, 20 Feb., 1962; *Northern News*, 26 Feb., 1962.

34. *Central African Mail* (formerly *African Mail*), 6 March, 1962.

35. *Ibid.*, 27 Feb., 1962.

36. *Ibid.*, 6 Mar., 1962.

37. *Ibid.*, 27 Mar., 1962.

38. Welensky, *op. cit.*, pp. 360–1.

39. *Northern News*, 23 April, 1962.

40. *Ibid.*, 12 May, 1962.

41. *Ibid.*, 3 May, 1962.

42. Informant 'X', a senior European official at the Mongu Boma, who asked that he not be identified.

43. See, e.g., Hall, *op. cit.*, p. 219, and D. C. Mulford, *The Northern Rhodesian Elections*, 1962, (Nairobi, 1964), p. 143.

44. Copy of letter from F. L. Suu, Y. Mupatu, and L. Mufungulwa to the Litunga, 27 Nov., 1962, in possession of Mr. Mupatu, The three men were among the founders of the new party.

45. Informant X.

46. Mr. L. Imasiku, the Paramount's private secretary.

47. Suu *et al.* to Litunga, 27 Nov., 1962, *op. cit.*

48. Messrs. L. Imasiku and Mupatu, and *Central African Mail*, 23 Oct., 1962.

49. *Central African Mail*, 23 Oct., 1962.

50. Mr. Imasiku.

51. *Northern News*, 4 Sept., 1962.

52. *Ibid.*

53. *Central African Mail*, 17 July, 1962 and 24 July, 1962.

54. Mulford, *op. cit.*, p. 90; Mr. H. Noyoo.

55. *Central African Mail*, 30 Oct., 1962. Many people of both races frequently described the Lozi system as a 'feudal' one. For the differences between European feudalism and the Lozi system, see Gluckman, *Politics, Law and Ritual*, p. 40.

56. *Northern News*, 8 May, 1962; Mulford, *op. cit.*, pp. 143–4.

57. T. Ranger, 'Tribalism and Nationalism: The Case of Barotseland', (unpublished typescript), p. 12.

58. Mulford, *op. cit.*, pp. 143–4.

59. Suu *et al.* to Litunga and the chiefs of all the District Kutas, 27 Nov., 1962, *op. cit.*

60. *Northern News*, 13 Dec., 1962.

61. Mr. C. Zaza.

62. Prince Lubita.

63. *Central African Mail*, 24 Dec., 1962.

64. Mr. Imasiku and *Central African Mail*, 29 Jan., 1963.

65. Rawlins (Acting RC), *Report*, 1963.

66. *Ibid.*, 11 July, 1963.

67. *Central African Mail*, 13 July, 1963, and Mr. H. Noyoo.

68. *Northern News*, 2 Aug., 1967.

69. Sir Mwanawina.

70. *Northern News*, 15 Aug., 1962.

71. Prince Lubita: *Central African Mail*, 23 March, 1963; *Northern News*, 1 Aug., 1963.

72. Middleton (RC) to Ministry of Native Affairs, 11 July, 1963, Boma Files, Resident Commissioners' Letters; *Northern News*, 20 Aug., and 22 Aug., 1963.

73. Mr. Mbanga Mutemwa and Chief Liatitima. The latter stood as a UNIP candidate in Sesheke District and the former was one of his campaign organizers.

74. *Northern News*, 22 Aug., 1963.

75. Rawlins (RC), *Report*, 1963.

76. *Central African Mail*, 24 Aug., 1963.

77. Informant X.

78. Mr. L. Imasiku, the Litunga's private secretary. Wilson stayed with Mr. Graebert of the Lealui PMS.

79. 'Historical Record of Assurances Given of Barotseland's Rights', undated, privately held.

80. 'The Lozi Case for a Protectorate', 1963, privately held.

81. 'Barotseland Constitution', 1963, privately held.

82. Rawlins, *Report*, 1963.

83. Informant X.

84. *Northern News*, 5 Sept., 1963.

85. *Ibid.*, and Mr. H. Noyoo.

86. *Central African Mail*, 31 Aug., 1963.

87. *Northern News*, 13 Sept., 1963; Rawlins, *Report*, 1963; Mr. H. Noyoo.

88. Rawlins, *Report*, 1963. As a result of the incipient riots, Mr. John Wilson was appointed by the Boma as Administrative Secretary to the BNG. He lived in the capital for almost a year, both to deter violence and to keep a close scrutiny on events.

89. Informant X.

90. Rawlins, *Report*, 1963.

91. Memorandum by the Barotse Government in Preparation for Negotiations with the Northern Rhodesian Government Regarding its Future Status (undated), Boma Files, Negotiations with Central Government Dossier.

92. *Northern News*, 11 June, 1965.

93. Informant X.

94. *Central African Mail*, 24 Jan., 1964. Arthur Wina defeated his opponents, e.g. 14,676 to 515.

95. Lubita alone cannot be considered a reliable source, but the fact of his journey is confirmed by Mr. L. Imasiku, personal secretary to the Litunga, and Informant X of the Mongu Boma.

96. Mr. Lifunana Imasiku.

97. Northern Rhodesian Labour Department, *Annual Report*, 1960, and Mr. Richard Bailey, WNLA Representative, Barotseland, 1950–65.

98. Lubita showed me a copy of this letter, undated, bearing the Litunga's official seal.

99. Which it in fact did in 1967.

100. Mr. Bailey of WNLA in Mongu denied this, but Lubita's claim is confirmed by Mr. Imasiku and Griffiths Mukande, Treasurer of the BNG until 1963.

101. The interviews with Messrs. Imasiku and Lubita were of course conducted separately.

102. Mr. H. Noyoo and *Northern News*, 25 March, 1964.

103. See fn. 91.

104. *Northern News*, 20 April, 1964.

105. L. K. Wilson to Litunga, 20 April, 1964, Boma Files, Negotiations with Central Government Dossier; Kaunda to Litunga, 20 April, 1964, *ibid.*

106. *Central African Mail*, 24 April, 1964.

107. Informant X and Chief Liatitima.

108. Later Political Assistant in Northern Province and Political Organizer in Barotseland, respectively.

109. Informant X.

110. *Central African Mail*, 8 May, 1964.

111. Informant X.

112. *Northern News*, 11 May, 1964.

113. Bell and Hudson to Litunga, 11 May, 1964, Boma Files, *op. cit.*; Acting RC Rawlins to Litunga, 11 May, 1964, *ibid.*

114. Minutes of an Extraordinary Meeting of the National Council, 12 May, 1964, *ibid.*

115. Mr. H. Noyoo and informant X.

116. The Barotseland Agreement 1964, Cmd. 2366, 19 May, 1964 (London, 1964).

117. Cited in Ngambela Noyoo to President Kaunda, 23 June, 1965, Boma Files, *op. cit.*, Mr. Zaza made the same comment to me.

118. I am indebted for much of the following data to Mr. John Stewart, Senior Provincial Local Government Officer from Oct., 1964, to Dec., 1965. He was the representative in Barotseland of the Ministry of Local Government, under the aegis of which most of the reforms were carried out.

119. A dispute of major proportions which was settled literally on the eve of independence hinged directly on conflicting interpretations of Lozi history. The new government won control of the country's mineral rights from the British South Africa Company at a cost substantially less than the Company had initially demanded (see Hall, *Zambia*, pp. 230–4).

Much of the Company's case rested upon its concessions with Lewanika which were deemed to cover the area of the Copperbelt, a claim quite properly disputed by the Zambian government (see *The British South Africa Company's Claims to Mineral Royalties in Northern Rhodesian* [Lusaka, 1964]). This study has earlier shown that Lewanika himself never claimed jurisdiction over the area that became the Copperbelt. In 1905, however, the Administration unilaterally shifted the boundary between North-Western and North-Eastern Rhodesia to the east. The Copperbelt thereby fell under the concessions granted by Lewanika which allowed the Company full mineral rights outside of the reserved area (see above, chapter 4). One may like to consider it poetic justice that the successful assault on the Company was led by the Lozi Minister of Finance, Arthur Wina.

It should be added that the Company, over the previous few years, had gone out of its way to ingratiate itself to Lealui. In 1960 it began donating apparently unsolicited and condition-free annual grants of £5000 to the Barotse Treasury for 'development purposes' (*African Mail*, 1 Nov., 1960). There is no evidence that this grant was given as an inducement to Mwanawina to grant mineral rights to the Company in an area in which it was interested. though in 1963 he did finally concede to the Company prospecting rights in the Luena Plains (Rawlins Report, 1963). Perhaps the grant was donated merely as a gesture of friendship, a gesture reciprocated on behalf of the Lozi by L. K. Wilson. For it was part of his legal opinion that Lewanika did have jurisdiction over the Copperbelt area, and that the Company accordingly had a legal right to the minerals in that area (*Central African Mail*, 31 Aug., 1963). This decision did little to improve relations between the traditionalists and the nationalists.

120. *Northern News*, 21 Dec., 1964.

121. Mr. Stewart.

122. *Ibid.*

123. *Central African Mail*, 14 May, 1965.

124. Mr. Stewart.

125. *Northern News*, 10 June, 1965.

126. *Ibid.*, 29 June, 1965.

127. Mr. Stewart.

128. *Zambian Mail* (formerly *Central African Mail*), 3 Sept., 1965.

129. John Stewart to the Litunga, 24 Sept., 1965, privately held.

130. *Times of Zambia* (formerly *Northern News*), 22 Sept., 1965.

131. Ngambela Noyoo to John Stewart, 20 Sept., 1965, privately held.

132. Prince Ngombala Libuta.

133. Mr. L. Imasiku; also Minutes of a meeting between Mr. John Stewart and 55 Chiefs and Indunas at Lealui, 27 Aug., 1965, taken by myself.

134. Mr. Imasiku.

135. *Ibid.*

136. *Times of Zambia*, 30 Oct., 1965.

137. Government of Zambia, Act No. 67 of 1965, 4 Oct., 1965.

138. *Times of Zambia*, 8 Sept., 1967.

139. Who for obvious reasons asked to remain anonymous.

140. *Times of Zambia*, 16 Dec., 1968.

141. *Zambia News*, 22 Dec., 1968; ANC received 47,964 votes, UNIP 30,242.

142. See, *inter alia*, Giovanni Arrighi and John S. Saul, 'Nationalism and Revolution in Sub-Saharan Africa', in R. Milliband and J. Saville, (eds.), *The Socialist Register, 1969* (London, 1969).

143. These revealing phrases are from an editorial in the *Times of Zambia*, 23 Dec., 1968.

144. In February, 1969, an ANC member of parliament from Barotse Province referred to rumours that the government intended to overthrow the Litunga at the Kuomboka ceremony in March (*Times of Zambia, 19 Feb., 1969*). He was then fiercely criticized by government members and not permitted to enter the chamber until he apologized, which he did, stating that he had been referring to 'unsubstantiated rumours', (*Ibid.*, 21 Feb., 1969).

145. I am grateful to Mr. Robert Molteno of the University of Zambia for pointing out to me that my pessimistic predictions were inaccurate in this regard; see my 'Zambia, Barotseland and the Liberation of Southern Africa', *Africa Today*, Aug.–Sept., 1969.

146. See Richard Hall, 'An Altered Alter Ego', *Guardian Weekly*, 28 Aug., 1969, and J. D. F. Jones, 'Pressures Facing Kaunda', *The Standard* (Tanzania), 30 Aug., 1969.

147. *The Times* (London), 13 Aug., 1969.

148. *Ibid.*, 14 Aug., 1969.

149. *Montreal Star*, 26 Aug., 1969.

150. *The Times* (London), 27 Aug., 1969.

151. *Times of Zambia*, 10 Oct., 1969.

152. *Ibid.*, 16 Oct., 1969.

153. *Zambia Mail*, 28 Oct., 1969.

154. As Cranford Pratt had observed as early as 1958, Barotseland

'has none of the influence or power *vis-à-vis* the Central Government which Buganda enjoys because of her dominant position economically, politically, and culturally within Uganda'; Low and Pratt, *Buganda and British Overrule*, p. 299.

155. The tragedy of Biafra needs no further underlining here.
156. *Times of Zambia*, 12 Dec., 1969.
157. *Globe & Mail*, (Toronto) 30 Jan., 1970.
158. *Zambia Mail*, 14 Dec., 1969.

# SOURCES

# A. A Note on Sources

This book has been based on both oral and written sources, though the balance between the two has been uneven. The period up to about the middle 1930s is based largely on written sources, supplemented by oral testimonies; for the final three decades, the reverse is on the whole true. Nevertheless, for the latter period, critical data was obtained from newspapers, the annual reports of the Provincial Resident Commissioner, the PMS archives in Sefula, and the Boma Files in Mongu. In fact, these written sources more substantially complemented oral data for the final thirty years than Lozi testimonies supplemented the written records for the earlier period. Indeed, it is probably true that, with one exception, Lozi informants did not qualitatively add to the information which was extracted from the written sources.

Significantly, the exception was an eyewitness to the events of 1884–5 and 1888 in Sesheke, Mr. L. B. Kalimukwa, younger brother of Sitwala Mulanziani, who supported Mataa against Lewanika during the rebellion of 1884–5. Similarly, the reason why Lozi informants proved so much more valuable for the later period was because most of them were eyewitnesses of and often participants in the events they discussed. To be sure, the accounts of participants are bound to be highly biased—not least when the interviewer is a relatively unfamiliar white man—and must be scrutinized very rigorously. Nevertheless, there can be no question that, in my experience, the testimonies of eyewitnesses proved infinitely more fruitful than what Vansina definies as 'oral tradition, proper'—hearsay accounts of the past.[1]

The Lozi, perhaps because they consider themselves a superior people, are very conscious of their history. A Lozi house servant working for a white trader or official in Mongu knows the names of his past Kings and their Ngambelas in a way that, for example, a middle-class Canadian would not recall the names of Canada's prime ministers or governors-general. Yet their knowledge is tightly circumscribed. Even amateur historians such as Messrs. Simalumba, Mupatu and Newo Zaza were unable (or unwilling) to shed light on a number of important questions. Neither they nor any other Lozi informant had ever heard of Silva Porto, and had minimal knowledge of the Helmore–Price expedition of 1860, Livingstone, Serpa Pinto, and Westbeech. More importantly, their knowledge of

231

the internal politics of the course was superficial. They were usually unable to explain the conflicting interests of various factions, and indeed, aside from those situations in which there was an open dispute within the National Council—such as during the negotiations for the Lochner Concession in 1890—tended to speak of the ruling class as a monolithic entity.

There seem to be several explanations for this superficial level of knowledge (if, again, we may assume it was not simply a function of their distrust of the alien interviewer). Partly it may be a result of the highly centralized nature of the Lozi state, wherein oral tradition is passed down through the members of the ruling class, and in consequence is the story of those who have been victorious; this of course is hardly a unique phenomena, as any historian of Europe can attest. Secondly, oral tradition, one is forced to conclude, recalls largely that which remains important to the present generation. Virtually any Lozi can testify to the autochthonous nature of the Lozi kingdoms, an interpretation which legitimizes the right of the present ruling family to hold office. For, although it is impossible to quantify, I believe that the large majority of Lozi in Barotseland are proud of their kingship and their heritage. Moreover, Coillard is remembered rather than Westbeech, in part of course because he lived for fifteen years longer and actually taught the fathers of several of my informants, but also because the PMS continues as an important institution in the lives of many Lozi. George Middleton, who failed, is barely recalled. For the same reason, informants recalled the Lochner Concession but had only the dimmest recollection of the Ware Concession of 1889. Again, to most Lozi, after 1890 the important political events were not the internecine conflicts within the ruling class but the united front of all Lozi against the onslaught of the Company's administrators.

In the same way, Lozi institutions which have disappeared are no longer remembered. Gluckman places great emphasis on the important role of the *makolo*—the non-territorial political sectors— in pre-twentieth century Lozi history. He indeed claims that Lewanika's attempt to reinstitute the *makolo* between 1878 and 1884 was one of the key reasons for his overthrow.[2] I have accepted this argument, even though no Lozi informant volunteered information about the *makolo*, and few of them could describe it when asked directly. Even in 1941, Gluckman observed that 'Older people recognize their attachment to their hereditary sector head . . . but some young men do not know to which sector they belong'.[3] Today, not even the old men know their sector, and I believe the reason is this: though the *makolo* system had not functioned since the nineteenth century, a number of indunas still bore the titles of *makolo* heads in 1941 when Gluckman began his research. Six years later, as part of the government's enforced programme of reforms of the Barotse government, these titles were abolished since their bearers had no obvious function in the BNG. Two decades later, the entire concept of the sector system was forgotten by Lozi informants. In 1965, the traditional National Council was abolished by the UNIP government. It is not at all inconceivable that students who in the future try to record Lozi traditions—Lozi students not excluded—will find that their informants will know as little about the Council as mine did about the *makolo*.

Finally, oral tradition has been greatly influenced—and it is perhaps not too much to say corrupted—by Adolph Jalla of the PMS's *History of the Barotse Nation*, first published in 1909. More like a Lozi bible than a conventional history, it may not unfairly be considered an official document of the ruling class and the PMS. His informants were Lewanika, Ngambela Mokamba and the senior indunas of the Lealui Kuta, and Jalla acknowledged that 'The history was read to the Kuta before it was published. It is wholly approved by the Kuta.'[4] As Charles White, a serious student of Zambian ethnohistory, has written:

> Lozi traditions as recorded by Jalla are in general a disappointing source of ethnohistorical data. They provide no corroboration for cross-references from other traditions, and in fact are in contradiction to them; they contain an unusual amount of miraculous fairy tales in comparison with analogous traditions. . . . One may suspect that these traditions involve an unusual degree of manipulation of history for reasons of dynastic prestige, since so little real history is provided in them. . . .[5]

In short, according to Jalla, Lewanika was the direct descendant of the first Lozi King who was the son of God.

At the same time, the *History* is tendentious as regards the PMS as well as the royal family. Referring to the strife and instability following Lewanika's return to the throne in 1885, Jalla comments:

> It really seemed as if the nation wished to commit suicide. But no. The Lord of pity intended to save it by bringing to it the Gospel of peace and love. In March 1886, the King of Kings sent his servant François Coillard to Barotseland, and through him the country began to be saved.[6]

The damage Jalla has done to attempts accurately to reconstruct Lozi history through oral tradition is incalculable. His book has

been read by every literate Lozi in the past half century. On numerous occasions I found informants using phrases taken directly from
Jalla. The members of the Sesheke Kuta frequently referred to their
copy in Silozi during my interview with them. One could not
always be sure whether this dependence on Jalla was not merely a
device to keep anything but the authorized version from the interviewer. At times, I sensed that this was so, but on several occasions
I was convinced that the informant had little else to relate. Most
Lozi are pleased that Jalla seems to confirm that their royal family
is directly descended from the son of god. But even the most sophisticated of them accept that murder and bloodshed were commonplace
after the 1885 counter-rebellion, information which Jalla received
not from the royal family but from the semi-hysterical reports of
his colleague, Coillard.

To be sure, Coillard's voluminous outpourings cannot be over-
looked by the historian. From 1884 to 1890 his journals and letters
stored in Paris provide the only regular source of written observations about Barotseland. Since they had never previously been used,
one expected them to be the key evidence for the period. Unfortunately for the historian, however, they epitomize what Gray has
called the 'uncomprehending comments of European observers' of
African life during the last half of the nineteenth century.[7] Nor do
his unpublished journals and diaries go far to adding to the information which was provided in *On The Threshold of Central Africa*. It is
of great interest that in 1878, when he was still a supplicant hoping
for permission to establish a mission in Barotseland, Coillard's
comments on Lozi life and society were on the whole favourable.
This, I believe, is because he wanted to be able to prove to his friends
in Europe, upon whom he had to rely for financial backing, that
Barotseland was a fruitful area for mission work. Immediately upon
his return in 1884, however, having found his initial finances in
Europe and believing he was now welcome in the country, his
point of view dramatically shifted. 'I have studied heathenism at
close quarters in Basutoland as among the Zulu and other tribes',
he wrote, 'but here it surpasses all conception. . . . [Here one finds]
all that is hideous and odious in paganism. . . .'[8]

This was before the rebellion, before the bloodshed and murder.
The explanation for this *volte face* lies, I believe, with Coillard rather
than with the changed circumstances in Barotseland. For now that
his mission had been established, he had to demonstrate to his
sponsors in Europe the vital necessity for continuing his crusade to
end what he considered the 'savagery' and immorality of the Lozi.

Sharing, to begin with, the prejudices of most Europeans in

Africa during this period, needing to prove his indispensability in bringing 'civilization' to the heathens, Coillard's perspective of Lozi life and politics was no more detached and impartial than that today's social scientists. Nor did the circumstances of the Lozi political scene create a climate in which he felt sufficiently comfortable to begin providing a less distorted view of the situation. Coillard's time in the Barotse Valley may roughly be divided into two: 1885 to 1893, when he feared that the mission would be ejected from the country; and 1894 to his death in 1904, after Lewanika determined that the mission was to remain. During the first period, Coillard could see nothing but the machinations of what he unrevealingly called 'the pagan conservative party'; it was led by induna Nalabutu, whose motives and interests he never understood beyond the fact that the 'party' was hostile to the mission and to British protection upon which the PMS had begun to rely for its safety. At the same time, he consistently referred to Lewanika contemptuously as a 'weather-cock', believing him weak and labile, wholly refusing to see that the King was caught in an impossible position between the factions in the Kuta. During the latter period, Coillard and the King developed a warm, personal relationship. Lewanika, however, refused to the end to convert to Christianity, and Coillard's disappointment was so profound that once again he allowed his personal prejudices to colour his observations. So bitter was he, in fact, that he opposed Lewanika's trip to England in 1902,[9] almost certainly for vindictive reasons. From first to last, therefore, his role, as Gann has said, was that of 'the self-confessed "Micah" and moral critic of the Barotse and their ways'.[10]

The obvious question follows, can any of Coillard's data be relied upon? The answer seems to be that it may be used with the utmost caution in two ways: first, by checking it against Lozi traditions and other contemporary written sources; and secondly, by attempting to place his comments in their proper perspective. For example, we may take it that the 'pagan conservative party' was that faction in the Kuta which feared that Lewanika would collude with his white allies, including the missionaries, to limit the powers of his traditional advisers. Similarly, we can see that Lewanika's erratic attitude towards the mission was a product of his insecurity, caught between those indunas who opposed British protection and his belief that he needed Coillard to establish and maintain communication with the British government.

Nevertheless, the problems remain difficult Westbeech and Coillard, for example, both claimed to be playing a key role in Sesheke at the end of 1885, yet neither of them ever refers to the presence of the other. Frank Lochner's interpretations of Lozi political problems obviously came direct from Coillard. Middleton was wholly hostile to the Company. And oral tradition is unable to illuminate most of the problems of interpretation which result.

Nor were Coillard's missionary colleagues more forthcoming. Their letters from Barotseland, held in the mission's Paris headquarters, were clearly intended for publication in the several PMS journals. Their contents, in consequence, were intended not so much to edify their readers as to sustain their enthusiasm for contributing funds. They largely eschewed matters political, concentrating instead on the health and welfare of the missionaries and their families, financial problems of the mission, the latest baptism, or any recrudescence—real or imagined—of 'primitive heathensim' which might be the latest gossip on the mission stations. Since there were entire years when the Paris archives' files turned up not a single piece of new or relevant information, their circumscription by a fifty-year rule can hardly be considered critical to the historian.

Like those of the mission, the records of the government self-evidently reflect the interests of their writers. Since Barotseland–North-Western Rhodesia loomed relatively large in the eyes of Rhodes and the Company from about 1889 to about 1905, there is a large quantity of official records for this period, which are important in establishing the relationship between the King and his white overlords even if they provide few insights into local politics in Barotseland. By 1905, however, with Company authority effectively established, interest in the Lozi as such abruptly declined. 'The days of great events at the Zambesi are probably past', a missionary understood. 'We have come to 'the day of the small things'.'[11] As Lewanika and the Lozi lost their earlier role as 'the centre on which the successful development of the north depended . . . Barotseland was bound to sink more and more into the political and economic background'.[12] The consequence of the consolidation of white rule for the historian of Barotseland as of many other African peoples[13] was simply the dwindling number of political reports produced by government and Company officials; even a perfunctory glance at the indices of the African (South) volumes of the Colonial Office verifies how few are the rewards to be gleaned from such sources.

Similarly, reports from district officers tended to concentrate on local administrative problems such as taxation, new buildings for the Boma, and the like, to the exclusion of ongoing political issues. A number of crises—or, often, rumours of crises—at the capital produced further material, such as the alleged attempts to overthrow Lewanika in 1905 and 1911, and Yeta's prolonged dispute with George Lyons from 1919 to 1924. But such incidents were very much the exception, and in any event created the impression that the history of Barotseland consisted of a more or less regular series of crises and conflicts.

I have deliberately emphasized the inadequacies of both the oral and written sources for the period until about World War II. I hope it does not follow that no reconstruction of Lozi history before 1939 is therefore possible; it does follow that much of that reconstruction must be tentative, and that many questions must remain unanswered. Nevertheless, for all its inadequacies, the quantity of material from which to work is relatively large, however dubious its quality. All of it had to be analysed with rigorous care, cross-checking wherever possible the evidence of the various sources.

The evidence for the years from the war to the present is considerably more valuable, for three reasons. As has already been said, the testimonies of observers of or participants in Lozi politics since, say, the attempted coup against Yeta in 1937, were detailed and indispensable, at times indeed even indiscreet. Secondly, I was allowed access to the files in the Mongu Boma which had not yet been deposited in the National Archives in Lusaka. These contained a number of dossiers throwing great light on Yeta's forced abdication, the machinations involved in the dismissal of Ngambela Wina, the activities of the Mongu African Association, and the attempts by the Lozi ruling class to resist integration with Zambia.

Thirdly, I was able to see copies of reports which had been sent from Barotseland to Paris by the missionaries from about 1935 to 1959. These reflect the critical role played by simple chance in the historians's task. Many of the PMS missionaries were politically indifferent. The writer of these reports, however, J. P. Burger, was highly politically oriented, and always kept *au courant* with affairs in the capital through his unique role as a friend of the Boma, the ruling class, and the black intelligentsia. This role is clear in his letters, and was confirmed to me by his colleague, Etienne Berger. Burger, for example, provided information about the attempt to overthrow Yeta in 1937 which I found nowhere else; his data, combined with the testimonies of a number of alleged participants, made possible a coherent—and perhaps even an accurate—reconstruction of the event.

Similarly, he exposed the collusion between Lealui and the Boma in the appointment of the Rawlins Commission of 1957, the purpose of which was to justify the *status quo*. We can now see that the failure of the Commission to lead to substantial reforms in the Native Government helped force conservative opponents of Mwanawina into the hands of UNIP. Yet the very existence of the Commission is barely recalled by most Lozi, for reasons already implied: it resulted in no positive action, so there is little to remember about it any longer.

There is a second inadequacy in the testimonies of eyewitnesses and participants. They too lacked a proper perspective, and were unable to see the larger themes and currents emerging from particular incidents or ongoing events. Thus I found among my Lozi informants little grasp of the impact on African self-consciousness of the Second World War or of the migrants who were returning home from their awakening experiences on the Witwatersrand mines. Here it was European informants—missionaries—who were able to point out this impact since they were more alive to changes taking place in their adopted society.

Finally, no historian can begin to understand Barotseland's past without a thorough grounding in the many works of Gluckman published as a result of his field work in the 1940s. Gluckman, unfortunately, has never himself written a general history of Barotseland, though his works are replete with allusions to the past. It is difficult to know what kind of history he would have produced, for many of his informants were members of the ruling class. Gluckman freely acknowledges in conversation what he rarely states in his books: that he was treated by the Lozi as a *mulena*—'lord'—and that one of his chief assistants was Mwendaweli Lewanika, half-brother of the present Litunga, who later became chief of the Mankoya Kuta and, as I saw during my time in Lealui, one of the fiercest traditionalists in the ruling class. Moreover, as an American Scholar[14] and I both discovered, many Lozi today consider that Gluckman received a great deal of false and inaccurate information, and that the 'truth' was not revealed to him. It must also be pointed out that Gluckman does not make it clear in his books that the largest proportion of his field work was done in unique circumstances, that is, when Yeta was paralysed and the Ngambela was acting as Paramount Chief. His reconstruction of the Lozi political structure was consequently largely derived from hearsay accounts rather than from his own observations.

Nevertheless, one would very much have liked to have had Gluckman as an informant for the decade of the 1940s. He was in close touch with the Boma and with the ruling class, and must possess considerable knowledge of the period. Precisely how much he knows, however, cannot be deduced from his writings. For example, he writes: '. . . British insistence on reforming their [Lozi] administration in the interests of efficiency and economy has appeared to the people as an attack on the 'house of kingship' itself. The councillors who gave way to this attack have been discharged by the whole nation, after the death of the Paramount Chief who agreed to the reforms.'[15] The reference of course is to the dismissal of Ngambela Wina and Francis Suu by Mwanawina when he succeeded Imwiko in 1948. The point is that the interpretation is that of the ruling clique, and, as we have argued in chapter seven, Mwanawina's reasons for dismissing the two men were in fact personal rather than constitutional. Whether Gluckman offers this interpretation because he believed the rationalizations of his ruling-class informants, or because he was using a specific historical incident to illustrate an analytical generalization, is not known; perhaps he will yet produce the work which will give us the answer.

Again, one must reiterate that while this brief analysis of my sources has deliberately emphasized their inadequacies, it does not necessarily follow that no valid reconstruction of Lozi history is possible. All sources, after all, are biased, written as well as oral, those dealing with England as well as those concerning Zambia. This chapter has tried to indicate the peculiar nature of the biases of the sources available for writing the history of a part of Africa. It is also clear that the next necessary step for a more intensive study of Barotseland's history must be a more concerted effort to collect oral tradition than I was able to do, and as Roland Oliver has said, 'it is obvious that this is something which will be done mainly, and done best, by Africans themselves'.[16] And, of course, Dr. Mutumba Bull of the University of Zambia is already active in this area.

In the meanwhile, a pattern emerges from the general question of how written European and oral Lozi sources have complemented each other in the writing of this book. For the cumulative effect of Lozi testimonies was to evoke a qualitatively different interpretation of the main themes and problems in the modern history of Barotseland from that suggested by the written sources.

From the latter, one conjures up an image of a chaotic, savage society, which is saved from itself by Christianity, the Company and the Queen; it then exists contentedly for more than half a century in its isolation as a 'living museum', until peace and harmony are disrupted in the 1960s by 'outside agitators'.

The Lozi picture is substantially different. A wise King, perceiving the significance of the Scramble, takes the initiative in requesting British protection. He is deceived into 'selling' his country instead to a commercial company, which deprives him of most of his customary powers and his country of its empire. When Britain finally assumes direct overrule, the new King requests the restoration of the powers stolen from his father, but in vain. Here Lozi interpretations diverge. Opponents of UNIP saw the refusal to allow Barotseland to secede from Zambia as the final betrayal by Britain of its treaties with Lewanika. Nationalist supporters in the middle 1960s saw Mwanawina as a reactionary, refusing to allow the Lozi to take their proper places as leaders of a developing, progressive Zambia as the great modernizer, Lewanika, would have wished.

In a sense, both Lozi interpretations are valid. The European view distorts reality beyond recognition. As with that of most African peoples, the history of the Lozi cannot be reconstructed on the basis of the writings of Europeans alone, and historians rejoice that, across the larger part of the continent, it is no longer being attempted.

## REFERENCES

1. Jan Vansina, *Oral Tradition: A Study in Historical Methodology*, (trans. by H. M. Wright, London, 1965), pp. 20–1.

2. Gluckman, *The Ideas in Barotse Jurisprudence*, pp. 69–70.

3. Gluckman, *Economy of the Central Barotse Plain*, p. 98.

4. Jalla, *History of the Barotse Nation*, introduction.

5. White, 'The Ethnohistory of the Upper Zambesi', *African Studies*, Vol. XXI, No. 1, 1962, p. 12.

6. Jalla, *op. cit.*, p. 52.

7. Richard Gray, 'East Africa Without the Whites', review article in *Race*, Oct., 1964. Vol. vi, No. 2, p. 162.

8. Coillard, Journal, 4 Sept., 1884, and *Threshold*, p. 150.

9. Coillard, Journal, 30 Jan., 1901.

10. Gann, *History of Northern Rhodesia*, p. 30.

11. *News from Barotseland*, No. 34, May, 1908, p. 1.

12. Bradley, 'Statesmen: Coryndon and Lewanika', *African Observer*, Vol. iv, No. 5, Sept., 1936, pp. 53–5, Sept., 1936, pp. 53–4.

13. Barnes, e.g., met precisely the same difficulty in attempting to reconstruct the modern history of the Fort Jameson Ngoni; see Barnes, *Politics in a Changing Society*, p. 116.

14. Dr. Philip Silverman of the Department of Anthropology, City College of New York. It should be said that Silverman also shrewdly suggests that Lozi are probably now saying the same thing about him and me. See his *Local Elites and the Image of a Nation: The Incorporation of Barotseland within Zambia*, (unpublished Ph.D. thesis, Cornell University, 1968).

15. Gluckman, *Seven Tribes*, p. 39.

16. R. Oliver, 'After the Oxford History', SOAS Seminar Paper, 27 Oct., 1965, p. 7.

# B. ORAL SOURCES

## (i) *Lozi informants (data to November 1965)*

### L. A. AMBANWA

Born 1896 at Lealui. Attended Lealui PMS school under Adolph Jalla. Father, Akatama, was induna at Lealui. Mother, member of royal family, sister of late chief Lubinda, son of King Lewanika. Became *silalo* induna 1934–6 then transferred as induna to Mwandi Kute, Sesheke District. 1964 became Chief Judge, Mwandi Kuta.

### MUIMUI ANAKANDI

Born 1901 in Lealui. Father was induna Namamba in Lealui from 1875 until his death in 1931. Educated Sefula PMS school for five years. 1925 became Head Teacher at Loatile (Lealui) PMS school. 1929 appointed induna Nambayo at Lealui. Lost title after alleged implication in plot against Yeta in 1937. Returned to his village. 1963 appointed by Mwanawina as one of the nominated members of the Barotse National Council.

### MUBUKWANU MATAA IMANDI

Born 1905 in Lealui. Father, the grandson of Mulambwa's grand-daughter, was induna in Lealui and Ngambela Mataa, 1921–9. Lewanika sent him to PMS schools in Basutoland for four years and then to Zonnebloem College, Cape Town, where he reached the equivalent of GCE. Returned 1917 as interpreter and secretary to Yeta and the National Council until 1929, when both he and his father were dismissed after being acquitted of a murder charge and they returned to their village. 1941, was recalled to Lealui by Ngambela Wina to rejoin the Kuta. Appointed Labour induna for Barotseland, 1943. 1945, Imwiko appointed Imandi to be one of the Lozi members of the African Representative Council and promoted to Induna Inyamawina. 1948, made Education Induna for Barotse-land and remained with the African Representative Council until 1950. Later promoted to Induna Imandi. Resumed his Education post in 1957 until April, 1965, when Departmental Indunas were abolished. Several times in 1963 and 1964 represented Lozi ruling class in negotiations with UNIP government.

### LIFUNANA AKABESWA IMASIKU

Born 1921 in Nalolo, son of Akabeswa Imasiku, a Seventh Day

Adventist school teacher who married Iliayamupu, daughter of Muyabango, daughter of Lewanika. His father became Ngamebela to Mwanawina, 1956–62. Lifunana Imasiku sent to SDA schools in Northern Rhodesia to Standard VI, then the SDA Training College in Bulawayo to Form II and stayed there for a further two years training teachers. 1942, returned as Head Teacher to SDA school at Liumba Hill. 1945–8, employed by Northern Rhodesian government. 1951, the Paramount Chief requested that he be transferred to the Barotse government as assistant private secretary to Mwanawina. After Daniel Mukoboto's mysterious death in 1961, Imasiku succeeded as Mwanawina's private secretary.

### INAMBAO INDOPU

Born about 1895 in Senanga, related to the royal family. Maternal grandfather was the brother of Lewanika's mother. Father was a Nalolo induna. Sent to Senanga PMS school until 1914. Became a house servant in Salisbury 1915–7. Returned to Senanga and worked as furniture maker. 1928 built a store for a European and started wood carving. The King appointed him to an indunaship and made him official royal carver.

### LISULU BATUKE KALIMUKWA

Born during Sipopa's reign about 100 years ago. Son of Kalimukwa Mulanziani, senior representative induna at Sesheke, who was succeeded by his eldest son, Sitwala Mulanziani. 1885 Lewanika returned from Mashi and Lisulu escaped with his brother Sitwala to Matokaland in the Southern Province. 1888 they returned seeking revenge but were driven back. Sitwala killed by the Ndebele and Lisulu was taken as slave by them. Escaped during the Ndebele uprising against British South Africa Company, 1896, and returned to Barotseland in company with Coryndon's band in 1897. Lewanika forgave him and he was allowed to retire to village Siwela near Sefula and has since been supported by relatives.

### J. K. KAPOTA

Born 1902 in Mabumbu near Mongu, son of village headman and *silalo* induna. Sent to Mabumbu PMS school, 1913–8, to standard III. Then spent four years at Sefula Teacher Training School to Form I. Taught at Luwamba Mission for one year and then joined the BSA Police in Southern Rhodesia for two years. Then worked as a store assistant in South-West Africa for eighteen months. Returned home in 1927 and taught for a year at Mabumbu school. Joined the government service as Boma clerk and court interpreter. 1947 appointed by Imwiko as induna Luyanga in Lealui, but after differences with Mwanawina, he resigned or was dismissed in 1951. Again became Boma clerk in Mongu, where he is still employed.

## MUTAMBEKWA KAWANA

Born c. 1888 in the Sesheke district. Father sent by Sipopa to be representative induna at Sesheke soon after the Kololo were overthrown in 1864. Sent to PMS school to standard II, then worked on the railways in Bulawayo for five years. Returned to Barotseland, then 1916 went to Livingstone for seven years until his father died and he returned to Sesheke and was made an induna. Later promoted to one of the senior titles in the Kuta. He retired in 1965. A relatively early supporter of UNIP.

## DANIEL KASINA KENDALA

Born 1921 in Yuba village near Limulunga. PMS schools to standard III. 1942, Jeanes School, Mazabuka, to standard VI. Joined Rhodesia Railways, Bulawayo, as porter, then assistant conductor. 1953, promoted to assistant train inspector. Father died 1954 and he returned to Barotseland to succeed as Mwene (Chief) Kendala— one of the two chiefs of the Mbunda living in Barotseland. Has since then been President of several minor Kutas, and also sits on the National Council in his capacity as Mbunda Chief. Considered a chief of the Lozi royal family.

## KAFUNDUKA MUBUKWANU LIATITIMA

Born 1902 in Lealui. A direct descendant of King Mulambwa. Silumelume, who was king after Mulambwa, was his great grandfather. His father was chief councillor of Lukulu Kuta. Educated to standard IV at PMS school, Mabumbu. 1922 joined his father at Lukulu and in 1925 succeeded him as Chief of Lukulu. Allegedly implicated in plot in 1937 against King Yeta and deprived of his chieftainship. Became farmer until 1944. Then dealt in various trading ventures until 1950, when he opened a store in Sesheke, which he left in 1960 to become an organizer of UNIP. Returned 1962 to Barotseland to campaign for Nalilungwe and Wina. Successfully stood for Sesheke in 1963 in the National Council (Katengo) election. Later appointed to Zambian House of Chiefs. Widely known as 'the uncle of UNIP'.

## MOBITAMWINDE LIBATI

Born 1906 in Mongu. Father a member of Lealui Kuta until he died in 1939. Mother a commoner. Educated at Sefula PMS school to

I

standard VI. Then worked in Livingstone until 1938. He succeeded his father and became District Education Induna, Mwandi (Sesheke) Kuta. Remained Education Officer until 1965 when the new government system abolished his post. Now village headman, Sesheke District.

### NGOMBALA LUBITA

Born 1929 at Lealui. His mother was Lewanika's daughter. Educated in Northern Rhodesia and South Africa to Form VI. Now claims to be doing correspondence course with Oxford for B.Sc. (Economics). 1950 became sales manager in a store in Bechuanaland. Arrested for gold smuggling and held for nine months. Returned to Northern Rhodesia and became clerk for the Municipal Council of Luanshya. Arrested 1959 as member of UNIP; freed, but lost his job. Became leading member of the Barotse Anti-Secession Movement, a UNIP organization. 1962, Munukayambwa Sipalo burnt by a petrol bomb. Lubita believed UNIP Bemba supporters responsible and quit UNIP to join the Sicaba Party, later becoming President. Sicaba became affiliated with ANC but the party was soon disbanded. Apparently undertook secret mission for Paramount Chief, early 1964 but then returned to UNIP.

### MWANA MALI

Born 1910 in Mwandi. Father, Mwanga, village headman. Mother a Subiya. Educated to standard II PMS school, Mwandi. 1942 became *silalo* induna—had been supervisor for Zambesi Sawmills Company in Livingstone since 1937. 1949 appointed induna of Mwandi (Sesheke) Kuta.

### GRIFFITHS MUSIALIKE MUKANDE

Born 1912 at Namaenya, near Sefula. Father an evangelist, converted by Coillard. Mother a relative of an induna. Educated at Sefula PMS and Bulawayo to 1934. Worked as accounts clerk, then became District Treasurer to Imwiko until latter became Paramount Chief, and he was promoted to Central Treasurer for the Barotse government until 1963. Sent to Oxford University for six months course on Local Government. Joined Sicaba Party 1962 and stood unsuccessfully as one of its candidates in the 1962 national election. Quit 1963 when he learnt it was financed by Welensky's United Federal Party. Now has a store in Lifelo village, Mongu District.

### YUYI WAMUNYIMA MUPATU

Born 1898. Father was head bodyguard to Lewanika. After attending

Sefula PMS school, Lewanika sent him to Lovedale College in South Africa, together with two of the King's own sons, until 1914. Returned to Barotseland as store assistant. 1915, taught at Barotse National School until 1926 when a new headmaster, Holland, lowered the syllabus. Mupatu objected and lost his job. Sent to another school near Livingstone. Returned to Barotseland in 1929 and was the first Lozi to own a trading store. 1934, the store was burnt down and he lost all his savings. 1936, Cotterell, the new principal, invited him to return to BNS, but first sent him to be trained as a teacher-supervisor at Jeanes School, Mazabuka. 1943 became trader again and also opened a school in Limulunga for underprivileged young men, 'Makapekwa School'—'the rejected'. 1949, Mwanawina appointed him Administrative Secretary to the BNG and induna responsible for education. He remained there until 1956—but saw more and more of the suffering of boys thrown out of school and asked to reopen his school. Permission was denied him by the Kuta and he returned to trading. Joined opposition to Mwanawina for a short time in mid-1950s, but kept applying for his school until 1963, when he was finally allowed to reopen it. Original member of the Sicaba Party but quit when he found it was financed by the United Federal Party. Claims to know much of oral tradition because of the Lozi custom that young boys must listen to the stories of the old men around the fires at night. Has himself written three short booklets on aspects of Lozi history.

## MBANGA MUTEMWA

Born 1929 in Lealui. His father, a senior induna titled Kalonga, was a Subiya and his mother a Lozi-Toka. Educated at PMS schools to standard VI, then Lovedale College, South Africa, for eighteen months. 1950, returned to Northern Rhodesia as Post Office clerk until 1965. Then became Regional Produce Buyer in Mongu for the Barotse Province Agricultural Rural Marketing Board. Joined Zambian African National Congress 1958; has remained active member of UNIP, helping in 1963 to organize the Barotseland Provincial Election. Also much interested in Lozi history and has completed an unpublished work, *The Ngambelas of Barotseland*.

## MUHALI MUTEMWA

Born 1922 in Nalolo. Mother's father was a cousin to Lewanika and member of the household of Mokwae of Nalolo and fought in the 1884–5 rebellion. Educated PMS school to standard VI and Teachers Training School at Sefula. Became primary school teacher in 1943 and has taught all over Barotseland. Came to Mwandi

Primary School, Sescheke District, in 1960. Learned most of his history from his mother's father.

## PARAMOUNT CHIEF MWANAWINA III

Fourth son of Lewanika. Born at Lealui. Early education at PMS schools. 1908 sent to Lovedale College, South Africa. Completed education 1913. Returned as secretary and interpreter to his father. Worked in close co-operation with the government for the war effort during the two world wars. His services were recognized by the award, in 1946, of the King's Silver Medal for chiefs and the coronation medal in 1953. A senior adviser of his brother Yeta until 1939. Then appointed Chief of Mankoya Kuta until 1948. Succeeded Imwiko as Paramount Chief, 1948 until 1969. His policies assured the destruction of the traditional Lozi ruling class once UNIP became the government.

## MOOKA NAWA

Born 1897, Senanga District. Father, Nawa, son of Chief Mosokatani of Choma District. Mother was daughter of Ngambela Silumba, Lewanika's Ngambela (1878–84). Attended PMS schools until 1911 and became a messenger. 1937, clerk at Ngoma Kuta. 1942, steward of Chief Imwiko at Mwandi. 1947, appointed agriculture induna at Mwandi Kuta, Sesheke District; remained induna at Mwandi until the present.

## ILUKUI NJEKWA

Born 1923 at Mongu. His father's grandfather was Njekwa, King Sipopa's Ngambela; his grandfather was induna in charge of a *silalo* and his father was chosen by Ngambela Mokamba to go to Barotse National School, where he learned to become a clerk and worked for Europeans in Bomas across Barotseland; but he died young and never attained indunaship. Educated Mabumbu and Lukona PMS schools to standard VI. After school in 1942 he worked for Mwanawina as his treasury clerk and private secretary in Mankoya Kuta in 1945. Joined central government as health clerk in Mongu 1952–6. Then worked in Bechuanaland as interpreter and clerk of the court. Eye trouble caused him to lose his job and he worked at various trades until employed as book-keeper for a retail store in Mongu, April, 1965.

## HASTINGS NDANGWA NOYOO

Born 1928 in Sikandi village, Mongu District. Father, an evangelist and teacher for the PMS and very distantly related to the first Ngambela Imbula. His mother also a commoner, although some of her ancestors were Ngambelas. Educated at PMS schools to standard VI. 1948, joined Lusaka Medical School for four years. Medical certificate held back for six months because of his opposition to Federation. Later became a medical assistant for the Ministry of Health in Mongu, which was taken over in 1956 by the Federal government. Noyoo, already a strong ANC supporter, resigned in protest and returned to open a shop in Barotseland. Active in underground UNIP circles until 1963. Elected as UNIP member to the Barotse National Council. Appointed assistant Ngambela March, 1964, and Ngambela December, 1964. Temporarily suspended from UNIP for refusing to follow party line, mid-1964.

## SAMUEL SHAPA

Born 1926 at Kalabo. Ancestors were indunas but parents were 'ordinary Lozi'. Educated at Seventh Day Adventist College, Rhodesia, and became a convert. Returned to Liumba Hill SDA Mission School as an evangelist and school supervisor. Ordained as pastor 1950. Field pastor in Mongu 1952–59. Transferred to Sitoti Mission and School, near Senanga, as acting director, manager of schools and pastor.

## NDAMBO SIMALUMBA

Born 1913 at Nalolo. Father a steward of Mokwae Matauka of Nalolo during Lewanika's reign and grandfather an induna. Educated Sefula and Lukona PMS schools to standard VI, then Normal School, Sefula, for three years. Started teaching 1935 and is now Headmaster since 1960 at Itufa PMS school. He is also an evangelist and runs both the school and the services on the station. An early supporter of UNIP. Profoundly interested in Lozi history, which he learnt from his father and grandfather and other people he has talked to. Considering writing a book on Lozi history.

## P. SOKA

Born 1916 in Mwandi. Father a Subiya, had an apparently important ruling position. Attended Mwandi PMS school to Sub B. Worked at Zambesi Sawmills Company 1934–49. Says he was appointed *silalo* induna 1945, although worked in Livingstone and Bulawayo until 1953. Appointed induna of Mwandi Kuta 1964.

## M. TIMWENDILA

Born 1909 in Mongu. Father, Lubinda, son of Lewanika, who was Lealui Natamoyo from 1934–45, and then Chief of Sesheke, 1946–66.

Mother's father village headman. Educated Barotse National School to standard IV. 1934 became inventory clerk, Zambesi Sawmills Company. 1939, Nkana Mines as Telephone operator. 1944, store clerk. When his father became Chief of Sesheke he was appointed induna of Mwandi Kuta.

## MUHELI WALUBITA

Born 1897 at Kazangula. Father Liashimba (Chief Councillor) to Imwiko at Sesheke. 1904, started school at Sesheke PMS then to Basutoland until 1916. Returned to Barotseland as clerk at Mwandi Kuta and private secretary to the Chief of Sesheke until 1935. 1936 helped set up Naliele as Kuta for Mankoya District. 1938 father died and he was appointed by the Paramount Chief to be Liashimba at Sesheke. 1945 went with Imwiko to Lealui and was appointed induna Kalonga—educational induna for Barotseland. 1947, induna for agricultural development. 1948 appointed Ngambela. 1956 resigned as Ngambela because of differences with Mwanawina.

## SHEMAKONO KALONGA WINA

Born 1878, son of a Lealui induna. 1893 PMS school, Kazangula, for five years. Then taken by Yeta as his kitchen boy. Returned PMS schools until 1902. Returned to Sesheke to work in Yeta's household, marrying one of Lewanika's daughters in 1905. After Yeta became King in 1916, he remained at Sesheke with Imwiko, having been appointed an induna. His father died in 1922 and Wina returned to Lealui to succeed him as Induna Wina Lioma. 1936 Daniel Akafuna took him to Balovale to be his Chief Councillor. Appointed in 1941 as Ngambela and acting Paramount Chief. Remained Ngambela under Imwiko, but dismissed by Mwanawina in 1948. Retired to village Namitomi, Mongu-Lealui District. Father of Arthur and Sikota Wina, members of the Zambian cabinet.

## ARTHUR MUBUKWANU ZAZA

Born 1919 in Mule village, near Sefula. His mother was a Matoka and his father a bodyguard to Lewanika who selected him to attend Coillard's first school at Sefula. Father among a small group which converted early and he became a PMS evangelist, preacher and teacher until his death in 1924. Arthur Zaza also went to Sefula PMS school from 1930–35 to standard III, then Lukona for upper primary education to standard VI. 1940–42 to Munali Secondary School (now called Hodgson Technical School) to Form II which was the highest education available in Northern Rhodesia at that time. Became recruiting agent (1942–43) for WNLA in Kalabo until offered a job by the Information Department in Lusaka as a broad-caster in the vernacular, and edited the Silozi part of *Mutende*, a fortnightly journal. 1949 he was transferred to Provincial Administra-tion, Barotseland, as head clerk at Namushakende Development Centre. 1956–60 accounts clerk in Mankoya for the Boma. 1961–62 head clerk for the Boma at Sesheke. 1962–64 chief clerk for the Boma at Senanga. September, 1964, sent to Staff Training College, Lusaka, to study finance and joined the Ministry of Local Govern-ment and Housing in May, 1965. Now District Local Government Officer in Samfya District.

## MUYUNDA CLEMENT ZAZA

Born 1901 at Sefula. Brother of Arthur Zaza (see above). Sent to Sefula PMS school to standard III, then did four years as a trainee teacher. Became school teacher at Sefula until 1926. Went to Belgian Congo for short while and returned on foot. Joined Senanga PMS school as area supervisor for four schools. Became head teacher in Sefula Girl's Primary School, then Lukona School. Returned to Sefula Normal School as assistant teacher until 1936. After wage dispute with PMS officials, went to Bechuanaland and became super-visor of eighteen schools. 1954, returned to Barotseland and became a cabinet-maker and one of the leaders of the opposition to Mwana-wina, 1953–59. Called upon to be Boarding Master at Munali Secondary School in Luska from 1960 until February, 1965, when President Kaunda appointed him Political Assistant to the Resident Minister of Barotse Province.

## NEWO ZAZA

Born 1910 in Mule village, Sefula. Brother of Arthur and Clement Zaza (see above). Educated to standard VI at Sefula PMS school. Then became a laboratory technician on the Copper Belt and later taught practical pathology in Lusaka, which he learnt from a local doctor. Did a South African correspondence course to Form III. 1945 returned to Mule and tried several trades and then was elected to the reformed Katengo Council, 1954–57. He was threatened with dismissal by the Litunga for being a leader of the anti-Mwanawina group. He was also a member of the District Education authority and Chairman of the School Council in Sefula. A well-known local historian. Has interviewed many old Lozi and has read C. Mackintosh, *Coillard of the Zambesi*.

## (ii) *Non-Lozi Informants* (*data to the end of 1965*)

RICHARD BAILEY
WNLA local representative in Barotseland, 1950–65.

ETIENNE BERGER
Paris Missionary Society, 1934–49, 1961–65.

MARIE BORLE
Paris Missionary Society, 1931–65.

MAURICE GRAEBERT
Paris Missionary Society, 1948–65.

KELVIN MLENGA
Editor, *Central African Mail* (Lusaka), 1964–66.

D. PITTET
Paris Missionary Society, 1948–65.

DANIEL SOKO
A Nyasa. Arrived Barotseland c. 1939. Runs shop in Mongu. Active member of the Mongu African Welfare Association 1943–51.

JOHN A. B. STEWART
Senior Provincial Local Government Officer, October, 1964, to December, 1965.

'x'
A senior European official at the Mongu, Boma, 1962–65, who asked that he should not be identified.

## C. Written Sources

### (i) Selected Published Unofficial Books and Pamphlets

Addison, J. T., *François Coillard*. Hartford, Conn., 1924.

Allan, W., *The African Husbandman*. Edinburgh, 1965.

Apthorpe, Raymond (ed.), *From Tribal Rule to Modern Government*. Lusaka, 1959.

Arnot, Frederick, S., *Missionary Travels in Central Africa*. London, 1914.

——, *Garenganze, or Seven Years Pioneer Mission Work in Central Africa*. London, 1889.

Baker, E., *The Life and Explorations of F. S. Arnot*, FRGS. London, 1921.

Baldwin, Arthur, *A Missionary Outpost in Central Africa*. London, 1914.

——, *Rev. Henry Buckenham, Pioneer Missionary*. London, 1920.

Barnes, John A., *Politics in a changing Society: A Political History of the Fort Jameson Ngoni*. Cape Town, 1954.

Beguin, Eugene, *Les Ma-rotse: Etude géographique et ethnographique du Haut-Zambèze*. Lausanne, 1903.

Bertrand, Alfred, *Kingdom of the Barotsi, Upper Zambesi*. London, 1898.

Bertrand, Alice E., *Alfred Bertrand, Explorer and Captain of Cavalry*. London, 1926.

Bouchet, J., *Comme l'Evangile agit au Zambèze*. Paris, 1922.

Brelsford, W. V., *The Tribes of Northern Rhodesia*. Lusaka, 1957.

——, *Generation of Men: The European Pioneers of Northern Rhodesia*. Lusaka, 1965.

Butt, G. E., *My Travels in North-Western Rhodesia*. London, 1909.

Chapman, James, *Travels in the Interior of South Africa*. 2 Vols. London, 1868.

Clark, Desmond J., *The Prehistory of Southern Africa*. London, 1959.

Clay, G. C. R., *History of the Mankoya District*. Rhodes–Livingstone Institute Communication, No. 4, Lusaka, 1946.

——, *Your Friend Lewanika, Litunga of Barotseland, 1842–1916*. London, 1968.

Coillard, François, *La Mission au Zambèze*. Paris, 1881.

——, *Zambesia: Work among the Barotse*. Glasgow, 1894.

——, *On The Threshold of Central Africa*. London, 1897.

Colson, E. and Gluckman, M. (eds.), *Seven Tribes of Central Africa*. London, 1951.

Cunnison, I. G., *The Luapula Peoples of Northern Rhodesia: Custom and History In Tribal Politics*. Manchester, 1959.

——, (ed. and trans.), *Historical Traditions of the Eastern Lunda*. RLI Communication, No. 23, 1962.

Davidson, J. W., *The Northern Rhodesian Legislative Council*. London, 1948.

Davis, J. M. (ed.), *Modern Industry and the African*. London, 1933.

Depelchin, H. and Croonenberghs, C., *Trois ans dans l'Afrique Australe . . . débuts de la Mission du Zambèze*, 2 Vols. Bruxelles, 1882–83.

Dieterlen, H., *François Coillard*. Paris, 1921.

Ellenberger, D. F., *History of the Basuto: Ancient and Modern*. Trans. by J. C. MacGregor, London, 1912.

Epstein, A. L., *Politics in an Urban African Community*. Manchester, 1958.

Fagan, Brian M. (ed.), *A Short History of Zambia*. Nairobi, 1966.

Favre, Edward, *François Coillard, 1834–1904*, 3 Vols. Paris, 1946.

Fortes, M., and Evans–Pritchard, E. E. (eds.), *African Political Systems*. London, 1940.

Fraenkel, Peter, *Wayaleshi*. London, 1959.

Franklin, Harry, *Unholy Wedlock: The Failure of the Central African Federation*. London, 1963.

Gann, Lewis H., *The Birth of a Plural Society: the Development of Northern Rhodesia under British South Africa Company: 1894–1914*. Manchester, 1958.

——, *A History of Northern Rhodesia: Early Days to 1953*. London, 1964.

Gelfand, Michael, *Northern Rhodesia in the Days of the Charter: a Medical and Social Study: 1878–1924*. Oxford, 1961.

——, *Livingstone the Doctor: His Life and Travels*. Oxford, 1957.

Gibbons, Alfred St. Hill, *Africa from South to North through Marotseland*. London, 1904.

——, *Exploration and Hunting in Central Africa: 1895–6*. London, 1898.

Gluckman, Max, *Economy of the Central Barotse Plain*. Rhodes–Livingstone Papers, No. 7, Livingstone, 1941.

——, *Administrative Organization of the Barotse Native Authorities, with a plan for reforming them*. Rhodes–Livingstone Institute, Communication No. 1, Livingstone, 1943.

——, *Essays on Lozi Land and Royal Property*. Rhodes–Livingstone Papers, No. 10, Livingstone, 1943.

——, *The Judicial Process Among the Barotse of Northern Rhodesia*. Manchester, 1955.

——, *Custom and Conflict in Africa*. Oxford, 1956.

——, *Order and Rebellion in Tribal Africa*. London, 1963.

——, *The Ideas of Barotse Jurisprudence*. New Haven, 1965.

——, *Politics, Law and Ritual in Tribal Society: Some Problems in Social Anthropology.* Oxford, 1965.

Goy, Mme. M. K., *Alone in Africa, or Seven Years on the Zambesi.* London, 1901.

Gray, Richard, *The Two Nations: Aspects of the Development of Race Relations in the Rhodesias and Nyasaland.* London, 1960.

Groves, C. P., *The Planting of Christianity in Africa*, Vol. iii. London, 1955, and Vol. iv, London, 1958.

Hailey, Lord, *Native Administration in the British African Territories: Part II, Central Africa.* London, 1950.

Hall, Richard, *Zambia.* London, 1965.

——, *The High Price of Principles.* London, 1969.

Hanna, A. J., *The Story of the Rhodesians and Nyasaland.* London, 1960.

Harding, Col. Colin, *Far Bugles.* 2nd edition, London, 1933.

——, *In Remotest Barotseland.* London, 1905.

——, *Frontier Patrols: a History of the British South Africa Police and other Rhodesian Forces.* London, 1937.

Hepburn, J. D., *Twenty Years in Khama's Country*, London, 1896.

Hole, H. M., *The Making of Rhodesia*, London, 1926.

——, *The Passing of the Black Kings*, London, 1932.

Holub, Emil, *Seven Years in South Africa*, 2 Vols. London, 1881.

Hubbard, Mary G., *African Gamble.* New York, 1937.

Jalla, Adolph, *Lewanika, Roi des Ba-Rotsi.* Geneva, 1902.

——, *Pionniers parmi le Ma-rotsi.* Florence, 1903.

——, *La Mission du Zambèze.* Paris, c. 1922.

——, *The History of the Barotse Nation (Litaba za Sicaba sa Ma-Lozi).* 6th edition, Lusaka, 1961.

Jalla, Louis, *Sur les Rives du Zambèze: Notes Ethnographiques.* Paris, 1928.

Johnston, James, *Reality versus Romance in South-Central Africa.* London, 1893.

Keatley, Patrick, *The Politics of Partnership: the Federation of Rhodesia and Nyasaland.* London, 1963.

Kuntz, Marthe, *Ombres et Lumières: Extraits du Journal d'une Institutrice, Missionaire au Zambèze, 1913–19*, 3rd edition. Paris, 1929.

Leverhulme Inter-Collegiate History Conference, *Historians in Tropical Africa.* Salisbury, 1960.

Lienard, J. L., *Notre Voyage au Zambèze.* Lausanne, 1899.

Livingstone, David, *Missionary Travels and Researches in South Africa.* London, 1957.

——, and Livingstone, Charles, *Narrative of an Expedition to the Zambesi and its Tributaries.* London, 1865.

Low, D. A. and Pratt, R. C., *Buganda and British Overrule*. London, 1960.

Luck, R. A., *Visit to Lewanika, King of the Barotse*. London, 1902.

MacConnachie, J., *An Artisan Missionary on the Zambesi: being the life story of William Thomson Waddell*. Edinburgh, 1910.

MacDonald, J. F., *Zambesi River*. London, 1955.

Mackintosh, C. W., *Yeta III, Paramount Chief of the Barotse, Northern Rhodesia: a sketch of his life*. London, 1937.

——, *The New Zanbesi Trail: a Record of Two Journeys to Northern Western Rhodesia: 1903–1920*. London, 1922.

——, *Coillard of the Zambesi: 1858–1904*. London, 1907.

——, *Lewanika, Paramount Chief of the Barotse and Allied Tribes, 1875–1916*. London, 1942.

——, *Some Pioneer Missions of Northern Rhodesia and Nyasaland*. Livingston, 1950.

MacNair, James I. (ed.), *Livingstone's Travels*. London, 1956.

Mason, Philip, *The Birth of a Dilemma: The Conquest and Settlement of Rhodesia*. London, 1958.

Mbikusita, Godwin, *The Paramount Chief Yeta IIIs' visit to England*. Lusaka, 1937.

McCulloch, M., *The Lunda, Luena and Related Tribes of North Western Rhodesia and adjoining Territories*. London, 1951.

*Mission Work on the Upper Zambesi*. Glasgow, 1888.

Mulford, David C., *The Northern Rhodesia General Election, 1962*. Nairobi, 1964.

——, *Zambia: The Politics of Independence, 1957–64*. London, 1967.

Omer-Cooper, John, D., *The Zulu Aftermath: Nineteenth-Century Revolution in Bantu Africa*. London, 1966.

Oswell, W. Edward, *Wm. Cotton Oswell: Hunter and Explorer*, 2 Vols. London, 1900.

Palmer, R. H., *Lewanika's Country*. Privately printed in Canada, 1955.

Peters, David U., *Land Usage in Barotseland*. Lusaka, 1960.

Pinto, A. de Serpa, *How I crossed Africa from the Atlantic to the Indian Ocean*, 2 Vols. London, 1881.

Reynolds, Barrie, *Magic, Divination and Witchcraft among the Barotse of Northern Rhodesia*. London, 1963.

Rotberg, Robert I., *The Rise of Nationalism in Central Africa: the Making of Malawi and Zambia, 1873–1964*. Harvard, 1965.

——, *Christian Missionaries and the Creation of Northern Rhodesia: 1880–1924*. Princeton, 1965.

Roux, André, *Dans la Grande Ile et au Bord du Zambèze*. Paris, 1948.

Roux, S. Le, *Pioneers and Sportsmen of South Africa*. Salisbury, 1939.

Schapera, I. (ed.), *Livingstone's Africa Journals: 1853-56*, 2 Vols. London, 1963.

—— (ed.), *Livingstone's Private Journals: 1851-53*. London, 1960.

Scott, E. D., *Some Letters from South Africa, 1894-1932*. Manchester, 1903.

Seaver, George, *David Livingstone, his Life and Letters*. London, 1957.

Selous, F. C., *Travel and Adventure in South-East Africa*. London, 1893.

Shillito, E., *François Coillard: a Wayfaring Man*. London, 1923.

Smith, E. W., *Great Lion of Bechuanaland: the Life and Times of Roger Price, Missionary*. London, 1957.

——, *The Blessed Missionaries*. Cape Town, 1950.

——, *The Ways of the White Field in Rhodesia: a Survey of Christian Enterprise in Northern and Southern Rhodesia*. London, 1928.

Smith, E. W., and Dale, A. M., *The Ila Speaking Peoples of Northern Rhodesia*, 2 Vols. London, 1920.

Stokes, Eric, and Brown, Richard (eds.), *The Zambesian Past: Studies in Central African History*. Manchester, 1966.

Stirke, D. E. C., *Barotseland: Eight Years among the Barotse*. London, 1922.

Tabler, Edward C. (ed.), *Trade and Travel in Early Barotseland: the Diaries of George Westbeech, 1885-88, and Captain Norman MacLeod, 1875-76*. London, 1963.

Thomson, J. Moffat, *Memorandum on the Native Tribes and Tribal Areas of Northern Rhodesia*. Lusaka, 1934.

Trapnell, C. G., and Clothier, J., *The Soils, Vegetations and Agricultural Systems of North Western Rhodesia*. Lusaka, 1937.

Turner, V. W., *The Lozi Peoples of North Western Rhodesia*. London, 1952.

Vansina, Jan, *Oral Tradition: a study in Historical Methodology*, trans. by H. M. Wright. London, 1965.

Wallis, J. P. R. (ed.), *The Zambesi Expedition of David Livingstone*. London, 1956.

—— (ed.), *The Barotseland Journal of James Stevenson-Hamilton: 1898-99*. London, 1953.

Welensky, Roy, *Welensky's 4,000 Days: The Life and Death of the Federation of Rhodesia and Nyasaland*. London, 1964.

White, C. M. N., *An Outline of Luvale Social and Political Organization*, Rhodes-Livingstone Paper No. 30. Manchester, 1960.

Woodhouse, C. M., and Lockhart, John G., *Cecil Rhodes*. London, 1963.

*Work for God in Central Africa: Mission to the Upper Zambesi*. Glasgow, 1891.

## (ii) *Selected Published Articles*

Apthorpe, R. J., 'Problems of African Political History: The Nsenga of Northern Rhodesia', *Rhodes–Livingstone Journal*, No. 28, 1960.

Akafuna, Ishee Kwandu Sikota, 'Lewanika in England, 1902', *Northern Rhodesian Journal*, Vol. II, No. 2, 1953.

Baxter, William T., 'The Concessions of Northern Rhodesia', *Occasional Papers of the National Archives of Rhodesia and Nyasaland*, No. 1, June, 1963.

Bradley, K., 'Statesmen: Coryndon and Lewanika in North Western Rhodesia', *African Observer*, Vol. 5, No. 5, Sept., 1936.

Brown, Richard, 'Aspects of the Scramble for Matabeleland', in Stokes and Brown (ed.), *Zambesian Past*. Manchester, 1966.

Burles, R. S., 'The Katengo Council Elections', *The Journal of African Administration*, Vol. 4, 1952.

Caplan, Gerald L., 'Barotseland's Scramble for Protection', *Journal of African History*, Vol. X, No. 2, 1969.

——, 'Barotseland: The Secessionist Challenge to Zambia', *Journal of Modern African Studies*, Vol. 6, No. 3, October, 1968.

——, 'Zambia ,Barotseland, and the Liberation of Southern Africa', *Africa Today*, Vol. 16, No. 4, Aug.–Sept., 1969.

Clay, G. C. R., 'Barotseland in the Nineteenth Century between 1801 and 1864', *Proceedings of the Conference on the History of the Central African Peoples*. Lusaka, 1963.

Coombe, Trevor, 'The Origins of Secondary Education in Zambia, Part I: Policy Making in the Thirties', *African Social Research* (formerly *Rhodes–Livingstone Journal*), No. 3, June, 1967.

——, 'The Origins of Secondary Education in Zambia, Part II, Anatomy of a Decision, 1934–36', *African Social Research*, No. 4, Dec., 1967.

——, 'The Origins of Secondary Education in Zambia, Part iii, Anatomy of a Decision, 1937–39', *African Social Research*, No. 5, June, 1968.

Cooper, C., 'Village Crafts in Barotseland', *The Rhodes–Livingstone Journal, Human Problems in British Central Africa*, No. xi, 1951.

Gann, L. H., 'The end of the Slave Trade in British Central Africa: 1889–1912', *Rhodes–Livingstone Journal*, No. xvi, 1954.

Gibbons, A. St. H., 'Journey in Marotse and Mashikolumbwe Countries', *Geographical Journal*, Vol. ix, No. 2, Feb., 1897.

——, 'Marotseland and the Tribes of the Upper Zambesi', *Proceedings of the Royal Colonial Institute*, No. xxix, 1897–98.

——, 'Exploration in Marotseland and Neighbouring Regions', *Geographical Journal*, Vol. xvii, No. 2, Feb., 1901.

Glennie, A. F. B., 'The Barotse System of Government', *The Journal of African Administration*, Vol. iv. No. 1, Jan., 1952.

——, 'The Administration Officer Today: Barotseland', *Corona*, Vol. ii, No. 3, March, 1959.

Gluckman, Max, 'Zambesi River Kingdom', *Libertas*, Vol. v, July, 1945.

——, 'Kingship and Marriage among the Lozi of Northern Rhodesia and the Zulu of Natal', in A. R. Radcliffe-Brown and Daryll Forde (ed.), *African Systems of Kinship and Marriage*. London, 1950.

——, 'African Land Tenure', *Rhodes–Livingstone Journal*, Vol. iii, June, 1945.

Heisler, Helmuth, 'Continuity and Change in Zambian Administration', *Journal of Local Administration, Overseas*, Vol. iv, No. 3. July, 1965.

Hudson, R. S. and Prescot, H. K., 'The Election of a "Ngambela" in Barotseland', *Man*, Vol. xxiv, No. 103, 1924.

Jordan, E. K., 'Mongu in 1908', *Northern Rhodesia Journal*, Vol. iv, No. 2, 1959.

Jones, Stanely, 'Mankoya in 1925 to 1927', *Northern Rhodesian Journal*, Vol. iv, No. 2, 1959.

Kuntz, Marthe, 'Education Indigène sur le Haut-Zambesi', *Le Monde Non Chrétien*, 1ere série, No. 3, 1932.

Lloyd, Peter C., 'The Political Structure of African Kingdoms: an Exploratory Model', Association of Social Anthropologists, *Political Systems and the Distribution of Power*. London, 1965.

Lawley, Arthur, 'From Bulawayo to the Victoria Falls: a Mission to King Lewanika', *Blackwood's Magazine*, Dec., 1898.

MacQueen, James, 'Journeys of Silva Porto with the Arabs from Benguela to Ibo and Mozambique through Africa, 1852–54', *Journals of the Royal Geographical Society*, Vol. xxx, 1860.

Mainga, Mutumba, 'The Lozi Kingdom', in B. Fagan (ed.) *A Short History of Zambia*. Nairobi, 1966.

——, 'The Origin of the Lozi: Some Oral Traditions', in Stokes and Brown, (ed.) *The Zambian Past*. Manchester, 1966.

Mortimer, M., 'History of the Barotse National School: 1907 to 1957', *The Northern Rhodesia Journal*, Vol. iii, No. 4, 1957.

Muuka, L. S., 'The Colonization of Barotseland in the Seventeenth Century', in Stokes and Brown (ed.) *The Zambesian Past*. Manchester, 1966.

Philpott, R., 'The Mulobezi-Mongu Labour Route', *Rhodes–Livingstone Institute Journal*, No. iii, June, 1945.

'Pula', 'The Barotse People and Some of their Customs', NADA, 1926.

Ranger, Terence, 'The "Ethiopian" Episode in Barotseland: 1900–1905', *Rhodes–Livingstone Journal*, No. xxxvii, June, 1965.

——, 'Traditional Authorities and the Rise of Modern Politics in Southern Rhodesia 1898–1930', in Stokes and Brown (ed.), *The Zambesian Past*. Manchester, 1966.

Read, Margaret, 'Migrant Labour and its Effects on Tribal Life', *International Labour Review*, Vol. xlv, July, 1942.

Roberts, Andrew, 'Migrations from the Congo (AD 1500 to 1850)', in B. Fagan (ed.), *A Short History of Zambia*. Nairobi, 1966.

Smith, E. W., 'Sebitwane and the Makololo', *African Studies*, Vol. xv, No. 2, 1956.

Stokes, Eric, 'Barotseland: the Survival of an African State', in Stokes and Brown (ed.), *The Zambesian Past*. Manchester, 1966.

Summers, Roger, and Gann, L. H., 'Robert Edward Codrington, 1869–1908', *The Northern Rhodesia Journal*, Vol. iii, 1956.

Thwaits, D. C., 'Trekking from Kalomo to Mongu in 1906', *The Northern Rhodesia Journal*, Vol. iii, No. 4, 1957.

Van Velsen, Jaap, 'Some Early Pressure Groups in Malawi', in Stokes and Brown (ed.), *The Zambesian Past*. Manchester, 1966.

——, 'Labour Migration as a Positive Factor in the Continuity of Tonga Tribal Society', *Economic Development and Cultural Change*, Vol. viii, 1960.

——, 'The Missionary factor among the Lakeside Tonga of Nyasaland', *Rhodes–Livingstone Journal*, Vol. xxvi, 1959.

——, 'Notes on the History of the Lakeside Tonga of Nyasaland', *African Studies*, Vol. xviii, No. 3, 1959.

Wallace, L. A., 'The Beginning of Native Administration in Northern Rhodesia', *Journal of the African Society*, Vol. xxi, 1922.

Watt, Nigel, 'Lewanika's Visit to Edinburgh', *Northern Rhodesia Journal*, Vol. ii, No. 1, 1953.

White, C. M. N., 'The Ethno-History of the Upper Zambesi', *African Studies*, Vol. xxi, No. 1, 1962.

——, 'The History of the Lunda–Lubale Peoples', *Rhodes–Livingstone Journal*, Vol. viii, 1949.

——, 'The Balovale peoples and their Historical Background', *Rhodes–Livingstone Journal*, No. 8, 1948.

## (iii) *Lozi Works*
### (translated by Mr. David Nyambe)

(a) PUBLISHED

Ikacana, N. S., *Litaba za Makwanga* [*The History of the Kwanga*]. Morija, Basutoland, 1964.

Mupatu, Y. W., *Bulozi Sapili* [*Barotseland in the Past*]. Cape Town, 1959.

——, *Mulambwa Santulu U Amuhela Bo Mweve*, [*King Mulambwa Welcomes the Mbunda Chiefs*]. London, 1958.

Nalilungwe, Mubiana, *Makolo Ki Ba* [*The Coming of the Kololo*]. Cape Town, 1958.

Sakubita, M. M., *Za Luna Li Lu Siile* [*Our Vanishing Past*]. London, 1958.

(b) UNPUBLISHED

Akafuna, Ishee Kwandu Sikota, *Makalelo a Bulena Bwa Silozi* [*The Origin of the Lozi Chieftainship*]. private typescript, Mongu, 1 Nov., 1959.

Mutemwa, Mbanga, *Lingambela za Meva Bulozi* [*The Ngambelas of Barotseland*], private typescript, Mongu, undated.

## (iv) *Unpublished Unofficial Works*

Maxwell Stamp Associates, *A History of the Mineral Rights of Northern Rhodesia*, 2 Vols. London, 1967.

Fortune, George, 'A Note on the Languages of Barotseland'. 1963, privately held.

Nyaywa, Kekelwa, 'The Definition of the Barotse Boundary', University College of Rhodesia and Nyasaland, Undergraduate Seminar Paper No. 9, 19 May, 1965.

Oliver, Roland, 'After the Oxford History: Historical Research in East Africa', School of Oriental and African Studies Seminar Paper, Oct., 1965.

Ranger, Terence, 'Tribalism and Nationalism: The Case of Barotseland', typescript, undated, privately held.

Silverman, Philip, *Local Elites and the Image of a Nation: The Incorporation of Barotseland within Zambia*. Unpublished Ph.D. thesis, Cornell University, 1968.

'A record of the Historical Assurances of Barotseland's Rights'. 1963, privately held.
'Constitution for the Independent Protectorate of Barotseland.' 1963, privately held.
'The Lozi Case for an Independent Protectorate'. 1963, privately held.

## (v) *Official Documents*

(a) PUBLISHED

*Agreement between Great Britain and Portugal Relative to Spheres of Influence North of the Zambesi*, C. 7032. London, 1893.

*Award of His Majesty the King of Italy respecting the Western Boundary of the Barotse Kingdom*, Cmnd. 2584. London, 1905.

Barotse Native Government, *Orders and Rules*. English Version, Lusaka, 1959.

*Memorandum on Native Policy in Northern Rhodesia* [Gardiner–Brown Report]. Lusaka, 1950.

*Northern Rhodesia: Proposals for Constitutional Change*, Cmnd. 1295. London, 1961.

*Northern Rhodesia: Social and Economic Progress of the People*, No. 1868. Lusaka, 1937.

Northern Rhodesian Government, *The British South Africa Company's Claims to Mineral Rights in Northern Rhodesia*. Lusaka, 1964.

*Northern Rhodesian Labour Department Annual Reports*.

*Northern Rhodesian Legislative Council Debates*. Lusaka.

*Proposals for Constitutional Change*, Northern Rhodesia Cmnd. 530. London, 1958.

'Reports on Barotseland', in *Northern Rhodesian Native Affairs Annual Reports*.

*Reports of the Advisory Commission on the Review of the Constitution of Rhodesia and Nyasaland* [Monckton Commission], Cmnd. 1148. London, 1960.

*Report of the Commission Appointed to Enquire into the Financial and Economic Position of Northern Rhodesia* [Pim–Milligan Report], Col. No. 145. London, 1938.

*Report of the Committee appointed to inquire into the Constitution of the Barotse Native Government together with the comments thereon of the National Council* [Rawlins Committee]. Lusaka, 1957.

*Rhodesia-Nyasaland Royal Commission Report* [Bledislow Commission], Cmnd. 5949. London, 1939.

*The Barotseland Agreement 1964*, Cmnd. 2366. London, 1964.

(b) UNPUBLISHED

Jones, G. S. 'Local Government Development with Special Reference to Barotseland', 19 July, 1958. Lusaka, privately held.

*Report of the Commission Appointed to Examine and Report Upon the Whole Question of the Past and Present Relations of the Paramount Chief of the Barotse Nation and the Chiefs Resident in the Balovale District both east and west of the Zambesi River, with Special Reference to the Ownership of Land and the Methods by which the Tribes have been Governed and to make Recommendations for the Future* [MacDonnell Commission]. Lusaka, 1939.


## (vi) *Newspapers and Periodicals*

*African Mail (Central African Mail)* (*Zambian Mail*), Lusaka.
*Journal des Missions Evangeliques*, Paris.
*Mutende*, Lusaka.
*News From Barotseland* (*News from Basutoland and Barotseland*), London.
*Northern News* (*Times of Zambia*), Ndola.
*Nouvelles du Zambèze*, Geneva.
*The Zambesi Mission Record*. London.


## (vii) *Archival Sources*

LONDON

British Museum. The Arthur Balfour Papers, Vol. xxvi, Correspondence between Balfour and Lord Selborne, 1904–22.
Methodist Missionary Society:
  (a) 'Minutes of the Primitive Methodist Church Foreign Missionary Committee', Vol. 34, Mashukulumbwe [Ila] Mission Minutes, 1894–1904.
  (b) Smith, E. W. (ed.), *The Journal of Andrew Baldwin, Pioneer Missionary in Northern Rhodesia* (typescript, 1953).

Public Record Office      FO    3  ⎫ North Zambesi
  Series (to 1914):        FO   93  ⎬ North-Western Rhodesia
                          FO   97  ⎩ Northern Rhodesia.
                          FO  403  ⎭

Colonial Office Library    CO African ⎫
  Series (to 1914):      (South) ⎪
              CO 417  ⎪ North Zambesia
              CO 455  ⎬North-western Rhodesia
              CO 468  ⎪ Northern Rhodesia.
              CO 743  ⎪
              CO 798  ⎭

OXFORD

Rhodes House. P. J. Law, Personal Letters from Northern Rhodesia, 1932–36, Mss. Afr. s. 393.

PARIS

Societé des Missions Evangéliques:
  (a) François Coillard, Journals and Notebooks.
  ——, Miscellaneous Letters.
  (b) Christina Coillard, Miscellaneous Letters and Journals.
  (c) 'Lettres Reçues', 1889–1914 (annual volumes).

SALISBURY

National Archives of Rhodesia:
  (a) *Historical Manuscripts:*
    P. F. Holland, 'History of the Barotse National School' (type-script, 1932).
    F. C. Quicke, 'Notes on a Journey through North Western Rhodesia 1898–99', QU 1/2
    François and Christina Coillard Papers, 7 vols., CO5.
    Diary of William Waddell, WA 1.
    Frank Worthington Papers, WO 3.
    H. Marshall Hole Papers, HO 1.
    George Westbeech Papers, WE 1.
    Catherine Mackintosh Papers, MA 18.
  (b) *Series (to 1923):*
    A   3 ⎫
    A  11 ⎬Administrator, North-Western Rhodesia.
    A  12 ⎭
    CT 1   British South Africa Company, Cape Town.
    HC 1–5 High Commissioner for South Africa.
    LO 6   British South Africa Company, London.
    RC 2–3 Resident Commissioner, Barotseland.

LUSAKA

National Archives of Zambia Series (to 1935):

A    1–3 Administrator, North-Western Rhodesia.
B    1    Barotseland, Miscellaneous.
IN   1    Secretary for Native Affairs, North-Western Rhodesia.
KDE  1–2 Barotseland, Miscellaneous, 1902–35.
KDE  8    Barotse Province Annual Reports, 1906–29.
IND  1–2 Kasempa District Reports.
KTO  1–3 Sesheke District Reports.
ZA   1    Barotseland, Miscellaneous.
ZA   7    Barotse Province Annual Reports and Tour Reports, 1929–34.

Box No. 356 – Special File of Historical Notes on Barotseland.
Box No. 1311 – Proposals for Constitutional Reform in Barotseland, 1946.

Institute for Social Research (formerly Rhodes–Livingstone Institute):
Barotseland Historical Manuscripts.
George Westbeech, 'Part of a Diary'.


MONGU

Barotse Province Files, Mongu Boma.


SEFULA

Societé des Missions Evangéliques, 'Correspondence avec le Directeur, 1933–59'.

# INDEX